Twentieth-Century
Short Story Explication:
Supplement I to Second Edition,
1967-1969

Compiled by
WARREN S. WALKER
Professor of English, Texas Tech University

THE SHOE STRING PRESS, INC.
1970

1. Short story - Bibliography.

Second Edition, Supplement I
© 1970, The Shoe String Press, Inc.
Library of Congress Catalog Card Number: 67-24192
ISBN: 1-208-01146-3

Printed in the United States of America

149912

PREFACE

The first edition of <u>Twentieth-Century Short Story Explication</u> (1961) was an attempt to list all of the significant interpretive studies of short fiction published from 1900 through 1960. Supplement I (1963) carried the bibliography forward to April 1, 1963; Supplement II (1965) advanced the bibliography to January 1, 1965. The second edition (1967) brought the listing of explications through 1966; in this present Supplement, entries have been carried forward through 1967, 1968, and 1969. Entries are limited to material written in English except for important articles in such readily available foreign-language journals as <u>Modern Language Notes, Monatshefte, Hispania, French Review,</u> and <u>Slavic and East European Journal.</u> The Index of Short Story Writers in this Supplement includes forty-eight authors explications of whose works appear in this bibliography for the first time. In cases where explications have been reprinted since the second edition of <u>Twentieth-Century Short Story Explication</u>, the original entry has been repeated in this Supplement to provide full documentation.

The term <u>short story</u> here has the same meaning it carries in the Wilson Company's <u>Short Story Index</u>: "... a brief narrative of not more than 150 average-size pages." By <u>explication</u> I suggest simply interpretation or explanation of the meaning of a story, including observations on theme, symbol, and structure. This excludes from the bibliography what are primarily studies of sources, biographical data, and background materials. Occasionally there are explicatory passages cited in works otherwise devoted to one of these external considerations.

Entries are as nearly complete as space will permit. The abbreviations for titles of journals are, wherever possible, those used in the Wilson indexes. The dates listed for the periodical entries are limited to the year dates only for those journals paged continuously throughout a volume; for those paged anew with each issue the complete date (quarter or month, and day where needed) is provided.

Where a volume paged continuously spans two calendar
years, the only year date given is the one applicable to the
pages listed in the particular entry. For all journal entries,
the pages cited indicate only the explicatory passages, not
the total lengths of the articles.

   I am indebted to several other scholarly works for
leads, especially to Abstracts of English Studies and to the
bibliographies that appear in Modern Fiction Studies and
PMLA. To well over 100 American publishers I wish to
express appreciation for their willingness to lend me copies
of their new books; to the reference librarians at Texas
Tech University Library, my gratitude for their patient
pursuit of elusive journals. I wish also to acknowledge the
encouragement and assistance of my wife, Barbara K.
Walker, in bringing this project to completion.

                         Warren S. Walker
                         Texas Technological University

JAMES AGEE

"The Morning Watch"
   Phillipson, J. S. "Character, Theme, and Symbol in
      'The Morning Watch,'" Western Hum R, XV (Autumn,
      1961), 359–367.

   Seib, Kenneth. James Agee: Promise and Fulfillment
      (Pittsburgh: Univ. of Pittsburgh Press, 1968), 69–73.

"A Mother's Tale"
   Seib, Kenneth. James Agee: Promise and Fulfillment
      (Pittsburgh: Univ. of Pittsburgh Press, 1968), 66–69.

"Six Days at Sea"
   Seib, Kenneth. James Agee: Promise and Fulfillment
      (Pittsburgh: Univ. of Pittsburgh Press, 1968), 62–66.

"The Waiting"
   Mizener, Arthur. A Handbook for Use with "Modern
      Short Stories: The Uses of Imagination, Revised Edi-
      tion" (New York: Norton, 1966), 88–90.

SCHMUEL YOSEF AGNON

"Agunot"
   Band, Arnold J. Nostalgia and Nightmare: A Study in
      the Fiction of S. Y. Agnon (Berkeley: Univ. of Cali-
      fornia Press, 1968), 57–63.

"And the Crooked Shall Become Straight"
   Band, Arnold J. Nostalgia and Nightmare: A Study in
      the Fiction of S. Y. Agnon (Berkeley: Univ. of Cali-
      fornia Press, 1968), 83–92.

"The Ascent of the Soul"
   Band, Arnold J. Nostalgia and Nightmare: A Study in
      the Fiction of S. Y. Agnon (Berkeley: Univ. of Cali-
      fornia Press, 1968), 80–81.

1

"Ascents and Descents"
> Band, Arnold J. Nostalgia and Nightmare: A Study in the Fiction of S. Y. Agnon (Berkeley: Univ. of California Press, 1968), 106–107.

"At the Death of Tsadik"
> Band, Arnold J. Nostalgia and Nightmare: A Study in the Fiction of S. Y. Agnon (Berkeley: Univ. of California Press, 1968), 280–281.

"At the Entrance of the Day"
> Band, Arnold J. Nostalgia and Nightmare: A Study in the Fiction of S. Y. Agnon (Berkeley: Univ. of California Press, 1968), 359–362.

"At Hemdat's"
> Band, Arnold J. Nostalgia and Nightmare: A Study in the Fiction of S. Y. Agnon (Berkeley: Univ. of California Press, 1968), 356–359.

"The Banished One"
> Band, Arnold J. Nostalgia and Nightmare: A Study in the Fiction of S. Y. Agnon (Berkeley: Univ. of California Press, 1968), 96–99.

"Beneath the Tree"
> Band, Arnold J. Nostalgia and Nightmare: A Study in the Fiction of S. Y. Agnon (Berkeley: Univ. of California Press, 1968), 277–278.

"The Betrothal Oath"
> Band, Arnold J. Nostalgia and Nightmare: A Study in the Fiction of S. Y. Agnon (Berkeley: Univ. of California Press, 367–382.

"The Candles"
> Band, Arnold J. Nostalgia and Nightmare: A Study in the Fiction of S. Y. Agnon (Berkeley: Univ. of California Press, 1968), 202–204.

"The Dead Child"
Band, Arnold J. Nostalgia and Nightmare: A Study in
the Fiction of S. Y. Agnon (Berkeley: Univ. of California Press, 1968), 271–272.

"A Different Face"
Band, Arnold J. Nostalgia and Nightmare: A Study in
the Fiction of S. Y. Agnon (Berkeley: Univ. of California Press, 1968), 257–260.

"A Different Talit"
Band, Arnold J. Nostalgia and Nightmare: A Study in
the Fiction of S. Y. Agnon (Berkeley: Univ. of California Press, 1968), 341–342.

"The Doctor and His Divorcée"
Band, Arnold J. Nostalgia and Nightmare: A Study in
the Fiction of S. Y. Agnon (Berkeley: Univ. of California Press, 1968), 254–257.

"The Document"
Band, Arnold J. Nostalgia and Nightmare: A Study in
the Fiction of S. Y. Agnon (Berkeley: Univ. of California Press, 1968), 209–210.

"Eternal Peace"
Band, Arnold J. Nostalgia and Nightmare: A Study in
the Fiction of S. Y. Agnon (Berkeley: Univ. of California Press, 1968), 411–412.

"The Face of the Face"
Band, Arnold J. Nostalgia and Nightmare: A Study in
the Fiction of S. Y. Agnon (Berkeley: Univ. of California Press, 1968), 331–333.

"Fathers and Sons"
Band, Arnold J. Nostalgia and Nightmare: A Study in
the Fiction of S. Y. Agnon (Berkeley: Univ. of California Press, 1968), 216–217.

"Fernheim"
Band, Arnold J. Nostalgia and Nightmare: A Study in
the Fiction of S. Y. Agnon (Berkeley: Univ. of California Press, 1968), 396–398.

"Friendship"
Band, Arnold J. Nostalgia and Nightmare: A Study in
the Fiction of S. Y. Agnon (Berkeley: Univ. of California Press, 1968), 206–209.

"From Dwelling to Dwelling"
Band, Arnold J. Nostalgia and Nightmare: A Study in
the Fiction of S. Y. Agnon (Berkeley: Univ. of California Press, 1968), 220–221.

"From Heaven"
Band, Arnold J. Nostalgia and Nightmare: A Study in
the Fiction of S. Y. Agnon (Berkeley: Univ. of California Press, 1968), 275–276.

"The Garment"
Band, Arnold J. Nostalgia and Nightmare: A Study in
the Fiction of S. Y. Agnon (Berkeley: Univ. of California Press, 1968), 405–406.

"Hemdat"
Band, Arnold J. Nostalgia and Nightmare: A Study in
the Fiction of S. Y. Agnon (Berkeley: Univ. of California Press, 1968), 364–366.

"The Home"
Band, Arnold J. Nostalgia and Nightmare: A Study in
the Fiction of S. Y. Agnon (Berkeley: Univ. of California Press, 1968), 217–220.

"Honoring Father"
Band, Arnold J. Nostalgia and Nightmare: A Study in
the Fiction of S. Y. Agnon (Berkeley: Univ. of California Press, 1968), 274–275.

"Ido and Enam"
> Band, Arnold J. Nostalgia and Nightmare: A Study in
> the Fiction of S. Y. Agnon (Berkeley: Univ. of Cali-
> fornia Press, 1968), 382–396.

"In the Forest and in the City"
> Band, Arnold J. Nostalgia and Nightmare: A Study in
> the Fiction of S. Y. Agnon (Berkeley: Univ. of Cali-
> fornia Press, 1968), 234–237.

"In the Heart of the Seas"
> Band, Arnold J. Nostalgia and Nightmare: A Study in
> the Fiction of S. Y. Agnon (Berkeley: Univ. of Cali-
> fornia Press, 1968), 262–270.

"In the Noontide of Her Day"
> Band, Arnold J. Nostalgia and Nightmare: A Study in
> the Fiction of S. Y. Agnon (Berkeley: Univ. of Cali-
> fornia Press, 1968), 115–118.

"The Kerchief"
> Band, Arnold J. Nostalgia and Nightmare: A Study in
> the Fiction of S. Y. Agnon (Berkeley: Univ. of Cali-
> fornia Press, 1968), 224–228.

"The Kidnappers"
> Band, Arnold J. Nostalgia and Nightmare: A Study in
> the Fiction of S. Y. Agnon (Berkeley: Univ. of Cali-
> fornia Press, 1968), 411.

"Kipurim"
> Band, Arnold J. Nostalgia and Nightmare: A Study in
> the Fiction of S. Y. Agnon (Berkeley: Univ. of Cali-
> fornia Press, 1968), 120–121.

"Knots"
> Band, Arnold J. Nostalgia and Nightmare: A Study in
> the Fiction of S. Y. Agnon (Berkeley: Univ. of Cali-
> fornia Press, 1968), 339–341.

"The Last Bus"
    Band, Arnold J. Nostalgia and Nightmare: A Study in
        the Fiction of S. Y. Agnon (Berkeley: Univ. of Cali-
        fornia Press, 1968), 204–206.

"Lawlessness"
    Band, Arnold J. Nostalgia and Nightmare: A Study in
        the Fiction of S. Y. Agnon (Berkeley: Univ. of Cali-
        fornia Press, 1968), 335–336.

"The Legend of the Scribe"
    Band, Arnold J. Nostalgia and Nightmare: A Study in
        the Fiction of S. Y. Agnon (Berkeley: Univ. of Cali-
        fornia Press, 1968), 109–113.

"The Letter"
    Band, Arnold J. Nostalgia and Nightmare: A Study in
        the Fiction of S. Y. Agnon (Berkeley: Univ. of Cali-
        fornia Press, 1968), 342–346.

"Like David They Fashioned Themselves Musical
Instruments"
    Band, Arnold J. Nostalgia and Nightmare: A Study in
        the Fiction of S. Y. Agnon (Berkeley: Univ. of Cali-
        fornia Press, 1968), 279–280.

"Miriam's Well"
    Band, Arnold J. Nostalgia and Nightmare: A Study in
        the Fiction of S. Y. Agnon (Berkeley: Univ. of Cali-
        fornia Press, 1968), 63–67.

"The Month of Tishre"
    Band, Arnold J. Nostalgia and Nightmare: A Study in
        the Fiction of S. Y. Agnon (Berkeley: Univ. of Cali-
        fornia Press, 1968), 68–73.

"Nights"
    Band, Arnold J. Nostalgia and Nightmare: A Study in
        the Fiction of S. Y. Agnon (Berkeley: Univ. of Cali-
        fornia Press, 1968), 74–75.

"Offerings for the Dead."
> Band, Arnold J. Nostalgia and Nightmare: A Study in the Fiction of S. Y. Agnon (Berkeley: Univ. of California Press, 1968), 76–77.

"On One Rock"
> Band, Arnold J. Nostalgia and Nightmare: A Study in the Fiction of S. Y. Agnon (Berkeley: Univ. of California Press, 1968), 228–229.

"On the Road"
> Band, Arnold J. Nostalgia and Nightmare: A Study in the Fiction of S. Y. Agnon (Berkeley: Univ. of California Press, 1968), 333–335.

"On the Tora"
> Band, Arnold J. Nostalgia and Nightmare: A Study in the Fiction of S. Y. Agnon (Berkeley: Univ. of California Press, 1968), 212–213.

"One Night"
> Band, Arnold J. Nostalgia and Nightmare: A Study in the Fiction of S. Y. Agnon (Berkeley: Univ. of California Press, 1968), 362–364.

"The Orchestra"
> Band, Arnold J. Nostalgia and Nightmare: A Study in the Fiction of S. Y. Agnon (Berkeley: Univ. of California Press, 1968), 336–339.

"Ovadia the Cripple"
> Band, Arnold J. Nostalgia and Nightmare: A Study in the Fiction of S. Y. Agnon (Berkeley: Univ. of California Press, 1968), 118–120.

"The Paths of Righteousness"
> Band, Arnold J. Nostalgia and Nightmare: A Study in the Fiction of S. Y. Agnon (Berkeley: Univ. of California Press, 1968), 104–105.

"The Sense of Smell"
    Band, Arnold J. <u>Nostalgia and Nightmare: A Study in
    the Fiction of S. Y. Agnon</u> (Berkeley: Univ. of Cali-
    fornia Press, 1968), 229–230.

"Sheepfolds"
    Band, Arnold J. <u>Nostalgia and Nightmare: A Study in
    the Fiction of S. Y. Agnon</u> (Berkeley: Univ. of Cali-
    fornia Press, 1968), 75–76.

"The Soil of Erets Yisrael"
    Band, Arnold J. <u>Nostalgia and Nightmare: A Study in
    the Fiction of S. Y. Agnon</u> (Berkeley: Univ. of Cali-
    fornia Press, 1968), 230–234.

"The Song That Was Sung"
    Band, Arnold J. <u>Nostalgia and Nightmare: A Study in
    the Fiction of S. Y. Agnon</u> (Berkeley: Univ. of Cali-
    fornia Press, 1968), 221–222.

"The Tale of a Goat"
    Band, Arnold J. <u>Nostalgia and Nightmare: A Study in
    the Fiction of S. Y. Agnon</u> (Berkeley: Univ. of Cali-
    fornia Press, 1968), 103–104.

"Tehila"
    Band, Arnold J. <u>Nostalgia and Nightmare: A Study in
    the Fiction of S. Y. Agnon</u> (Berkeley: Univ. of Cali-
    fornia Press, 1968), 406–409.

"To Father's House"
    Band, Arnold J. <u>Nostalgia and Nightmare: A Study in
    the Fiction of S. Y. Agnon</u> (Berkeley: Univ. of Cali-
    fornia Press, 1968), 210–212.

"To the Doctor"
    Band, Arnold J. <u>Nostalgia and Nightmare: A Study in
    the Fiction of S. Y. Agnon</u> (Berkeley: Univ. of Cali-
    fornia Press, 1968), 201–202.

"Twofold"
Band, Arnold J. Nostalgia and Nightmare: A Study in
the Fiction of S. Y. Agnon (Berkeley: Univ. of California Press, 1968), 213–216.

"A Whole Loaf"
Band, Arnold J. Nostalgia and Nightmare: A Study in
the Fiction of S. Y. Agnon (Berkeley: Univ. of California Press, 1968), 189–201.

"With Our Youth and With Our Aged"
Band, Arnold J. Nostalgia and Nightmare: A Study in
the Fiction of S. Y. Agnon (Berkeley: Univ. of California Press, 1968), 121–125.

ILSE AICHINGER

"The Bound Man"
Bedwell, Carol B. "Who Is the Bound Man? Toward an
Interpretation of Ilse Aichinger's 'Der Gefesselte,'"
Germ Q, XXXVIII (1956), 30–37.

"Eliza, Eliza"
Lübbren, Rainer. "Die Sprache der Bilder: Zu Ilse
Aichingers 'Eliza, Eliza,'" Neue Rundschau, LXXVI
(1965), 626–636.

"Spiegelgeschichte"
Bedwell, Carol. "The Ambivalent Image in Aichinger's
'Spiegelgeschichte,'" R Langues Vivantes, XXXIII
(1967), 362–363.

SHERWOOD ANDERSON

"Adventure"
Fussell, Edwin. "Winesburg, Ohio: Art and Isolation,"
Mod Fiction Stud, VI (1960), 111; reprinted in White,
Ray L., Ed. The Achievement of Sherwood Ander-

son: Essays in Criticism (Chapel Hill: Univ. of
North Carolina Press, 1966), 109; Ferres, John
H., Ed. Winesburg, Ohio: Text and Criticism (New
York: Viking, 1966), 392–393.

Joselyn, Sister M. "Sherwood Anderson and the Lyric
Story," in Langford, Richard, and William E. Taylor,
Eds. The Twenties: Poetry and Prose (Deland:
Everett Edwards, 1966), 72; reprinted in Ferres,
John H., Ed. Winesburg, Ohio: Text and Criticism
(New York: Viking, 1966), 450.

"The Book of the Grotesque"

Anderson, David D. "The Grotesques and George Willard," in Ferres, John H., Ed. Winesburg, Ohio:
Text and Criticism (New York: Viking, 1966), 421–
423; reprinted, with changes, in his Sherwood Anderson: An Introduction and Interpretation (New York:
Holt, Rinehart & Winston, 1967), 40–41.

Epifanio, San Juan. "Vision and Reality: A Reconsid-
eration of Sherwood Anderson's Winesburg, Ohio,"
Am Lit, XXXV (1963), 138–139; reprinted in Ferres,
John H., Ed. Winesburg, Ohio: Text and Criticism
(New York: Viking, 1966), 469–470.

Trilling, Lionel. "Sherwood Anderson," Kenyon R,
III (1941), 296–298; reprinted in his The Liberal
Imagination (New York: Viking, 1950), 26–28; An-
chor edition (New York: Doubleday, 1958), 37–38;
Aldridge, John W., Ed. Critiques and Essays on
Modern Fiction, 1920–1951 (New York: Ronald,
1952), 322–323; Revue des Lettres Modernes, Nos.
78–80 (1963), 15–17; Matlaw, Myron, and Leonard
Lief, Eds. Story and Critic (New York: Harper &
Row, 1963), 175–176; White, Ray L., Ed. The
Achievement of Sherwood Anderson: Essays in
Criticism (Chapel Hill: Univ. of North Carolina
Press, 1966), 216–217; Ferres, John H., Ed. Wines-
burg, Ohio: Text and Criticism (New York: Viking,
1966), 460–461.

"Death in the Woods"
 Guerin, Wilfred L. "'Death in the Woods': Sherwood
  Anderson's 'Cold Pastoral,'" Coll Engl Assoc Critic,
  XXX (May, 1968), 4–5.
 Joselyn, Sister Mary. "Some Artistic Dimensions of
  Sherwood Anderson's 'Death in the Woods,'" Stud
  Short Fiction, IV (1967), 252–259.

"Departure"
 Gold, Herbert. "The Purity and Cunning of Sherwood
  Anderson," Hudson R, X (1957), 553; reprinted in
  his The Age of Happy Problems (New York: Dial,
  1962), 62–63; Shapiro, Charles, Ed. Twelve Origi-
  nal Essays on Great American Novels (Detroit:
  Wayne State Univ. Press, 1958), 203; Ferres, John
  H., Ed. Winesburg, Ohio: Text and Criticism (New
  York: Viking, 1966), 399.

"Drink"
 Epifanio, San Juan. "Vision and Reality: A Reconsid-
  eration of Sherwood Anderson's Winesburg, Ohio,"
  Am Lit, XXXV (1963), 140–141.

"The Egg"
 Anderson, David D. Sherwood Anderson: An Introduc-
  tion and Interpretation (New York: Holt, Rinehart &
  Winston, 1967), 64–65.
 Mizener, Arthur, Ed. Modern Short Stories: The Uses
  of Imagination, Revised edition (New York: Norton,
  1967), 427–430.
 ————. A Handbook for Use with "Modern Short
  Stories: The Uses of Imagination, Revised Edition"
  (New York: Norton, 1966), 114–116.
 West, Michael D. "Sherwood Anderson's Triumph:
  'The Egg,'" Am Q, XX (1968), 675–693.

"Godliness"
 Anderson, David D. Sherwood Anderson: An Introduc-
  tion and Interpretation (New York: Holt, Rinehart &
  Winston, 1967), 45–46.

Laughlin, Rosemary M. "'Godliness' and the American Dream in Winesburg, Ohio," Twentieth-Century Lit, XIII (1967), 97–103.

Walcutt, Charles C. "Sherwood Anderson: Impressionism and the Buried Life," Sewanee R, LX (1952), 34–35; reprinted in his American Literary Naturalism, A Divided Stream (Minneapolis: Univ. of Minnesota Press, 1956), 227–228; Revue des Lettres Modernes, Nos. 78–80 (1963), 77–78; Ferres, John H., Ed. Winesburg, Ohio: Text and Criticism (New York: Viking, 1966), 436–437.

"Hands"

Anderson, David D. "The Grotesques and George Willard," in Ferres, John H., Ed. Winesburg, Ohio: Text and Criticism (New York: Viking, 1966), 424–425; reprinted, with changes, in his Sherwood Anderson: An Introduction and Interpretation (New York: Holt, Rinehart & Winston, 1967), 42.

Joselyn, Sister M. "Sherwood Anderson and the Lyric Story," in Langford, Richard, and William E. Taylor, Eds. The Twenties: Poetry and Prose (Deland: Everett Edwards, 1966), 71–72; Ferres, John H., Ed. Winesburg, Ohio: Text and Criticism (New York: Viking, 1966), 448–449.

"I'm a Fool"

Anderson, David D. Sherwood Anderson: An Introduction and Interpretation (New York: Holt, Rinehart & Winston, 1967), 71–73.

Dietrich, R. F., and Roger H. Sundell. Instructor's Manual for "The Art of Fiction" (New York: Holt, Rinehart & Winston, 1967), 47–53.

Walcutt, Charles C. "Sherwood Anderson: Impressionism and the Buried Life," Sewanee R, LX (1952), 39–40; reprinted in his American Literary Naturalism, A Divided Stream (Minneapolis: Univ. of Minnesota Press, 1956), 233; Revue des Lettres Modernes, Nos. 78–80 (1963), 84–85; Ferres, John H., Ed. Winesburg, Ohio: Text and Criticism (New York: Viking, 1966), 442.

"I Want to Know Why"
    Anderson, David D. Sherwood Anderson: An Introduc-
        tion and Interpretation (New York: Holt, Rinehart &
        Winston, 1967), 62–63.
    Rees, Robert A., and Barry Menikoff. A Manual to Ac-
        company "The Short Story: An Introductory Anthol-
        ogy" (Boston: Little, Brown, 1969), 10–11.

"Loneliness"
    Gold, Herbert. "The Purity and Cunning of Sherwood
        Anderson," Hudson R, X (1957), 551–552; reprinted
        in his The Age of Happy Problems (New York: Dial,
        1962), 61–62; Shapiro, Charles, Ed. Twelve Origi-
        nal Essays on Great American Novels (Detroit:
        Wayne State Univ. Press, 1958), 202–203; Ferres,
        John H., Ed. Winesburg, Ohio: Text and Criticism
        (New York: Viking, 1966), 398–399.

"A Man of Ideas"
    Epifanio, San Juan. "Vision and Reality: A Reconsid-
        eration of Sherwood Anderson's Winesburg, Ohio,"
        Am Lit, XXXV (1963), 151–152; reprinted in Ferres,
        John H., Ed. Winesburg, Ohio: Text and Criticism
        (New York: Viking, 1966), 478–479.

"The Man Who Became a Woman"
    Anderson, David D. Sherwood Anderson: An Introduc-
        tion and Interpretation (New York: Holt, Rinehart &
        Winston, 1967), 75–77.
    Gold, Herbert. "The Purity and Cunning of Sherwood
        Anderson," Hudson R, X (1957), 551–552; reprinted
        in his The Age of Happy Problems (New York: Dial,
        1962), 61; Shapiro, Charles, Ed. Twelve Original
        Essays on Great American Novels (Detroit: Wayne
        State Univ. Press, 1958), 201; Ferres, John H., Ed.
        Winesburg, Ohio: Text and Criticism (New York:
        Viking, 1966), 397–398.

"Mother"
   Anderson, David D. "The Grotesques and George Wil-
      lard," in Ferres, John H., Ed. Winesburg, Ohio:
      Text and Criticism (New York: Viking, 1966), 426–
      427; reprinted, with changes, in his Sherwood An-
      derson: An Introduction and Interpretation (New
      York: Holt, Rinehart & Winston, 1967), 43–44.

"Paper Pills"
   Anderson, David D. "The Grotesques and George Wil-
      lard," in Ferres, John H., Ed. Winesburg, Ohio:
      Text and Criticism (New York: Viking, 1966), 425–
      426; reprinted, with changes, in his Sherwood An-
      derson: An Introduction and Interpretation (New
      York: Holt, Rinehart & Winston, 1967), 42–43.
   Epifanio, San Juan. "Vision and Reality: A Recon-
      sideration of Sherwood Anderson's Winesburg,
      Ohio," Am Lit, XXXV (1963), 140–141; reprinted
      in Ferres, John H., Ed. Winesburg, Ohio: Text
      and Criticism (New York: Viking, 1966), 469–470.

"The Philosopher"
   Epifanio, San Juan. "Vision and Reality: A Reconsid-
      eration of Sherwood Anderson's Winesburg, Ohio,"
      Am Lit, XXXV (1963), 139–140; reprinted in Ferres,
      John H., Ed. Winesburg, Ohio: Text and Criticism
      (New York: Viking, 1966), 470–471.

"Queer"
   Anderson, David D. "The Grotesques and George Wil-
      lard," in Ferres, John H., Ed. Winesburg, Ohio:
      Text and Criticism (New York: Viking, 1966), 429–
      430; reprinted, with changes, in his Sherwood An-
      derson: An Introduction and Interpretation (New
      York: Holt, Rinehart & Winston, 1967), 48.
   Howe, Irving. "The Book of the Grotesque," Partisan
      R, XVIII (1951), 37–38; reprinted in his Sherwood
      Anderson (New York: William Sloane, 1951), 104–
      105; Westbrook, Max, Ed. The American Novel:
      Essays in Criticism (New York: Random House,

1966), 42–43; White, Ray L., Ed. The Achievement
of Sherwood Anderson: Essays in Criticism (Chapel
Hill: Univ. of North Carolina Press, 1966), 99; Fer-
res, John H., Ed. Winesburg, Ohio: Text and Criti-
cism (New York: Viking, 1966), 416–417.
————— "Sherwood Anderson, Winesburg, Ohio," in
Stegner, Wallace, Ed. The American Novel from
James Fenimore Cooper to William Faulkner (New
York: Basic Books, 1965), 162.

"Sophistication"
    Fussell, Edwin. "'Winesburg, Ohio': Art and Isolation,"
      Mod Fiction Stud, VI (1960), 112–113; reprinted in
      White, Ray L., Ed. The Achievement of Sherwood
      Anderson (Chapel Hill: Univ. of North Carolina Press,
      1966), 112–113; Ferres, John H., Ed. Winesburg,
      Ohio: Text and Criticism (New York: Viking, 1966),
      392–394.
    Joselyn, Sister M. "Sherwood Anderson and the Lyric
      Story," in Langford, Richard, and William E. Tay-
      lor, Eds. The Twenties: Poetry and Prose (Deland:
      Everett Edwards, 1966), 72; reprinted in Ferres,
      John H., Ed. Winesburg, Ohio: Text and Criticism
      (New York: Viking, 1966), 451.
    Walcutt, Charles C. "Sherwood Anderson: Impression-
      ism and the Buried Life," Sewanee R, LX (1952),
      37–38; reprinted in his American Literary Natural-
      ism, A Divided Stream (Minneapolis: Univ. of Min-
      nesota Press, 1956), 230–231; Revue des Lettres
      Modernes, Nos. 78–80 (1963), 81–82; White, Ray L.,
      Ed. The Achievement of Sherwood Anderson: Es-
      says in Criticism (Chapel Hill: Univ. of North Caro-
      lina Press, 1966), 163–164; Ferres, John H., Ed.
      Winesburg, Ohio: Text and Criticism (New York:
      Viking, 1966), 439–440.

"The Teacher"
    Walcutt, Charles C. "Sherwood Anderson: Impres-
      sionism and the Buried Life," Sewanee R, LX (1952),

35–36; reprinted in his American Literary Naturalism, A Divided Stream (Minneapolis: Univ. of Minnesota Press, 1956), 229–230; Revue des Lettres
Modernes, Nos. 78–80 (1963), 79–80; White, Ray L.,
Ed. The Achievement of Sherwood Anderson: Essays in Criticism (Chapel Hill: Univ. of North Carolina Press, 1966), 162–163; Ferres, John H., Ed.
Winesburg, Ohio: Text and Criticism (New York:
Viking, 1966), 438–439.

"The Thinker"
Epifanio, San Juan. "Vision and Reality: A Reconsid-
eration of Sherwood Anderson's Winesburg, Ohio,"
Am Lit, XXXV (1963), 150–151; reprinted in Ferres,
John H., Ed. Winesburg, Ohio: Text and Criticism
(New York: Viking, 1966), 477.
Joselyn, Sister M. "Sherwood Anderson and the Lyric
Story," in Langford, Richard, and William E. Tay-
lor, Eds. The Twenties: Poetry and Prose (Deland:
Everett Edwards, 1966), 72–73; reprinted in Ferres,
John H., Ed. Winesburg, Ohio: Text and Criticism
(New York: Viking, 1966), 451–452.
Walcutt, Charles C. "Sherwood Anderson: Impres-
sionism and the Buried Life," Sewanee R, LX (1952),
35–36; reprinted in his American Literary Natural-
ism, A Divided Stream (Minneapolis: Univ. of Min-
nesota Press, 1956), 228–229; Revue des Lettres
Modernes, Nos. 78–80 (1963), 79; White, Ray L., Ed.
The Achievement of Sherwood Anderson: Essays in
Criticism (Chapel Hill: Univ. of North Carolina
Press, 1966), 162; Ferres, John H., Ed. Winesburg,
Ohio: Text and Criticism (New York: Viking, 1966),
437–438.

"The Triumph of the Modern"
Anderson, David D. Sherwood Anderson: An Introduc-
tion and Interpretation (New York: Holt, Rinehart &
Winston, 1967), 73–74.

"The Untold Lie"
>   Gold, Herbert. "The Purity and Cunning of Sherwood
>   Anderson," Hudson R, X (1957), 551; reprinted in
>   his The Age of Happy Problems (New York: Dial,
>   1962), 60; Shapiro, Charles, Ed. Twelve Original
>   Essays on Great American Novels (Detroit: Wayne
>   State Univ. Press, 1958), 201; Ferres, John H., Ed.
>   Winesburg, Ohio: Text and Criticism (New York:
>   Viking, 1966), 397.
>   Thurston, Jarvis. "Anderson and 'Winesburg': Mysti-
>   cism and Craft," Accent, XVI (1956), 119–120; re-
>   printed in Ferres, John H., Ed. Winesburg, Ohio:
>   Text and Criticism (New York: Viking, 1966), 332–
>   333.

MARY AUSTIN

"The Bandit's Prayer"
>   Robinson, Cecil. With the Ears of Strangers: The
>   Mexican in American Literature (Tucson: Univ. of
>   Arizona Press, 1963), 232–233.

ISAAC BABEL

"Di Grasso"
>   Trilling, Lionel. The Experience of Literature (New
>   York: Holt, Rinehart & Winston, 1967), 713–715.

"In Odessa"
>   Frakes, James, and Isadore Traschen, Eds. Short
>   Fiction: A Critical Collection (Englewood Cliffs:
>   Prentice-Hall, 1959), 55–57; Second edition (1969),
>   53–55.

JAMES BALDWIN

"This Morning, This Evening, So Soon"
  Hagopian, John V. "This Morning, This Evening, So
    Soon," in Hagopian, John V., and Martin Dolch, Eds.
    Insight I: Analyses of American Literature (Frank-
    furt: Hirschgraben, 1962), 14–22; reprinted in Coll
    Lang Assoc J, VII (1963), 133–140; McKenzie, Bar-
    bara, Ed. The Process of Fiction (New York: Har-
    court, Brace & World, 1969), 451–456.

HONORÉ DE BALZAC

"Gambara"
  Citron, Jean-Pierre. "'Gambara,' Strunz et Beethoven,"
    Année Balzacienne (1967), 165–170.
  Pugh, Anthony R. "Balzac's Beethoven: A Note on
    'Gambara,'" Romance Notes, VIII (1966), 43–46.

"Gobseck"
  Cherry, Adrian. "Balzac's 'Gobseck': A Character
    Study of a Usurer," Lang Q, V, i–ii (1967), 5–14.

"La Grande Bretèche"
  Godin, Henri. "Le cadran solaire de 'La Grande
    Bretèche,'" Année Balzacienne (1967), 346–349.

"The Vicar of Tours"
  Hoffman, Leon-François. "Eros en filigraine: 'Le
    curé de Tours,'" Année Balzacienne (1967), 89–105.
  Jean-Bérard, Suzanne. "Encore la maison du 'Curé de
    Tours,'" Année Balzacienne (1968), 197–210.

BARBEY d'AUREVILLY

"Le Cachet d'onyx"
  Rogers, Brian G. "Two Short Stories by Barbey d'Aure-
    villy," Mod Lang R, LX (1965), 516–519.

"Lea"
   Rogers, Brian G. "Two Short Stories by Barbey
      d'Aurevilly," Mod Lang R, LX (1965), 516–519.

SAMUEL BECKETT

"L'Calamant"
   Federman, Raymond. Journey into Chaos: Samuel
      Beckett's Early Fiction (Berkeley: Univ. of Cali-
      fornia Press, 1965), 179–180, 191–192.

"Dante and the Lobster"
   Federman, Raymond. Journey into Chaos: Samuel
      Beckett's Early Fiction (Berkeley: Univ. of Cali-
      fornia Press, 1965), 51–52.

"L'Expulsé"
   Federman, Raymond. Journey into Chaos: Samuel
      Beckett's Early Fiction (Berkeley: Univ. of Cali-
      fornia Press, 1965), 186–187.

"La Fin"
   Federman, Raymond. Journey into Chaos: Samuel
      Beckett's Early Fiction (Berkeley: Univ. of Cali-
      fornia Press, 1965), 180–181, 190–191.

"Love and Lethe"
   Federman, Raymond. Journey into Chaos: Samuel
      Beckett's Early Fiction (Berkeley: Univ. of Cali-
      fornia Press, 1965), 45–46.

"Premier Amour"
   Federman, Raymond. Journey into Chaos: Samuel
      Beckett's Early Fiction (Berkeley: Univ. of Cali-
      fornia Press, 1965), 178–179.

"A Wet Night"
   Federman, Raymond. Journey into Chaos: Samuel
      Beckett's Early Fiction (Berkeley: Univ. of Cali-
      fornia Press, 1965), 37–38.

"What a Misfortune"
    Federman, Raymond. Journey into Chaos: Samuel
       Beckett's Early Fiction (Berkeley: Univ. of Cali-
       fornia Press, 1965), 49–50.

SAUL BELLOW

"Address by Gooley MacDowell to the Hasbeens Club of
Chicago"
    Tanner, Tony. Saul Bellow (Edinburgh: Oliver and
       Boyd, 1965), 39–41; American edition (New York:
       Barnes & Noble, 1965), 39–41.

"A Father-to-Be"
    Clayton, John J. Saul Bellow: In Defense of Man
       (Bloomington: Indiana Univ. Press, 1968), 54–56.
    Demarest, David P. "The Theme of Discontinuity in
       Saul Bellow's Fiction: 'Looking for Mr. Green' and
       'A Father-to-Be,'" Stud Short Fiction, VI (1969),
       181–185.
    Freedman, Ralph. "Saul Bellow: The Illusion of En-
       vironment," Wisconsin Stud Contemporary Lit, I
       (1960), 57; reprinted in Malin, Irving, Ed. Saul
       Bellow and the Critics (New York: New York Univ.
       Press, 1967), 59–60.
    Tanner, Tony. Saul Bellow (Edinburgh: Oliver and
       Boyd, 1965), 59–60; American edition (New York:
       Barnes & Noble, 1965), 59–60.

"The Gonzaga Manuscripts"
    Clayton, John J. Saul Bellow: In Defense of Man
       (Bloomington: Indiana Univ. Press, 1968), 13–14.
    Tanner, Tony. Saul Bellow (Edinburgh: Oliver and
       Boyd, 1965), 61; American edition (New York:
       Barnes & Noble, 1965), 61.

"Looking for Mr. Green"
    Clayton, John J. Saul Bellow: In Defense of Man
       (Bloomington: Indiana Univ. Press, 1968), 21–22.

Demarest, David P. "The Theme of Discontinuity in
Saul Bellow's Fiction: 'Looking for Mr. Green' and
'A Father-to-Be,'" Stud Short Fiction, VI (1969),
176–181.
Tanner, Tony. Saul Bellow (Edinburgh: Oliver and
Boyd, 1965), 60–61; American edition (New York:
Barnes & Noble, 1965), 60–61.

"Seize the Day"
Chase, Richard. "The Adventures of Saul Bellow: The
Progress of a Novelist," Commentary, XXVII (1959),
326–327; reprinted in Malin, Irving, Ed. Saul Bel-
low and the Critics (New York: New York Univ. Press,
1967), 30–33.
Clayton, John J. Saul Bellow: In Defense of Man (Bloom-
ington: Indiana Univ. Press, 1968), 69–74, 128–134.
Davis, Robert G. "The American Individualist Tradi-
tion: Bellow and Styron," in Balakian, Nona, and
Charles Simmons, Eds. The Creative Present
(Garden City: Doubleday, 1963), 124–127.
Fiedler, Leslie. "Saul Bellow," Prairie Schooner,
XXXI (1957), 108; reprinted in Malin, Irving, Ed.
Saul Bellow and the Critics (New York: New York
Univ. Press, 1967), 7–8.
Fossum, Robert H. "The Devil and Saul Bellow," in
Panichas, George A., Ed. Mansions of the Spirit:
Essays in Literature and Religion (New York: Haw-
thorn, 1967), 349–353.
Freedman, Ralph. "Saul Bellow: The Illusion of En-
vironment," Wisconsin Stud Contemporary Lit, I
(1960), 55–57; reprinted in Malin, Irving, Ed.
Saul Bellow and the Critics (New York: New York
Univ. Press, 1967), 57–59.
Galloway, David D. "The Absurd Man as Picaro: The
Novels of Saul Bellow," Texas Stud Lit & Lang, VI
(1964), 241–244; reprinted in his The Absurd Hero
in American Fiction (Austin: Univ. of Texas Press,
1966), 104–110.

Geismar, Maxwell. American Moderns: From Rebel-
    lion to Conformity (New York: Hill & Wang, 1958),
    218–223; reprinted in Malin, Irving, Ed. Saul Bel-
    low and the Critics (New York: New York Univ.
    Press, 1967), 19–23.
Hall, James. The Lunatic Giant in the Drawing Room
    (Bloomington: Indiana Univ. Press, 1968), 159–163.
Harper, Howard M. Desperate Faith (Chicago: Univ.
    of Chicago Press, 1967), 32–39.
Hassan, Ihab. "Five Faces of a Hero," Critique, III
    (Summer, 1960), 31–32.
Howe, Irving, Ed. Classics of Modern Fiction (New
    York: Harcourt, Brace & World, 1968), 457–466.
Levenson, J. C. "Bellow's Dangling Men," Critique,
    III (Summer, 1960), 8–10; reprinted in Malin, Irving,
    Ed. Saul Bellow and the Critics (New York: New
    York Univ. Press, 1967), 44–46.
Morrow, Patrick. "Threat and Accommodation: The
    Novels of Saul Bellow," Midwest Q, VIII (1967),
    391–394.
Schulz, Max F. Radical Sophistication: Studies in Con-
    temporary Jewish-American Novelists (Athens: Ohio
    Univ. Press, 1969), 120–126.
Stock, Irvin. "The Novels of Saul Bellow," Southern R,
    III (1967), 27–31.
Tanner, Tony. Saul Bellow (Edinburgh: Oliver and
    Boyd, 1965), 61–70; American edition (New York:
    Barnes & Noble, 1965), 61–70.
Trachtenberg, Stanley. "Saul Bellow's Luftmenschen:
    The Compromise with Reality," Critique, IX, iii
    (1967), 49–52.
Trowbridge, Clinton W. "Water Imagery in 'Seize the
    Day,'" Critique, IX, iii (1967), 62–73.
Weiss, Daniel. "Caliban on Prospero: A Psychoanalytic
    Study on the Novel 'Seize the Day,' by Saul Bellow,"
    Am Imago, XIX (1962), 277–306; reprinted in Malin,
    Irving, Ed. Psychoanalysis and American Fiction
    (New York: Dutton, 1965), 279–307; Malin, Irving,
    Ed. Saul Bellow and the Critics (New York: New
    York Univ. Press, 1967), 114–141.

"A Sermon by Doctor Pep"
Tanner, Tony. Saul Bellow (Edinburgh: Oliver and
Boyd, 1965), 38–39; American edition (New York:
Barnes & Noble, 1965), 38–39.

STEPHEN VINCENT BENÉT

"The Devil and Daniel Webster"
Walsh, Thomas F. "The 'Noon Wine' Devils," Georgia
R, XXII (1968), 90–96.

WERNER BERGENGRUEN

"Die Wunderbare Schreibmaschine"
Bedwell, Carol B. "The Disappointing Miracle in Wer-
ner Bergengruen's 'Die Wunderbare Schreibmaschine,'"
Stud Short Fiction, V (1967), 12–17.

ITZHAK D. BERKOVITZ

"Cut Off"
Rabinovich, Isaiah. Major Trends in Modern Hebrew
Fiction, trans. M. Roston (Chicago: Univ. of Chicago
Press, 1968), 156–158.

"Feivka's Day of Judgment"
Rabinovich, Isaiah. Major Trends in Modern Hebrew
Fiction, trans. M. Roston (Chicago: Univ. of Chicago
Press, 1968), 150–156.

"The Uprooted"
Rabinovich, Isaiah. Major Trends in Modern Hebrew
Fiction, trans. M. Roston (Chicago: Univ. of Chicago
Press, 1968), 158–164.

AMBROSE BIERCE

"An Occurrence at Owl Creek Bridge"
Crane, John Kenny. "Crossing the Bar Twice: Post-
Mortem Consciousness in Bierce, Hemingway, and
Golding," Stud Short Fiction, VI (1969), 361–376.

HEINRICH BÖLL

"Christmas Every Day"
Frakes, James, and Isadore Traschen, Eds. Short
Fiction: A Critical Collection (Englewood Cliffs:
Prentice-Hall, 1959), 176–177; Second edition
(1969), 184–185.

"In the Valley of the Thundering Hooves"
Smith, G. Ralph. Review of 18 Stories, Stud Short
Fiction, IV (1967), 356–357.

"Murke's Collected Silences"
Sonnenfeld, Albert. "'They That Have Not Heard Shall
Understand': A Study of Heinrich Böll," in Mooney,
Harry J., and Thomas F. Staley, Eds. The Shape-
less God: Essays on Modern Fiction (Pittsburgh:
Univ. of Pittsburgh Press, 1968), 187–188.

JORGE L. BORGES

"Abenjacán the Bojarí, Dead in His Labyrinth"
Murillo, L. A. "The Labyrinths of Jorge Luis Borges,
An Introduction to the Stories of El Aleph," Mod
Lang Q, XX (1959), 262–263.
Wheelock, Carter. The Mythmaker: A Study of Motif
and Symbol in the Short Stories of Jorge Luis Borges
(Austin: Univ. of Texas Press, 1969), 165–168.

"The Aleph"
  Wheelock, Carter. The Mythmaker: A Study of Motif
    and Symbol in the Short Stories of Jorge Luis Borges
    (Austin: Univ. of Texas Press, 1969), 32–39.

"The Approach to Almotásim"
  Christ, Ronald. The Narrow Act: Borges' Art of Allu-
    sion (New York: New York Univ. Press, 1969), 94–
    130.
  Wheelock, Carter. The Mythmaker: A Study of Motif
    and Symbol in the Short Stories of Jorge Luis Borges
    (Austin: Univ. of Texas Press, 1969), 149–153.

"Averroes' Search"
  Wheelock, Carter. The Mythmaker: A Study of Motif
    and Symbol in the Short Stories of Jorge Luis Borges
    (Austin: Univ. of Texas Press, 1969), 156–158.

"The Babylonian Lottery"
  Isaacs, Neil D. "The Labyrinth of Art in Four 'Ficciones'
    of Jorge Luis Borges," Stud Short Fiction, VI (1969),
    383–386.
  Weber, Frances W. "Borges's Stories: Fiction and Phi-
    losophy," Hispanic R, XXXVI (1968), 130–132.
  Wheelock, Carter. The Mythmaker: A Study of Motif
    and Symbol in the Short Stories of Jorge Luis Borges
    (Austin: Univ. of Texas Press, 1969), 108–119.
  Zaniello, Thomas. "Outopia in Jorge Luis Borges'
    Fiction," Extrapolation, IX (1967), 9–11.

"Biography of Tadeo Isidoro Cruz"
  Wheelock, Carter. The Mythmaker: A Study of Motif
    and Symbol in the Short Stories of Jorge Luis Borges
    (Austin: Univ. of Texas Press, 1969), 155–156.

"The Circular Ruins"
  Wheelock, Carter. The Mythmaker: A Study of Motif
    and Symbol in the Short Stories of Jorge Luis Borges
    (Austin: Univ. of Texas Press, 1969), 48–53.

"The Cult of the Phoenix"
 Wheelock, Carter. The Mythmaker: A Study of Motif
   and Symbol in the Short Stories of Jorge Luis Borges
   (Austin: Univ. of Texas Press, 1969), 55–62.

"The Dead Man"
 Wheelock, Carter. The Mythmaker: A Study of Motif
   and Symbol in the Short Stories of Jorge Luis Borges
   (Austin: Univ. of Texas Press, 1969), 85–89.

"Death and the Compass"
 Murillo, L. A. The Cyclical Night: Irony in James
   Joyce and Jorge Luis Borges (Cambridge: Harvard
   Univ. Press, 1968), 187–194.
 Wheelock, Carter. The Mythmaker: A Study of Motif
   and Symbol in the Short Stories of Jorge Luis Borges
   (Austin: Univ. of Texas Press, 1969), 90–91.

"Deutsches Requiem"
 Wheelock, Carter. The Mythmaker: A Study of Motif
   and Symbol in the Short Stories of Jorge Luis Borges
   (Austin: Univ. of Texas Press, 1969), 160–164.

"Emma Zunz"
 Murillo, L. A. The Cyclical Night: Irony in James Joyce
   and Jorge Luis Borges (Cambridge: Harvard Univ.
   Press, 1968), 195–203.
 Wheelock, Carter. The Mythmaker: A Study of Motif
   and Symbol in the Short Stories of Jorge Luis Borges
   (Austin: Univ. of Texas Press, 1969), 139–143.

"The End"
 Wheelock, Carter. The Mythmaker: A Study of Motif
   and Symbol in the Short Stories of Jorge Luis Borges
   (Austin: Univ. of Texas Press, 1969), 98–102.

"Examination of the Work of Herbert Quain"
 Wheelock, Carter. The Mythmaker: A Study of Motif
   and Symbol in the Short Stories of Jorge Luis Borges
   (Austin: Univ. of Texas Press, 1969), 119–120.

"Funes the Memorious"
Hollander, Robert, and Sidney E. Lind, Eds. The Art
of the Story: An Introduction (New York: American
Book, 1968), 385–387.
Wheelock, Carter. The Mythmaker: A Study of Motif
and Symbol in the Short Stories of Jorge Luis Borges
(Austin: Univ. of Texas Press, 1969), 121–122.

"The Garden of Forking Paths"
Himelblau, Jack. "El arte de Jorge Luis Borges visto
en su 'El jardin de senderos que se bifurcan,'" Re-
vista Hispanica Moderna, XXXII (1966), 37–42.
Isaacs, Neil D. "The Labyrinth of Art in Four 'Fic-
ciones' of Jorge Luis Borges," Stud Short Fiction,
VI (1969), 392–394.
Murillo, L. A. The Cyclical Night: Irony in James
Joyce and Jorge Luis Borges (Cambridge: Harvard
Univ. Press, 1968), 135–184.
Weber, Frances W. "Borges's Stories: Fiction and
Philosophy," Hispanic R, XXXVI (1968), 135–138.
Wheelock, Carter. The Mythmaker: A Study of Motif
and Symbol in the Short Stories of Jorge Luis Borges
(Austin: Univ. of Texas Press, 1969), 119–121.

"The House of Asterion"
Wheelock, Carter. The Mythmaker: A Study of Motif
and Symbol in the Short Stories of Jorge Luis Borges
(Austin: Univ. of Texas Press, 1969), 147–149.

"The Immortal"
Christ, Ronald. The Narrow Act: Borges' Art of Allu-
sion (New York: New York Univ. Press, 1969), 192–
228.
Murillo, L. A. The Cyclical Night: Irony in James
Joyce and Jorge Luis Borges (Cambridge: Harvard
Univ. Press, 1968), 215–242.
Weber, Frances W. "Borges's Stories: Fiction and
Philosophy," Hispanic R, XXXVI (1968), 132–135.

Wheelock, Carter. The Mythmaker: A Study of Motif
and Symbol in the Short Stories of Jorge Luis Borges
(Austin: Univ. of Texas Press, 1969), 129–134.

"The Library of Babel"
Huck, Wilbur, and William Shanahan, Eds. The Mod-
ern Short Story (New York: American Book, 1968),
115–116.
Isaacs, Neil D. "The Labyrinth of Art in Four 'Fic-
ciones' of Jorge Luis Borges," Stud Short Fiction,
VI (1969), 386–387.
Janssens, Marcel. "Jorge Luis Borges en de biblio-
theek van Babel," Dietsche Warande en Belfort,
CXIII (1968), 216–220.
Wheelock, Carter. The Mythmaker: A Study of Motif
and Symbol in the Short Stories of Jorge Luis Borges
(Austin: Univ. of Texas Press, 1969), 158–160.
Zaniello, Thomas. "Outopia in Jorge Luis Borges'
Fiction," Extrapolation, IX (1967), 11–13.

"The Man on the Threshold"
Wheelock, Carter. The Mythmaker: A Study of Motif
and Symbol in the Short Stories of Jorge Luis Borges
(Austin: Univ. of Texas Press, 1969), 168–171.

"The Maker"
Wheelock, Carter. The Mythmaker: A Study of Motif
and Symbol in the Short Stories of Jorge Luis Borges
(Austin: Univ. of Texas Press, 1969), 177–178.

"The Other Death"
Wheelock, Carter. The Mythmaker: A Study of Motif
and Symbol in the Short Stories of Jorge Luis Borges
(Austin: Univ. of Texas Press, 1969), 174–175.

"The Parable of the Palace"
Zaniello, Thomas. "Outopia in Jorge Luis Borges' Fiction," Extrapolation, IX (1967), 7–9.

"The Secret Miracle"
   Wheelock, Carter. The Mythmaker: A Study of Motif
      and Symbol in the Short Stories of Jorge Luis Borges
      (Austin: Univ. of Texas Press, 1969), 143-147.

"The Shape of the Sword"
   Wheelock, Carter. The Mythmaker: A Study of Motif
      and Symbol in the Short Stories of Jorge Luis Borges
      (Austin: Univ. of Texas Press, 1969), 171-173.

"The South"
   Wheelock, Carter. The Mythmaker: A Study of Motif
      and Symbol in the Short Stories of Jorge Luis Borges
      (Austin: Univ. of Texas Press, 1969), 175-177.

"Theme of the Traitor and the Hero"
   Scholes, Robert. Elements of Fiction (New York: Ox-
      ford Univ. Press, 1968), 83-88.
   Wheelock, Carter. The Mythmaker: A Study of Motif
      and Symbol in the Short Stories of Jorge Luis Borges
      (Austin: Univ. of Texas Press, 1969), 173-174.

"The Theologians"
   Murillo, L. A. "The Labyrinths of Jorge Luis Borges,
      An Introduction to the Stories of El Aleph," Mod Lang
      Q, XX (1959), 263-264.
   Wheelock, Carter. The Mythmaker: A Study of Motif
      and Symbol in the Short Stories of Jorge Luis Borges
      (Austin: Univ. of Texas Press, 1969), 83-85.

"Three Versions of Judas"
   Wheelock, Carter. The Mythmaker: A Study of Motif
      and Symbol in the Short Stories of Jorge Luis Borges
      (Austin: Univ. of Texas Press, 1969), 164-165.

"Tlön, Uqbar, Orbis Tertius"
   Harss, Luis, and Barbara Dohmann. Into the Main-
      stream (New York: Harper & Row, 1967), 125-126.

Isaacs, Neil D. "The Labyrinth of Art in Four 'Fic-
ciones' of Jorge Luis Borges," Stud Short Fiction,
VI (1969), 387–392.
Weber, Frances W. "Borges's Stories: Fiction and
Philosophy," Hispanic R, XXXVI (1968), 127–130.
Wheelock, Carter. The Mythmaker: A Study of Motif
and Symbol in the Short Stories of Jorge Luis Borges
(Austin: Univ. of Texas Press, 1969), 93–98.
Zaniello, Thomas. "Outopia in Jorge Luis Borges' Fic-
tion," Extrapolation, IX (1967), 13–15.

"The Wait"
Wheelock, Carter. The Mythmaker: A Study of Motif and
Symbol in the Short Stories of Jorge Luis Borges
(Austin: Univ. of Texas Press, 1969), 134–139.

"The Writing of the Lord" [same as "The God's Script"]
Murillo, L. A. "The Labyrinths of Jorge Luis Borges,
An Introduction to the Stories of El Aleph," Mod
Lang Q, XX (1959), 264–266; expanded and reprinted
in his The Cyclical Night: Irony in James Joyce and
Jorge Luis Borges (Cambridge: Harvard Univ. Press,
1968), 203–213.
Wheelock, Carter. The Mythmaker: A Study of Motif
and Symbol in the Short Stories of Jorge Luis Borges
(Austin: Univ. of Texas Press, 1969), 122–128.

"The Zahir"
Wheelock, Carter. The Mythmaker: A Study of Motif
and Symbol in the Short Stories of Jorge Luis Borges
(Austin: Univ. of Texas Press, 1969), 32–39.

ELIZABETH BOWEN

"The Happy Autumn Fields"
Lynskey, Winifred, Ed. Reading Modern Fiction, Sec-
ond edition (New York: Scribner, 1957), 41–42;
Fourth edition (1968), 41–42.

KAY BOYLE

"Evening at Home"
   Stuckey, W. J. "The Heart Is Not Enough," Critique,
      IX, ii (1967), 85–85.

"They Weren't Going to Die"
   Lynskey, Winifred, Ed. Reading Modern Fiction, Sec-
      ond edition (New York: Scribner, 1957), 48–49;
      Fourth edition (1968), 48–49.

GEORG BÜCHNER

"Lenz"
   West, Ray B. The Art of Writing Fiction (New York:
      Crowell, 1968), 163–168.

IVAN BUNIN

"The Gentleman from San Francisco"
   Proffer, Carl R., Ed. From Karamzin to Bunin: An
      Anthology of Russian Short Stories (Bloomington:
      Indiana Univ. Press, 1969), 44–49.

JAMES BRANCH CABELL

"The Choices"
   Tarrant, Desmond. James Branch Cabell: The Dream
      and the Reality (Norman: Univ. of Oklahoma Press,
      1967), 125–127.

"In Necessity's Mortar"
   Tarrant, Desmond. James Branch Cabell: The Dream
      and the Reality (Norman: Univ. of Oklahoma Press,
      1967), 148–151.

"In the Second April"
    Tarrant, Desmond. James Branch Cabell: The Dream
        and the Reality (Norman: Univ. of Oklahoma Press,
        1967), 169–174.

"The Rat-Trap"
    Tarrant, Desmond. James Branch Cabell: The Dream
        and the Reality (Norman: Univ. of Oklahoma Press,
        1967), 124–125.

"The Sestina"
    Tarrant, Desmond. James Branch Cabell: The Dream
        and the Reality (Norman: Univ. of Oklahoma Press,
        1967), 115–120.

"Simon's Hour"
    Tarrant, Desmond. James Branch Cabell: The Dream
        and the Reality (Norman: Univ. of Oklahoma Press,
        1967), 164–169.

"The Tenson"
    Tarrant, Desmond. James Branch Cabell: The Dream
        and the Reality (Norman: Univ. of Oklahoma Press,
        1967), 120–124.

GEORGE W. CABLE

"Attalie Brouillard"
    Rubin, Louis D. George W. Cable: The Life and Times
        of a Southern Heretic (New York: Pegasus, 1969),
        195–196.

"Belles Demoiselles Plantation"
    Rubin, Louis D. George W. Cable: The Life and Times
        of a Southern Heretic (New York: Pegasus, 1969),
        50–52.

"The Entomologist"
    Rubin, Louis D. George W. Cable: The Life and Times
        of a Southern Heretic (New York: Pegasus, 1969),
        240–241.

"Gregory's Island" [retitled "The Solitary"]
   Rubin, Louis D. George W. Cable: The Life and Times
      of a Southern Heretic (New York: Pegasus, 1969),
      239–240.

"Jean-ah Poquelin"
   Rubin, Louis D. George W. Cable: The Life and Times
      of a Southern Heretic (New York: Pegasus, 1969),
      56–57.

"Madame Déliceuse"
   Rubin, Louis D. George W. Cable: The Life and Times
      of a Southern Heretic (New York: Pegasus, 1969),
      55–56.

"Posson Jone'"
   Rubin, Louis D. George W. Cable: The Life and Times
      of a Southern Heretic (New York: Pegasus, 1969),
      54–55.

"'Sieur George"
   Rubin, Louis D. George W. Cable: The Life and Times
      of a Southern Heretic (New York: Pegasus, 1969),
      46–50.

"'Tite Poulette"
   Rubin, Louis D. George W. Cable: The Life and Times
      of a Southern Heretic (New York: Pegasus, 1969),
      52–54.

MORLEY CALLAGHAN

"Ancient Lineage"
   Conron, Brandon. "Morley Callaghan as a Short Story
      Writer," J Commonwealth Lit, No. 3 (1967), 61–62.

"A Cap for Steve"
   Conron, Brandon. Morley Callaghan (New York: Twayne,
      1966), 151–152; reprinted in his "Morley Callaghan
      as a Short Story Writer," J Commonwealth Lit, No. 3
      (1967), 73.

"A Country Passion"
    Conron, Brandon. "Morley Callaghan as a Short Story
       Writer," J Commonwealth Lit, No. 3 (1967), 60–61.

"The Faithful Wife"
    Conron, Brandon. Morley Callaghan (New York: Twayne,
       1966), 99–100; reprinted in his "Morley Callaghan
       as a Short Story Writer," J Commonwealth Lit, No.
       3 (1967), 68–69.

"Getting on in the World"
    Conron, Brandon. Morley Callaghan (New York: Twayne,
       1966), 150–151; reprinted in his "Morley Callaghan
       as a Short Story Writer," J Commonwealth Lit, No.
       3 (1967), 72–73.

"A Girl with Ambition"
    Conron, Brandon. Morley Callaghan (New York: Twayne,
       1966), 39–41; reprinted in his "Morley Callaghan as
       a Short Story Writer," J Commonwealth Lit, No. 3
       (1967), 62–63.

"It Had to be Done"
    Conron, Brandon. Morley Callaghan (New York: Twayne:
       1966), 149–150; reprinted in his "Morley Callaghan
       as a Short Story Writer," J Commonwealth Lit, No.
       3 (1967), 72.

"A Predicament"
    Conron, Brandon. Morley Callaghan (New York: Twayne,
       1966), 35–36; reprinted in his "Morley Callaghan as
       a Short Story Writer," J Commonwealth Lit, No. 3
       (1967), 63–64.

"A Sick Call"
    Conron, Brandon. "Morley Callaghan as a Short Story
       Writer," J Commonwealth Lit, No. 3 (1967), 69.

"Two Fishermen"
    Conron, Brandon. Morley Callaghan (New York: Twayne,
       1966), 105–106; reprinted in his "Morley Callaghan

as a Short Story Writer," J Commonwealth Lit, No.
3 (1967), 69–70.

ALBERT CAMUS

"The Adulterous Woman"
  Rhein, Phillip H. Albert Camus (New York: Twayne,
    1969), 120–121.

"The Exile and the Kingdom"
  Rhein, Phillip H. Albert Camus (New York: Twayne,
    1969), 116–130.

"The Fall"
  Ames, Sanford. "'La chute': From Summitry to Spe-
    leology," French R, XXXIX (1966), 559–566.
  Babbage, Stuart B. The Mark of Cain: Studies in Lit-
    erature and Theology (Grand Rapids: Eerdmans,
    1966), 56–61.
  Friedman, Maurice. Problematic Rebel: An Image of
    Modern Man (New York: Random House, 1963), 330–
    332.
  Kirk, Irina. "Dramatization of Consciousness in Camus
    and Dostoevsky," Bucknell R, XVI (March, 1968),
    96–104.
  Locke, F. W. "The Metamorphoses of Jean-Baptiste
    Clamence," Symposium, XXI (1967), 306–315.
  Madden, David. "Ambiguity in Albert Camus' 'The
    Fall,'" Mod Fiction Stud, XII (1966), 461–472.
  Rhein, Phillip H. Albert Camus (New York: Twayne,
    1969), 104–115.
  Royce, Barbara. "'La chute' and 'Saint Genet': The
    Question of Guilt," French R, XXXIX (1966), 709–
    716.
  Trahan, Elizabeth. "Clamence vs. Dostoevsky: An Ap-
    proach to 'La Chute,'" Comp Lit, XVIII (1966), 337–
    350.

Van Kaam, Adrian, and Kathleen Healy. The Demon
and the Dove (Pittsburgh: Duquesne Univ. Press,
1967), 225–258.
Whartenby, H. Allen. "The Interlocutor in 'La Chute':
A Key to Its Meaning," PMLA, LXXXIV (1968),
1326–1333.

"The Guest"
Grobe, Edwin P. "The Psychological Structure of
Camus's 'L'Hote,'" French R, XL (1966), 357–376.
Hollander, Robert, and Sidney E. Lind, Eds. The Art
of the Story: An Introduction (New York: American
Book, 1968), 367–368.
Rhein, Phillip H. Albert Camus (New York: Twayne,
1969), 125–126.
Showalter, English. "Camus' Mysterious Guests: A
Note on the Value of Ambiguity,'" Stud Short Fiction,
IV (1967), 348–350.
Shrodes, Caroline, Justine Van Gundy, and Joel Dorius.
Instructor's Manual for "Reading for Understanding"
(New York: Macmillan, 1968), 40–42.
Trilling, Lionel. The Experience of Literature (New
York: Holt, Rinehart & Winston, 1967), 794–796.

"Jonas, or the Artist at Work"
Rhein, Phillip H. Albert Camus (New York: Twayne,
1969), 126–128.

"The Stranger"
Amash, Paul J. "The Choice of an Arab in 'L' Étranger,'"
Romance Notes, IX (1967), 6–7.
Champigny, Robert J. Sur un héros païen (Paris: Li-
brairie Gallimard, 1959), passim.
Falk, Eugene H. Types of Thematic Structure: The
Nature and Function of Motifs in Gide, Camus, and
Sartre (Chicago: Univ. of Chicago Press, 1967), 52–
115.
Frohock, W. M. Style and Temper: Studies in French
Fiction, 1925–1960 (Cambridge: Harvard Univ. Press,
1966), 107–113.

Hackel, Sergei. "Raskolnikov Through the Looking-Glass: Dostoevsky and Camus's 'L'Étranger,'" Contemporary Lit, IX (1968), 189–209.

Madden, David. "Camus' 'The Stranger': An Achievement in Simultaneity," Renascence, XX (1968), 186–197.

Matthews, J. H. "From Naturalism to the Absurd: Edmond de Goncourt and Albert Camus," Symposium, XXII (1968), 241–255.

Morreale, Gerald. "Meursault's Absurd Act," French R, XL (1967), 456–462.

Parker, Emmett. Albert Camus: The Artist in the Arena (Madison: Univ. of Wisconsin Press, 1965), 42–45; paperback edition (1966), 42–45.

Pickens, Rupert T., and James D. Tedder. "Liberation in Suicide: Meursault in the Light of Dante," French R, XLI (1968), 524–531.

Rhein, Phillip H. Albert Camus (New York: Twayne, 1969), 33–41.

Smith, Albert B. "Eden as Symbol in Camus' 'L'Étranger,'" Romance Notes, IX (1967), 1–5.

R. V. CASSILL

"And in My Heart"
Roberts, David. "The Short Fiction of R. V. Cassill," Critique, IX (1967), 62–65.

"This Hand, These Talons"
Roberts, David. "The Short Fiction of R. V. Cassill," Critique, IX (1967), 58–62.

WILLA CATHER

"The Best Years"
Bush, Sargent. "'The Best Years': Willa Cather's Last Story and Its Relation to Her Canon," Stud Short Fiction, V (1968), 269–274.

"The Bohemian Girl"
  Schneider, Sister Lucy. "Willa Cather's Early Stories
    in the Light of Her 'Land-Philosophy,'" Midwest Q,
    IX (1967), 87–92.

"The Clemency of the Court"
  Schneider, Sister Lucy. "Willa Cather's Early Stories
    in the Light of Her 'Land-Philosophy,'" Midwest Q,
    IX (1967), 79–80.

"Coming, Aphrodite!"
  Jones, Howard M.   The Bright Medusa (Urbana: Univ.
    of Illinois Press, 1952), 17–21; reprinted in Schroeter,
    James, Ed. Willa Cather and Her Critics (Ithaca:
    Cornell Univ. Press, 1967), 237–240.

"The Enchanted Bluff"
  Schneider, Sister Lucy. "Willa Cather's Early Stories
    in the Light of Her 'Land-Philosophy,'" Midwest Q,
    IX (1967), 87.

"Eric Hermannson's Soul"
  Schneider, Sister Lucy. "Willa Cather's Early Stories
    in the Light of Her 'Land Philosophy,'" Midwest Q,
    IX (1967), 82–85.

"Lou, the Prophet"
  Schneider, Sister Lucy. "Willa Cather's Early Stories
    in the Light of Her 'Land-Philosophy,'" Midwest Q,
    IX (1967), 77–79.

"Neighbor Rosicky"
  Daiches, David. Willa Cather: A Critical Introduction
    (Ithaca: Cornell Univ. Press, 1951), 157–158; re-
    printed in Schroeter, James, Ed. Willa Cather and
    Her Critics (Ithaca: Cornell Univ. Press, 1967), 87–
    88.

"Old Mrs. Harris"
  Daiches, David. Willa Cather: A Critical Introduction
    (Ithaca: Cornell Univ. Press, 1951), 158–166; re-

printed in Schroeter, James, Ed. Willa Cather and
Her Critics (Ithaca: Cornell Univ. Press, 1967), 88–
93.

"On the Divide"
  Schneider, Sister Lucy. "Willa Cather's Early Stories
  in the Light of Her 'Land-Philosophy,'" Midwest Q,
  IX (1967), 80–82.

"Paul's Case"
  Lynskey, Winifred, Ed. Reading Modern Fiction (New
  York: Scribner, 1952), 81–83; Second edition (1957),
  81–83; Third edition (1962), 81–83; Fourth edition
  (1968), 81–83.

"The Sculptor's Funeral"
  Jones, Howard M. The Bright Medusa (Urbana: Univ.
  of Illinois Press, 1952), 15–17; reprinted in Schroeter,
  James, Ed. Willa Cather and Her Critics (Ithaca:
  Cornell Univ. Press, 1967), 236–237.

"Two Friends"
  Daiches, David. Willa Cather: A Critical Introduction
  (Ithaca: Cornell Univ. Press, 1951), 166–168; re-
  printed in Schroeter, James, Ed. Willa Cather and
  Her Critics (Ithaca: Cornell Univ. Press, 1967), 93–
  94.

"A Wagner Matinée"
  Schneider, Sister Lucy. "Willa Cather's Early Stories
  in the Light of Her 'Land-Philosophy,'" Midwest Q,
  IX (1967), 85–87.

ADELBERT VON CHAMISSO

"Peter Schlemihl"
  Neumarkt, Paul. "Chamisso's 'Peter Schlemihl': A
  Literary Approach in Terms of Analytical Psychol-
  ogy," Lit & Psych, XVII (1967), 120–127.

JOHN CHEEVER

"The Enormous Radio"
  Kendle, Burton. "Cheever's Use of Mythology in 'The
    Enormous Radio,'" Stud Short Fiction, IV (1967),
    262–264.

ANTON CHEKHOV

"Anna on the Neck"
  Proffer, Carl R., Ed. From Karamzin to Bunin: An
    Anthology of Russian Short Stories (Bloomington:
    Indiana Univ. Press, 1969), 35–38.

"The Bet"
  Shrodes, Caroline, Justine Van Gundy, and Joel Dorius.
    Instructor's Manual for "Reading for Understanding"
    (New York: Macmillan, 1968), 11–13.

"The Black Monk"
  Rossbacker, Peter. "The Function of Insanity in Čexov's
    'The Black Monk' and Gogol's 'Notes of a Madman,'"
    Slavic & East European J, XIII (1969), 191–199.

"The Darling"
  Proffer, Carl R., Ed. From Karamzin to Bunin: An
    Anthology of Russian Short Stories (Bloomington:
    Indiana Univ. Press, 1969), 39–41.

"A Doctor's Visit"
  Hingley, Ronald. Chekhov: A Biographical and Criti-
    cal Study (London: Allen and Unwin, 1950), 156–158;
    Second edition (1966), 160–162; American edition
    (New York: Barnes & Noble, 1966), 160–162.

"A Dreary Story" [same as "A Tedious Tale"]
  Hingley, Ronald. Chekhov: A Biographical and Criti-
    cal Study (London: Allen and Unwin, 1950), 100–103;
    Second edition (1966), 106–109; American edition
    (New York: Barnes & Noble, 1966), 106–109.

"Enemies"
   Trilling, Lionel. The Experience of Literature (New
   York: Holt, Rinehart & Winston, 1967), 556-559.

"Gooseberries"
   Dickinson, Leon T. Suggestions for Teachers of "In-
   troduction to Literature" (New York: Holt, Rine-
   hart & Winston, 1967), 59-60.
   Dietrich, R. F., and Roger H. Sundell. Instructor's
   Manual for "The Art of Fiction"(New York: Holt,
   Rinehart & Winston, 1967), 40-44.
   Hollander, Robert, and Sidney E. Lind, Eds. The Art
   of the Story: An Introduction (New York: American
   Book, 1968), 201-202.
   Proffer, Carl R., Ed. From Karamzin to Bunin: An
   Anthology of Russian Short Stories (Bloomington:
   Indiana Univ. Press, 1969), 38-39.
   Schorer, Mark, Ed. The Story: A Critical Collection
   (New York: Prentice-Hall, 1950), 62-64; Second
   edition (Englewood Cliffs: Prentice-Hall, 1967),
   54-57; reprinted in Locke, Louis G., William M.
   Gibson, and George Arms, Eds. Introduction to
   Literature, Fifth edition (New York: Holt, Rinehart
   & Winston, 1967), 307-309.

"Gusev"
   Frakes, James R., and Isadore Traschen, Eds. Short
   Fiction: A Critical Collection (Englewood Cliffs:
   Prentice-Hall, 1959), 68-70; Second edition (1969),
   67-69.

"Heartache"
   Proffer, Carl R., Ed. From Karamzin to Bunin: An
   Anthology of Russian Short Stories (Bloomington:
   Indiana Univ. Press, 1969), 34-35.

"The Kiss"
   Hingley, Ronald. Chekhov: A Biographical and Critical
   Study (London: Allen and Unwin, 1950), 73-76; Second
   edition (1966), 81-83; American edition (New York:
   Barnes & Noble, 1966), 81-83.

"The Man in a Case" [same as "The Man in a Shell"]
   Conrad, Joseph L. "Čexov's 'The Man in a Shell':
   Freedom and Responsibility," Slavic & East Euro-
   pean J, X (1966), 400–410.

"My Life"
   Hingley, Ronald. Chekhov: A Biographical and Criti-
   cal Study (London: Allen and Unwin, 1950), 161–164;
   Second edition (1966), 164–168; American edition
   (New York: Barnes & Noble, 1966), 164–168.

"Sleepy"
   Struve, Gleb. "On Chekhov's Craftmanship: The Anatomy of a Story," Slavic R, XX (1961), 471–476.

"The Steppe"
   Hingley, Ronald. Chekhov: A Biographical and Criti-
   cal Study (London: Allen and Unwin, 1950), 77–81;
   Second edition (1966), 84–88; American edition (New
   York: Barnes & Noble, 1966), 84–88.

"The Teacher of Literature"
   Hingley, Ronald. Chekhov: A Biographical and Criti-
   cal Study (London: Allen and Unwin, 1950), 206–209;
   Second edition (1966), 206–209; American edition
   (New York: Barnes & Noble, 1966), 206–209.

"Ward No. 6"
   Hingley, Ronald. Chekhov: A Biographical and Criti-
   cal Study (London: Allen and Unwin, 1950), 151–156;
   Second edition (1966), 155–159; American edition
   (New York: Barnes & Noble, 1966), 155–159.

KATE CHOPIN

"Athénaïse"
   Seyersted, Per. Kate Chopin: A Critical Biography
   (Baton Rouge: Louisiana State Univ. Press, 1969),
   112–115.

"Charlie"
  Seyersted, Per. <u>Kate Chopin: A Critical Biography</u>
    (Baton Rouge: Louisiana State Univ. Press, 1969),
    183–184.

"Miss McEnders"
  Seyersted, Per. <u>Kate Chopin: A Critical Biography</u>
    (Baton Rouge: Louisiana State Univ. Press, 1969),
    96–97.

"Ozème's Holiday"
  Seyersted, Per. <u>Kate Chopin: A Critical Biography</u>
    (Baton Rouge: Louisiana State Univ. Press, 1969),
    123–125.

"A Point at Issue"
  Seyersted, Per. <u>Kate Chopin: A Critical Biography</u>
    (Baton Rouge: Louisiana State Univ. Press, 1969),
    105–108.

"Regret"
  Seyersted, Per. <u>Kate Chopin: A Critical Biography</u>
    (Baton Rouge: Louisiana State Univ. Press, 1969),
    125–130.

"The Storm"
  Seyersted, Per. <u>Kate Chopin: A Critical Biography</u>
    (Baton Rouge: Louisiana State Univ. Press, 1969),
    164–169.

"The Story of an Hour"
  Seyersted, Per. <u>Kate Chopin: A Critical Biography</u>
    (Baton Rouge: Louisiana State Univ. Press, 1969),
    57–59.

"Wiser Than a God"
  Seyersted, Per. <u>Kate Chopin: A Critical Biography</u>
    (Baton Rouge: Louisiana State Univ. Press, 1969),
    104–105.

WALTER VAN TILBURG CLARK

"The Wind and the Snow of Winter"
  West, Ray B. The Art of Writing Fiction (New York:
  Crowell, 1968), 181–187.

JOSEPH CONRAD

"Amy Foster"
  Graver, Lawrence. Conrad's Short Fiction (Berkeley:
    Univ. of California Press, 1969), 104–108.
  Meyer, Bernard C. Joseph Conrad: A Psychoanalytic
    Biography (Princeton: Princeton Univ. Press, 1967),
    171–173, 178–181.
  Palmer, John A. Joseph Conrad's Fiction: A Study in
    Literary Growth (Ithaca: Cornell Univ. Press, 1968),
    83–85.
  Schorer, Mark, Ed. The Story: A Critical Anthology
    (New York: Prentice-Hall, 1950), 243–246; Second
    edition (Englewood Cliffs: Prentice-Hall, 1967), 198–
    201.

"An Anarchist"
  Fleishman, Avrom. Conrad's Politics: Community and
    Anarchy in the Fiction of Joseph Conrad (Baltimore:
    Johns Hopkins Press, 1967), 138–139.
  Graver, Lawrence. Conrad's Short Fiction (Berkeley:
    Univ. of California Press, 1969), 132–135.
  Palmer, John A. Joseph Conrad's Fiction: A Study in
    Literary Growth (Ithaca: Cornell Univ. Press, 1968),
    121–122.

"Because of the Dollars"
  Graver, Lawrence. Conrad's Short Fiction (Berkeley:
    Univ. of California Press, 1969), 172–174.
  Palmer, John A. Joseph Conrad's Fiction: A Study in
    Literary Growth (Ithaca: Cornell Univ. Press, 1968),
    238–240.

"The Black Mate"
  Graver, Lawrence. Conrad's Short Fiction (Berkeley:
    Univ. of California Press, 1969), 1-4.

"The Brute"
  Graver, Lawrence. Conrad's Short Fiction (Berkeley:
    Univ. of California Press, 1969), 130-133.

"Il Conde"
  Fleishman, Avrom. Conrad's Politics: Community and
    Anarchy in the Fiction of Joseph Conrad (Baltimore:
    Johns Hopkins Press, 1967), 141-142.
  Graver, Lawrence. Conrad's Short Fiction (Berkeley:
    Univ. of California Press, 1969), 141-144.
  Meyer, Bernard C. Joseph Conrad: A Psychoanalytic
    Biography (Princeton: Princeton Univ. Press, 1967),
    196-197.
  Schwarz, Daniel R. "The Self-Deceiving Narrator of
    Conrad's 'Il Conde,'" Stud Short Fiction, VI (1969),
    187-193.

"The Duel"
  Fleishman, Avrom. Conrad's Politics: Community and
    Anarchy in the Fiction of Joseph Conrad (Baltimore:
    Johns Hopkins Press, 1967), 140-141.
  Graver, Lawrence. Conrad's Short Fiction (Berkeley:
    Univ. of California Press, 1969), 144-147.
  Meyer, Bernard C. Joseph Conrad: A Psychoanalytic
    Biography (Princeton: Princeton Univ. Press, 1967),
    198-201.
  Palmer, John A. Joseph Conrad's Fiction: A Study in
    Literary Growth (Ithaca: Cornell Univ. Press, 1968),
    233-235.

"The End of the Tether"
  Graver, Lawrence. Conrad's Short Fiction (Berkeley:
    Univ. of California Press, 1969), 113-119.
  Palmer, John A. Joseph Conrad's Fiction: A Study in
    Literary Growth (Ithaca: Cornell Univ. Press, 1968),
    79-80.

"Falk"

Graver, Lawrence. Conrad's Short Fiction (Berkeley:
Univ. of California Press, 1969), 99–104.

Meyer, Bernard C. Joseph Conrad: A Psychoanalytic
Biography (Princeton: Princeton Univ. Press, 1967),
168–170.

Palmer, John A. Joseph Conrad's Fiction: A Study in
Literary Growth (Ithaca: Cornell Univ. Press, 1968),
85–89.

"Freya of the Seven Isles"

Fleishman, Avrom. Conrad's Politics: Community and
Anarchy in the Fiction of Joseph Conrad (Baltimore:
Johns Hopkins Press, 1967), 118–120.

Graver, Lawrence. Conrad's Short Fiction (Berkeley:
Univ. of California Press, 1969), 163–169.

Meyer, Bernard C. Joseph Conrad: A Psychoanalytic
Biography (Princeton: Princeton Univ. Press, 1967),
223–224.

Palmer, John A. Joseph Conrad's Fiction: A Study in
Literary Growth (Ithaca: Cornell Univ. Press, 1968),
231–233.

"Gaspar Ruiz"

Fleishman, Avrom. Conrad's Politics: Community and
Anarchy in the Fiction of Joseph Conrad (Baltimore:
Johns Hopkins Press, 1967), 135–137.

Graver, Lawrence. Conrad's Short Fiction (Berkeley:
Univ. of California Press, 1969), 125–130.

"Heart of Darkness"

Canario, John W. "The Harlequin in 'Heart of Darkness,"
Stud Short Fiction, IV (1967), 225–233.

Collins, Harold R. "Kurtz, the Cannibals, and the Sec-
ond-Rate Helmsman," Western Hum R, VIII (1954),
299–310; reprinted in Dean, Leonard, Ed. Joseph
Conrad's "Heart of Darkness": Backgrounds and
Criticisms (Englewood Cliffs: Prentice-Hall, 1960),
149–159; reprinted in part in Walker, Franklin, Ed.
Heart of Darkness and The Secret Sharer (New York:
Bantam, 1969), 227–230.

Crews, Frederick. "The Power of Darkness," Partisan R, XXXIV (1967), 518–525.

Dahl, James C. "Kurtz, Marlow, Conrad and the Human Heart of Darkness," Stud Literary Imagination, I (October, 1968), 33–40.

Dietrich, R. F., and Roger H. Sundell. Instructor's Manual for "The Art of Fiction" (New York: Holt, Rinehart & Winston, 1967), 92–101.

Fleishman, Avrom. Conrad's Politics: Community and Anarchy in the Fiction of Joseph Conrad (Baltimore: Johns Hopkins Press, 1967), 89–97.

Garrett, Peter K. Scene and Symbol from George Eliot to James Joyce: Studies in Changing Fictional Mode (New Haven: Yale Univ. Press, 1969), 164–172.

Graver, Lawrence. Conrad's Short Fiction (Berkeley: Univ. of California Press, 1969), 77–88.

Guerard, Albert J. Conrad the Novelist (Cambridge: Harvard Univ. Press, 1958), 33–48; reprinted in Dean, Leonard, Ed. Joseph Conrad's "Heart of Darkness": Backgrounds and Criticisms (Englewood Cliffs: Prentice-Hall, 1960), 166–177; Harkness, Bruce, Ed. Conrad's "Heart of Darkness" and the Critics (San Francisco: Wadsworth, 1960), 111–119; Schorer, Mark, Ed. Modern British Fiction: Essays in Criticism (New York: Oxford Univ. Press, 1961), 110–118; Kimbrough, Robert, Ed. Heart of Darkness (New York: Norton, 1963), 168–176; Guerard, Albert, et al., Eds. The Personal Voice (Philadelphia: Lippincott, 1964), 464–474; reprinted in part in Walker, Franklin, Ed. Heart of Darkness and The Secret Sharer (New York: Bantam, 1969), 224–227.

————, Ed. The Heart of Darkness and The Secret Sharer (New York: New American Library, 1950), 13–14.

Guetti, James. The Limits of Metaphor: A Study of Melville, Conrad, and Faulkner (Ithaca: Cornell Univ. Press, 1967), 46–68.

Gurko, Leo. Joseph Conrad: Giant in Exile (New York: Macmillan, 1962), 148–163; reprinted in part in Kim-

brough, Robert, Ed. Heart of Darkness (New York:
    Norton, 1963), 218–223; reprinted in part in Walker,
    Franklin, Ed. Heart of Darkness and The Secret
    Sharer (New York: Bantam, 1969), 231–235.
————. The Two Lives of Joseph Conrad (New York:
    Crowell, 1965), 128–129.
Karl, Frederick R. "Introduction to the Danse Macabre:
    Conrad's 'Heart of Darkness,'" Mod Fiction Stud,
    XIV (1968), 143–156.
Kauvar, Gerald B. "Marlow as Liar," Stud Short Fic-
    tion, V (1968), 290–292.
Ketterer, David. "'Beyond the Threshold' in Conrad's
    'Heart of Darkness,'" Texas Stud Lit & Lang, XI
    (1969), 1013–1022.
Lemon, Lee T. Approaches to Literature (New York:
    Oxford Univ. Press, 1969), 213–219.
McCall, Dan. "The Meaning in Darkness: A Response
    to a Psychoanalytical Study of Conrad," Coll Engl,
    XXIX (1968), 620–627.
Madden, David. "Romanticism and the Hero-Witness
    Relationship in Four Conrad Stories," Ohio Univ R,
    X (1968), 12–16.
Maud, Ralph. "The Plain Tale of 'Heart of Darkness,'"
    Hum Assoc Bull, XVII, ii (1966), 13–17.
Mellard, James. "Myth and Archetype in 'Heart of
    Darkness,'" Tennessee Stud Lit, XIII (1968), 1–15.
Meyer, Bernard C. Joseph Conrad: A Psychoanalytic
    Biography (Princeton: Princeton Univ. Press, 1967),
    154–159.
Mizener, Arthur. A Handbook for Use with "Modern
    Short Stories: The Uses of Imagination, Revised
    Edition" (New York: Norton, 1966), 1–8.
Nicolaisen, Von Peter. "Die Darstellung der Wildnis
    in Joseph Conrads 'Heart of Darkness,'" Die Neu-
    eren Sprachen, XVII (1968), 265–281.
Ruthven, K. K. "The Savage God: Conrad and Lawrence,"
    Critical Q, X (1968), 41–46.
Steinmann, Martin, and Gerald Willen, Eds. Literature
    for Writing (Belmont: Wadsworth, 1962), 288–289;
    Second edition (1967), 291.

Stephens, R. C. "'Heart of Darkness': Marlow's 'Spectral Moonshine,'" Essays in Criticism, XIX (1969), 273–284.

Stewart, J. I. M. Joseph Conrad (New York: Dodd, Mead, 1968), 77–85.

"The Idiots"
Graver, Lawrence. Conrad's Short Fiction (Berkeley: Univ. of California Press, 1969), 5–10.

"The Informer"
Fleishman, Avrom. Conrad's Politics: Community and Anarchy in the Fiction of Joseph Conrad (Baltimore: Johns Hopkins Press, 1967), 137–138.

Graver, Lawrence. Conrad's Short Fiction (Berkeley: Univ. of California Press, 1969), 139–141.

Palmer, John A. Joseph Conrad's Fiction: A Study in Literary Growth (Ithaca: Cornell Univ. Press, 1968), 122–124.

Walton, James. "Mr. X's 'Little Joke': The Design of Conrad's 'The Informer,'" Stud Short Fiction, IV (1967), 322–333.

"The Inn of the Two Witches"
Meyer, Bernard C. Joseph Conrad: A Psychoanalytic Biography (Princeton: Princeton Univ. Press, 1967), 226–227.

Palmer, John A. Joseph Conrad's Fiction: A Study in Literary Growth (Ithaca: Cornell Univ. Press, 1968), 237–238.

"Karain"
Fleishman, Avrom. Conrad's Politics: Community and Anarchy in the Fiction of Joseph Conrad (Baltimore: Johns Hopkins Press, 1967), 120–121.

Graver, Lawrence. Conrad's Short Fiction (Berkeley: Univ. of California Press, 1969), 29–34.

Palmer, John A. Joseph Conrad's Fiction: A Study in Literary Growth (Ithaca: Cornell Univ. Press, 1968), 75–77.

"The Lagoon"
  Graver, Lawrence. Conrad's Short Fiction (Berkeley:
    Univ. of California Press, 1969), 25-29.

"An Outpost of Progress"
  Graver, Lawrence. Conrad's Short Fiction (Berkeley:
    Univ. of California Press, 1969), 10-14.
  Meyer, Bernard C. Joseph Conrad: A Psychoanalytic
    Biography (Princeton: Princeton Univ. Press, 1967),
    122-123.
  Palmer, John A. Joseph Conrad's Fiction: A Study in
    Literary Growth (Ithaca: Cornell Univ. Press, 1968),
    77-78.
  Stewart, J. I. M. Joseph Conrad (New York: Dodd,
    Mead, 1968), 75-77.

"The Planter of Malata"
  Graver, Lawrence. Conrad's Short Fiction (Berkeley:
    Univ. of California Press, 1969), 174-178.
  Meyer, Bernard C. Joseph Conrad: A Psychoanalytic
    Biography (Princeton: Princeton Univ. Press, 1967),
    227-228.
  Palmer, John A. Joseph Conrad's Fiction: A Study in
    Literary Growth (Ithaca: Cornell Univ. Press, 1968),
    240-242.

"Prince Roman"
  Fleishman, Avrom. Conrad's Politics: Community and
    Anarchy in the Fiction of Joseph Conrad (Baltimore:
    Johns Hopkins Press, 1967), 143-146.

"The Return"
  Graver, Lawrence. Conrad's Short Fiction (Berkeley:
    Univ. of California Press, 1969), 34-41.

"The Secret Sharer"
  Curley, Daniel. "The Writer and His Use of Material:
    The Case of 'The Secret Sharer,'" Mod Fiction Stud,
    XIII (1967), 179-194.

Dussinger, Gloria R. "'The Secret Sharer': Conrad's Psychological Study," Texas Stud Lit & Lang, X (1969), 599–608.

Gilley, Leonard. "Conrad's 'The Secret Sharer,'" Midwest Q, VIII (1967), 319–330.

Graver, Lawrence. Conrad's Short Fiction (Berkeley: Univ. of California Press, 1969), 149–158.

Guerard, Albert. Conrad the Novelist (Cambridge: Harvard Univ. Press, 1958), 21–29; reprinted in Harkness, Bruce, Ed. Conrad's "Secret Sharer" and the Critics (Belmont: Wadsworth, 1962), 59–74; Guerard, Albert, et al., Eds. The Personal Voice (Philadelphia: Lippincott, 1964), 458–464; Duhamel, P. Albert, and Richard E. Hughes, Eds. Literature: Form and Function (Englewood Cliffs: Prentice-Hall, 1965), 416–419; reprinted in part in Walker, Franklin, Ed. Heart of Darkness and The Secret Sharer (New York: Bantam, 1969), 220–224.

————. Ed. The Heart of Darkness and The Secret Sharer (New York: New American Library, 1950), 9–12.

————. Joseph Conrad (New York: New Directions, 1947), 38–42.

————, Ed. Stories of the Double (Philadelphia: Lippincott, 1967), 12–14.

Hollander, Robert, and Sidney E. Lind, Eds. The Art of the Story: An Introduction (New York: American Book, 1968), 159–160.

Howe, Irving, Ed. Classics of Modern Fiction (New York: Harcourt, Brace & World, 1968), 271–280.

Lynskey, Winifred, Ed. Reading Modern Fiction (New York: Scribner, 1952), 147–149; Second edition (1957), 147–149; Third edition (1962), 147–149; Fourth edition (1968), 147–149.

Madden, David. "Romanticism and the Hero-Witness Relationship in Four Conrad Stories," Ohio Univ R, X (1968), 10–12.

Palmer, John A. Joseph Conrad's Fiction: A Study in Literary Growth (Ithaca: Cornell Univ. Press, 1968), 221–230.

Shrodes, Caroline, Justine Van Gundy, and Joel Dorius.
 Instructor's Manual for "Reading for Understanding"
 (New York: Macmillan, 1968), 10–11.
Stewart, J. I. M. Joseph Conrad (New York: Dodd, Mead,
 1968), 232–240.
Trilling, Lionel. The Experience of Literature (New
 York: Holt, Rinehart & Winston, 1967), 621–623.

"The Shadow Line"
 Graver, Lawrence. Conrad's Short Fiction (Berkeley:
 Univ. of California Press, 1969), 178–192.
 Meyer, Bernard C. Joseph Conrad: A Psychoanalytic
 Biography (Princeton: Princeton Univ. Press, 1967),
 229–230.
 Palmer, John A. Joseph Conrad's Fiction: A Study in
 Literary Growth (Ithaca: Cornell Univ. Press, 1968),
 245–249.
 Stewart, J. I. M. Joseph Conrad (New York: Dodd, Mead,
 1968), 240–247.

"A Smile of Fortune"
 Fleishman, Avrom. Conrad's Politics: Community and
 Anarchy in the Fiction of Joseph Conrad (Baltimore:
 Johns Hopkins Press, 1967), 115–118.
 Graver, Lawrence. Conrad's Short Fiction (Berkeley:
 Univ. of California Press, 1969), 158–163.
 Kirschner, Paul. "Conrad and Maupassant: Moral Soli-
 tude and 'A Smile of Fortune,'" R Engl Lit, VII (1966),
 62–77.
 Meyer, Bernard C. Joseph Conrad: A Psychoanalytic
 Biography (Princeton: Princeton Univ. Press, 1967),
 80–84.
 Palmer, John A. Joseph Conrad's Fiction: A Study in
 Literary Growth (Ithaca: Cornell Univ. Press, 1968),
 230–231.

"The Tale"
 Graver, Lawrence. Conrad's Short Fiction (Berkeley:
 Univ. of California Press, 1969), 193–198.

Meyer, Bernard C. Joseph Conrad: A Psychoanalytic
Biography (Princeton: Princeton Univ. Press, 1967),
237–238.

Palmer, John A. Joseph Conrad's Fiction: A Study in
Literary Growth (Ithaca: Cornell Univ. Press, 1968),
257–259.

Williams, Porter. "Story and Frame in Conrad's 'The
Tale,'" Stud Short Fiction, V (1968), 179–185.

"Tomorrow"
Graver, Lawrence. Conrad's Short Fiction (Berkeley:
Univ. of California Press, 1969), 108–113.

"Typhoon"
Graver, Lawrence. Conrad's Short Fiction (Berkeley:
Univ. of California Press, 1969), 94–99.

Meyer, Bernard C. Joseph Conrad: A Psychoanalytic
Biography (Princeton: Princeton Univ. Press, 1967),
162–163.

Palmer, John A. Joseph Conrad's Fiction: A Study in
Literary Growth (Ithaca: Cornell Univ. Press, 1968),
80–83.

Stewart, J. I. M. Joseph Conrad (New York: Dodd, Mead,
1968), 86–90.

"The Warrior's Soul"
Fleishman, Avrom. Conrad's Politics: Community and
Anarchy in the Fiction of Joseph Conrad (Baltimore:
Johns Hopkins Press, 1967), 146–147.

Graver, Lawrence. Conrad's Short Fiction (Berkeley:
Univ. of California Press, 1969), 193–198.

"Youth"
Graver, Lawrence. Conrad's Short Fiction (Berkeley:
Univ. of California Press, 1969), 70–77.

Krieger, Murray. "Conrad's 'Youth': A Naive Open-
ing to Art and Life," Coll Engl, XX (1959), 275–280;
reprinted in Timko, Michael, and Clinton F. Oliver,
Eds. Thirty-Eight Short Stories (New York: Knopf,
1968), 50–57.

Madden, David. "Romanticism and the Hero-Witness
Relationship in Four Conrad Stories," Ohio Univ R,
X (1968), 8–10.

JACK CONROY

"The Siren"
Larsen, Erling. "Jack Conroy's The Disinherited, or,
The Way It Was," in Madden, David, Ed. Proletarian
Writers of the Thirties (Carbondale: Southern Illin-
ois Univ. Press, 1968), 90–93.

BENJAMIN CONSTANT

"Adolphe"
Fairlie, Alison. "The Art of Constant's 'Adolphe': Cre-
ation of Character," Forum Mod Lang Stud, II (1966),
253–263.
————. "The Art of Constant's 'Adolphe': Structure
and Style," French Stud (1966), 226–242.
————. "The Art of Constant's 'Adolphe': The Styl-
ization of Experience," Mod Lang R, LXII (1967),
31–47.
Oliver, Andrew. "Cécile et la genese d' 'Adolphe,'"
Revue des Sciences Humaines, CXX (1967), 5–28.
Scott, Malcolm. "The Romanticism of 'Adolphe,'"
Nottingham French Stud, VI (1967), 58–66.

PETER COWAN

"The Empty Street"
Barnes, John. "New Tracks to Travel: The Stories of
White, Porter and Cowan," Meanjin Q, XXV (1966),
168.

STEPHEN CRANE

"The Angel Child"
  Solomon, Eric. Stephen Crane: From Parody to Re-
    alism (Cambridge: Harvard Univ. Press, 1966),
    209–210; reprinted in Bassan, Maurice, Ed. Stephen
    Crane: A Collection of Critical Essays (Englewood
    Cliffs: Prentice-Hall, 1967), 170–171.

"The Blue Hotel"
  Davison, Richard A. "Crane's 'Blue Hotel' Revisited:
    The Illusion of Fate," Mod Fiction Stud, XV (1969),
    537–539.
  Gibson, Donald B. The Fiction of Stephen Crane (Car-
    bondale: Southern Illinois Univ. Press, 1968), 106–
    109.
  Grenberg, Bruce L. "Metaphysics of Despair: Stephen
    Crane's 'The Blue Hotel,'" Mod Fiction Stud, XIV
    (1968), 203–213.
  Johnson, George W. "Stephen Crane's Metaphor of De-
    corum," PMLA, LXXVIII (1963), 254–255; reprinted
    in Bassan, Maurice, Ed. Stephen Crane: A Collec-
    tion of Critical Essays (Englewood Cliffs: Prentice-
    Hall, 1967), 75–77.
  Lynskey, Winifred, Ed. Reading Modern Fiction (New
    York: Scribner, 1952), 173–175; Second edition (1957),
    173–175; Third edition (1962), 173–175; Fourth edi-
    tion (1968), 173–175.
  Martin, Jay. Harvests of Change: American Literature,
    1865–1914 (Englewood Cliffs: Prentice-Hall, 1967),
    66–68.
  Rees, Robert A., and Barry Menikoff. A Manual to Ac-
    company "The Short Story: An Introductory An-
    thology" (Boston: Little, Brown, 1969), 4–5.
  VanDerBeets, Richard. "Character as Structure: Ironic
    Parallel and Transformation in 'The Blue Hotel,'"
    Stud Short Fiction, V (1968), 294–295.
  Weinig, Sister Mary Anthony. "Heroic Convention in
    'The Blue Hotel,'" Stephen Crane Newsletter, II,
    iii (Spring, 1968), 6–8.

Weiss, Daniel. "The Red Badge of Courage," Psycho-
    analytic R, LII (1965), 477–483; reprinted in Bassan,
    Maurice, Ed. Stephen Crane: A Collection of Criti-
    cal Essays (Englewood Cliffs: Prentice-Hall, 1967),
    154–164.

"The Bride Comes to Yellow Sky"
    Bernard, Kenneth. "'The Bride Comes to Yellow Sky':
        History As Elegy," Engl Record, XVII (April, 1967),
        17–20.
    Cazemajou, Jean. Stephen Crane (Minneapolis: Univ.
        of Minnesota Press, 1969), 26–27.
    Johnson, George W. "Stephen Crane's Metaphor of De-
        corum," PMLA, LXXVIII (1963), 254.
    Martin, Jay. Harvests of Change: American Literature,
        1865–1914 (Englewood Cliffs: Prentice-Hall, 1967),
        65–66.
    West, Ray B. The Art of Writing Fiction (New York:
        Crowell, 1968), 134–140.

"An Experiment in Misery"
    Bassan, Maurice. "The Design of Stephen Crane's
        Bowery 'Experiment,'" Stud Short Fiction, I (1964),
        129–132; reprinted in Bassan, Maurice, Ed. Stephen
        Crane: A Collection of Critical Essays (Englewood
        Cliffs: Prentice-Hall, 1967), 118–122.
    Gibson, Donald B. The Fiction of Stephen Crane (Car-
        bondale: Southern Illinois Univ. Press, 1968), 53–54.

"The Five White Mice"
    Weiss, Daniel. "The Red Badge of Courage," Psycho-
        analytic R, LII (1965), 476–477.

"Four Men in a Cave"
    Gibson, Donald B. The Fiction of Stephen Crane (Car-
        bondale: Southern Illinois Univ. Press, 1968), 6–7.

"George's Mother"
    Cazemajou, Jean. Stephen Crane (Minneapolis: Univ.
        of Minnesota Press, 1969), 16–17.

Gibson, Donald B. The Fiction of Stephen Crane (Carbondale: Southern Illinois Univ. Press, 1968), 40–52.

"The Holler Tree"
Gibson, Donald B. The Fiction of Stephen Crane (Carbondale: Southern Illinois Univ. Press, 1968), 17–18.

"A Little Pilgrimage"
Monteiro, George. "Whilomville as Judah: Crane's 'A
Little Pilgrimage,'" Renascence, XIX (1967), 184–
189.
Solomon, Eric. Stephen Crane: From Parody to Real-
ism (Cambridge: Harvard Univ. Press, 1966), 226–
228; reprinted in Bassan, Maurice, Ed. Stephen
Crane: A Collection of Critical Essays (Englewood
Cliffs: Prentice-Hall, 1967), 175–176.

"The Lover and the Telltale"
Solomon, Eric. Stephen Crane: From Parody to Real-
ism (Cambridge: Harvard Univ. Press, 1966), 213–
216; reprinted in Bassan, Maurice, Ed. Stephen
Crane: A Collection of Critical Essays (Englewood
Cliffs: Prentice-Hall, 1967), 173–175.

"Lynx-Hunting"
Solomon, Eric. Stephen Crane: From Parody to Real-
ism (Cambridge: Harvard Univ. Press, 1966), 210–
213; reprinted in Bassan, Maurice, Ed. Stephen
Crane: A Collection of Critical Essays (Englewood
Cliffs: Prentice-Hall, 1967), 171–173.

"Maggie: A Girl of the Streets"
Cazemajou, Jean. Stephen Crane (Minneapolis: Univ.
of Minnesota Press, 1969), 14–16.
Martin, Jay. Harvests of Change: American Literature,
1865–1914 (Englewood Cliffs: Prentice-Hall, 1967),
57–59.
Pizer, Donald. "Stephen Crane's 'Maggie' and American
Naturalism," Criticism, VII (1965), 168–175; re-

printed in his Realism and Naturalism in Nineteenth-
Century American Literature (Carbondale: Southern
Illinois Univ. Press, 1966), 121–131; Bassan, Mau-
rice, Ed. Stephen Crane: A Collection of Critical
Essays (Englewood Cliffs: Prentice-Hall, 1967),
110–117.

Taylor, Gordon O. The Passages of Thought: Psychological Representation in the American Novel 1870–
1900 (New York: Oxford Univ. Press, 1969), 111–119.

"The Men in the Storm"
Gibson, Donald B. The Fiction of Stephen Crane (Carbondale: Southern Illinois Univ. Press, 1968), 54–55.

"The Monster"
Cazemajou, Jean. Stephen Crane (Minneapolis: Univ.
of Minnesota Press, 1969), 29–30.
Gibson, Donald B. The Fiction of Stephen Crane (Carbondale: Southern Illinois Univ. Press, 1968), 136–
140.

"A Mystery of Heroism"
Johnson, George W. "Stephen Crane's Metaphor of De-
corum," PMLA, LXXVIII (1963), 252–253.
Witherington, Paul. "Stephen Crane's 'A Mystery of
Heroism': Some Redefinitions," Engl J, LVIII (1969),
201–204.

"The Open Boat"
Buitenhuis, Peter. "The Essentials of Life: 'The Open
Boat' as Existentialist Fiction," Mod Fiction Stud,
V (1959), 243–250; reprinted in Merritt, Travis R.,
Ed. Style and Substance (New York: Harcourt, Brace
& World, 1969), 422–430.
Colvert, James B. "Style and Meaning in Stephen
Crane's 'The Open Boat,'" Univ Texas Stud Engl,
XXXVII (1958), 34–45; reprinted in Sutherland, Wil-
liam O., and Robert L. Montgomery, Eds. The
Reader: A Study of Form and Content (Boston:

Little, Brown, 1960), 527–537; Merritt, Travis R.,
  Ed. Style and Substance (New York: Harcourt,
  Brace & World, 1969), 430–441.
Dendinger, Lloyd N. "Stephen Crane's Inverted Use
  of Key Images of 'The Rime of the Ancient Mariner,'"
  Stud Short Fiction, V (1968), 192–194.
Frederick, John T. "The Fifth Man in 'The Open
  Boat,'" Coll Engl Assoc Critic, XXX (May, 1968),
  1, 12–14.
Gibson, Donald B. The Fiction of Stephen Crane
  (Carbondale: Southern Illinois Univ. Press, 1968),
  127–135.
Hollander, Robert, and Sidney E. Lind, Eds. The Art
  of the Story: An Introduction (New York: American
  Book, 1968), 214–215.
Huck, Wilbur, and William Shanahan, Eds. The Modern
  Short Story (New York: American Book, 1968), 3–5.
Kissane, Leedice. "Interpretation Through Language:
  A Study of the Metaphors in Stephen Crane's 'The
  Open Boat,'" Rendezvous, I (1966), 18–22.
Martin, Jay. Harvests of Change: American Literature,
  1865–1914 (Englewood Cliffs: Prentice-Hall, 1967),
  68–69.
Stallman, Robert W. "The Land-Sea Irony in 'The
  Open Boat,'" Coll Engl Assoc Critic, XXX (May,
  1968), 15.
Stein, William B. "Stephen Crane's Homo Absurdus,"
  Bucknell R, VIII (May, 1959), 170–173; reprinted in
  Bassan, Maurice, Ed. Stephen Crane: A Collection
  of Critical Essays (Englewood Cliffs: Prentice-Hall,
  1967), 150–153.
Steinmann, Martin, and Gerald Willen, Eds. Literature
  for Writing (Belmont: Wadsworth, 1962), 153; Second edition (1967), 145.

"The Price of the Harness"
  Weiss, Daniel. "The Red Badge of Courage," Psychoanalytic R, LII (1965), 475–476.

"The Upturned Face"
Gibson, Donald B. The Fiction of Stephen Crane (Carbondale: Southern Illinois Univ. Press, 1968), 103–104.
Johnson, George W. "Stephen Crane's Metaphor of Decorum," PMLA, LXXVIII (1963), 252–253.

ISAK DINESEN

"Alkmene"
Harrington, David V. "Isak Dinesen's 'Alkmene,'" Discourse, IX (1966), 471–480.

"The Cardinal's First Tale"
Johannesson, Eric O. The World of Isak Dinesen (Seattle: Univ. of Washington Press, 1961), 11–13.

"The Cardinal's Third Tale"
Johannesson, Eric O. The World of Isak Dinesen (Seattle: Univ. of Washington Press, 1961), 122–124.

"The Caryatids"
Johannesson, Eric O. The World of Isak Dinesen (Seattle: Univ. of Washington Press, 1961), 60–62.

"Copenhagen Season"
Johannesson, Eric O. The World of Isak Dinesen (Seattle: Univ. of Washington Press, 1961), 104–106.

"The Deluge at Norderney"
Johannesson, Eric O. The World of Isak Dinesen (Seattle: Univ. of Washington Press, 1961), 71–75.

"The Dreamers"
Johannesson, Eric O. The World of Isak Dinesen (Seattle: Univ. of Washington Press, 1961), 63–64.

"The Invincible Slaveowners"
  Johannesson, Eric O. The World of Isak Dinesen
  (Seattle: Univ. of Washington Press, 1961), 106–108.

"The Monkey"
  Johannesson, Eric O. The World of Isak Dinesen
  (Seattle: Univ. of Washington Press, 1961), 55–59.

"The Old Chevalier"
  Johannesson, Eric O. The World of Isak Dinesen
  (Seattle: Univ. of Washington Press, 1961), 95–98.

"The Sailor-Boy's Tale"
  Trilling, Lionel. The Experience of Literature (New
  York: Holt, Rinehart & Winston, 1967), 723–725.

"Sorrow-Acre"
  Johannesson, Eric O. The World of Isak Dinesen
  (Seattle: Univ. of Washington Press, 1961), 99–104.

"The Supper at Elsinore"
  Johannesson, Eric O. The World of Isak Dinesen
  (Seattle: Univ. of Washington Press, 1961), 62–63.

"Tempests"
  Johannesson, Eric O. The World of Isak Dinesen
  (Seattle: Univ. of Washington Press, 1961), 88–89.

FYODOR DOSTOEVSKY

"Another Man's Wife and the Husband Under the Bed"
  Mochulsky, Konstantin. Dostoevsky: His Life and Work,
  trans. Michael A. Minihan (Princeton: Princeton
  Univ. Press, 1967), 82–83.

"A Christmas Tree and a Wedding"
  Mochulsky, Konstantin. Dostoevsky: His Life and Work,
  trans. Michael A. Minihan (Princeton: Princeton
  Univ. Press, 1967), 91–92.

"The Double"
Guerard, Albert J., Ed. Stories of the Double (Phila-
delphia: Lippincott, 1967), 5-8.
Mochulsky, Konstantin. Dostoevsky: His Life and Work,
trans. Michael A. Minihan (Princeton: Princeton
Univ. Press, 1967), 40-68.

"The Dream of a Ridiculous Man"
Proffer, Carl R., Ed. From Karamzin to Bunin: An
Anthology of Russian Short Stories (Bloomington:
Indiana Univ. Press, 1969), 21-24.

"The Eternal Husband"
Mochulsky, Konstantin. Dostoevsky: His Life and Work,
trans. Michael A. Minihan (Princeton: Princeton
Univ. Press, 1967), 382-403.

"A Faint Heart"
Mochulsky, Konstantin. Dostoevsky: His Life and Work,
trans. Michael A. Minihan (Princeton: Princeton
Univ. Press, 1967), 84-89.

"The Gambler"
Mochulsky, Konstantin. Dostoevsky: His Life and Work,
trans. Michael A. Minihan (Princeton: Princeton
Univ. Press, 1967), 314-333.

"The Grand Inquisitor"
Arisian, Khoren. "The Grand Inquisitor Revisited: An
Inquiry into the Character of Human Freedom,"
Crane R, IX (1967), 149-158.
Carver, Wayne. "The Grand Inquisitor's Long March,"
Univ Denver Q, I (1966), 41-49.
Cox, Roger L. "Dostoevsky's Grand Inquisitor," Cross
Currents, XVII (1967), 427-444.
Lawrence, D. H. Phoenix, ed. E. D. McDonald (New
York: Viking, 1936), 283-291; reprinted in his Se-
lected Literary Criticism, ed. Anthony Beal (London:
Heineman, 1955), 233-241; American edition (New
York: Viking, 1961), 233-241; Wellek, René, Ed.

Dostoevsky: A Collection of Critical Essays (Engle-
wood Cliffs: Prentice-Hall, 1962), 90–97; Freed-
man, Morris, and Paul B. Davis, Eds. Controversy
in Literature (New York: Scribner, 1968), 77–83.
Mochulsky, Konstantin. Dostoevsky: His Life and Work,
trans. Michael A. Minihan (Princeton: Princeton
Univ. Press, 1967), 617–623.
Neumann, Harry. "Milton's Adam and Dostoyevsky's
Inquisitor on the Problem of Freedom Before God,"
Personalist, XLVIII (1967), 317–327.
Riemer, Neal. "Some Reflections on 'The Grand In-
quisitor' and Modern Democratic Theory," Ethics,
LXVII (1957), 49–57; reprinted in Freedman, Morris,
and Paul B. Davis, Eds. Controversy in Literature
(New York: Scribner, 1968), 84–92.
Trilling, Lionel. The Experience of Literature (New
York: Holt, Rinehart & Winston, 1967), 482–485.

"The Landlady"
Mochulsky, Konstantin. Dostoevsky: His Life and Work,
trans. Michael A. Minihan (Princeton: Princeton
Univ. Press, 1967), 73–81.
Neuhauser, R. "'The Landlady': A New Interpretation,"
Canadian Slavonic Papers, X (1968), 42–67.

"A Little Hero"
Mochulsky, Konstantin. Dostoevsky: His Life and Work,
trans. Michael A. Minihan (Princeton: Princeton
Univ. Press, 1967), 138–144.

"Mr. Prokharchin"
Mochulsky, Konstantin. Dostoevsky: His Life and Work,
trans. Michael A. Minihan (Princeton: Princeton
Univ. Press, 1967), 40–68.

"Notes from Underground"
Friedman, Maurice. Problematic Rebel: An Image of
Modern Man (New York: Random House, 1963), 99–
109.

Goodheart, Eugene. The Cult of the Ego (Chicago:
    Univ. of Chicago Press, 1968), 90–104.
Howe, Irving, Ed. Classics of Modern Fiction (New
    York: Harcourt, Brace & World, 1968), 7–12.
Kirk, Irina. "Dramatization of Consciousness in Camus
    and Dostoevsky," Bucknell R, XVI (March, 1968),
    96–104.
Mochulsky, Konstantin. Dostoevsky: His Life and Work,
    trans. Michael A. Minihan (Princeton: Princeton
    Univ. Press, 1967), 242–269.
Shestov, Lev. Dostoevsky, Tolstoy and Nietzsche,
    trans. Spencer Roberts (Athens: Ohio Univ. Press,
    1969), 169–173.
Simons, John D. "The Nature of Suffering in Schiller
    and Dostoevsky," Comp Lit, XIX (1967), 163–164.
Van Ghent, Dorothy, and Joseph S. Brown, Eds. Conti-
    nental Literature: An Anthology, II (Philadelphia:
    Lippincott, 1968), 1323–1325.

"A Novel in Nine Letters"
    Mochulsky, Konstantin. Dostoevsky: His Life and Work,
        trans. Michael A. Minihan (Princeton: Princeton
        Univ. Press, 1967), 43.

"Uncle's Dream"
    Mochulsky, Konstantin. Dostoevsky: His Life and Work,
        trans. Michael A. Minihan (Princeton: Princeton
        Univ. Press, 1967), 155–181.

"White Nights"
    Mochulsky, Konstantin. Dostoevsky: His Life and Work,
        trans. Michael A. Minihan (Princeton: Princeton
        Univ. Press, 1967), 92–98.

THEODORE DREISER

"Typhoon"
    McAleer, John J. Theodore Dreiser: An Introduction
        and Interpretation (New York: Holt, Rinehart & Win-
        ston, 1968), 145–146.

"The Victor"
    McAleer, John J. Theodore Dreiser: An Introduction
    and Interpretation (New York: Holt, Rinehart & Win-
    ston, 1968), 116–117.

ANNETTE VON DROSTE-HÜLSHOFF

"Die Judenbüche"
    Rölleke, Heinz. "Erzähltes Mysterium-Studie zur
    'Judenbüche' der Annette von Droste-Hülshoff,"
    Deutsche Vierteljahrsschrift für Literaturwissen-
    schaft und Geistesgeschichte, XLII (1968), 399–426.

LORD DUNSANY

"The Two Bottles of Relish"
    Dietrich, R. F., and Roger H. Sundell. Instructor's
    Manual for "The Art of Fiction" (New York: Holt,
    Rinehart & Winston, 1967), 24–28.

MARIA EDGEWORTH

"Angelina; ou, L'Amie Inconnue"
    Colby, Robert A. Fiction with a Purpose (Bloomington:
    Indiana Univ. Press, 1967), 48–49.

GEORGE ELIOT

"The Lifted Veil"
    Hurley, Edward. "'The Lifted Veil': George Eliot as
    Anti-Intellectual," Stud Short Fiction, V (1968), 257–
    262.

WILLIAM FAULKNER

"Barn Burning"

Dickinson, Leon T. Suggestions for Teachers of "Introduction to Literature" (New York: Holt, Rinehart & Winston, 1967), 68–69.

Franklin, Phyllis. "Sarty Snopes and 'Barn Burning,'" Mississippi Q, XXI (1968), 189–193.

Shrodes, Caroline, Justine Van Gundy, and Joel Dorius. Instructor's Manual for "Reading for Understanding" (New York: Macmillan, 1968), 25–26.

Steinmann, Martin, and Gerald Willen, Eds. Literature for Writing (Belmont: Wadsworth, 1962), 202–203; Second edition (1967), 199–200.

Trilling, Lionel. The Experience of Literature (New York: Holt, Rinehart & Winston, 1967), 745–748.

"The Bear"

Adams, Richard P. Faulkner: Myth and Motion (Princeton: Princeton Univ. Press, 1968), 145–149.

Bradford, Melvin E. "The Gum Tree Scene: Observations on the Structure of 'The Bear,'" Southern Hum R, I (1967), 141–150.

Guetti, James. The Limits of Metaphor: A Study of Melville, Conrad, and Faulkner (Ithaca: Cornell Univ. Press, 1967), 158–163.

McDonald, Walter R. "Faulkner's 'The Bear': The Sense of Its Structure," Engl Record, XVIII (December, 1967), 2–7.

Merton, Thomas. "'Baptism in the Forest': Wisdom and Initiation in William Faulkner," in Panichas, George A., Ed. Mansions of the Spirit: Essays in Literature and Religion (New York: Hawthorn, 1967), 29–34.

Richardson, Kenneth E. Form and Faith in the Novels of William Faulkner (The Hague: Mouton, 1967), 45–61.

Rosenfield, Claire. "New World, Old Myths," in Jobes, Katharine T., Ed. Twentieth Century Interpretations of "The Old Man and the Sea" (Englewood Cliffs: Prentice-Hall, 1968), 41–55.

Stewart, Randall. American Literature and Christian
Doctrine (Baton Rouge: Louisiana State Univ. Press,
1958), 136–139; reprinted in his Regionalism and
Beyond: Essays of Randall Stewart, ed. George Core
(Nashville: Vanderbilt Univ. Press, 1968), 205–208.
————. "Hawthorne and Faulkner," Coll Engl, XVII
(1956), 260; reprinted in his Regionalism and Be-
ond: Essays of Randall Stewart, ed. George Core
(Nashville: Vanderbilt Univ. Press, 1968), 131.
Warren, Joyce W. "The Role of Lion in Faulkner's
'The Bear': Key to a Better Understanding," Arizona
Q, XXIV (1968), 252–260.

"A Courtship"
Howell, Elmo. "Inversion and the 'Female' Principle:
William Faulkner's 'A Courtship,'" Stud Short Fiction,
IV (1967), 308–314.

"Delta Autumn"
Mizener, Arthur, Ed. Modern Short Stories: The Uses
of Imagination, Revised edition (New York: Norton,
1967), 545–550.

"Elly"
Bradford, Melvin E. "Faulkner's 'Elly': An Expose,"
Mississippi Q, XXI (1968), 179–187.

"An Error in Chemistry"
Hunt, Joel A. "Thomas Mann and Faulkner: Portrait
of a Magician," Wisconsin Stud Contemporary Lit,
VIII (1967), 431–436.

"The Fire and the Hearth"
Mizener, Arthur. A Handbook for Use with "Modern
Short Stories: The Uses of Imagination, Revised Edi-
tion" (New York: Norton, 1966), 135–140.

"A Justice"
Howell, Elmo. "Sam Fathers: A Note on Faulkner's 'A
Justice,'" Tennessee Stud Lit, XII (1967), 149–153.

"Old Man"
  Feaster, John. "Faulkner's 'Old Man': A Psychoan-
    alytical Approach," Mod Fiction Stud, XIII (1967),
    89–93.
  Howell, Elmo. "William Faulkner and the Plain People
    of Yoknapatawpha County," J Mississippi Hist, XXIV
    (1962), 82–85.
  Richardson, Kenneth E. Form and Faith in the Novels
    of William Faulkner (The Hague: Mouton, 1967),
    96–99.

"Raid"
  Mizener, Arthur. A Handbook for Use with "Modern
    Short Stories: The Uses of Imagination, Revised
    Edition" (New York: Norton, 1966), 143–149.

"Red Leaves"
  Frakes, James R., and Isadore Traschen, Eds. Short
    Fiction: A Critical Collection (Englewood Cliffs:
    Prentice-Hall, 1959), 42–44; Second edition (1969),
    40–42.

"A Rose for Emily"
  Howell, Elmo. "A Note on Faulkner's Emily as a Tragic
    Heroine," Serif, III (September, 1966), 13–15.
  Jäger, Dietrich. "Der 'verheimlichte Raum' in Faulk-
    ners 'A Rose for Emily' und Brittings 'Der Schneck-
    enweg,'" Literatur in Wissenschaft und Unterricht
    (Kiel), I (1968), 108–116.
  Stafford, T. J. "Tobe's Significance in 'A Rose for
    Emily,'" Mod Fiction Stud, XIV (1969), 451–453.
  West, Ray B. The Art of Writing Fiction (New York:
    Crowell, 1968), 197–203.

"Shingles for the Lord"
  Howell, Elmo. "Faulkner's Country Church: A Note
    on 'Shingles for the Lord,'" Mississippi Q, XXI
    (1968), 205–210.

"Spotted Horses"
  Greiner, Donald J. "Universal Snopesism: The Sig-
    nificance of 'Spotted Horses,'" Engl J, LVII (1968),
    1133-1137.

"That Evening Sun"
  Sanders, Barry. "Faulkner's Fire Imagery in 'That
    Evening Sun,'" Stud Short Fiction, V (1967), 69-71.

"There Was a Queen"
  Bradford, Melvin. "Certain Ladies of Quality: Faulk-
    ner's View of Women and the Evidence of 'There
    Was a Queen,'" Arlington Q, I (Winter, 1968), 112-
    139.

"Was"
  Bradford, Melvin. "All the Daughters of Eve: 'Was'
    and the Unity of Go Down, Moses," Arlington Q, I
    (1967), 28-37.

"Wash"
  Stewart, Jack F. "Apotheosis and Apocalypse in Faulk-
    ner's 'Wash,'" Stud Short Fiction, VI (1969), 586-600.
  Tuso, Joseph F. "Faulkner's 'Wash,'" Explicator,
    XXVII (1968), Item 17.

MORDEKHAI ZE'EV FEIERBERG

"In the Evening"
  Rabinovich, Isaiah. Major Trends in Modern Hebrew
    Fiction, trans. M. Roston (Chicago: Univ. of Chicago
    Press, 1968), 51-52.

"The Shadows"
  Rabinovich, Isaiah. Major Trends in Modern Hebrew
    Fiction, trans. M. Roston (Chicago: Univ. of Chicago
    Press, 1968), 54-55.

LESLIE FIEDLER

"The First Spade in the West"
Schulz, Max F. Radical Sophistication: Studies in Con-
temporary Jewish-American Novelists (Athens:
Ohio Univ. Press, 1969), 168–170.

RUDOLPH FISHER

"Miss Cynthie"
Turpin, Waters E. "Four Short Fiction Writers of the
Harlem Renaissance: Their Legacy of Achievement,"
Coll Lang Assoc J, XI (1967), 62–64.

F. SCOTT FITZGERALD

"Author's House"
Mizener, Arthur, Ed. Afternoon of an Author: A Selec-
tion of Uncollected Stories and Essays by F. Scott
Fitzgerald (Princeton: Princeton Univ. Press, 1957),
183; reprinted, with changes, in his "The Maturity
of F. Scott Fitzgerald," Sewanee R, LXVII (1959),
663–665; reprinted, with additions, in his The Sense
of Life in the Modern Novel (Boston: Houghton Mifflin, 1963), 190–192.

"Babylon Revisited"
Edenbaum, Robert I. "'Babylon Revisited': A Psycho-
logical Note on F. Scott Fitzgerald," Lit & Psych,
XVIII (1968), 27–29.
Lynskey, Winifred, Ed. Reading Modern Fiction,
Fourth edition (New York: Scribner, 1968), 204–206.
Mizener, Arthur. A Handbook for Use with "Modern
Short Stories: The Uses of Imagination, Revised Edi-
tion" (New York: Norton, 1966), 10–14.
Sklar, Robert. F. Scott Fitzgerald: The Last Laocoön
(New York: Oxford Univ. Press, 1967), 243–245.

"The Diamond as Big as the Ritz"
    Sklar, Robert. F. Scott Fitzgerald: The Last Laocoön
    (New York: Oxford Univ. Press, 1967), 140–147.

"Jacob's Ladder"
    Sklar, Robert. F. Scott Fitzgerald: The Last Laocoön
    (New York: Oxford Univ. Press, 1967), 228–229.

"May Day"
    Sklar, Robert. F. Scott Fitzgerald: The Last Laocoön
    (New York: Oxford Univ. Press, 1967), 73–78.

"The Offshore Pirate"
    Sklar, Robert. F. Scott Fitzgerald: The Last Laocoön
    (New York: Oxford Univ. Press, 1967), 68–71.

"One Trip Abroad"
    Sklar, Robert. F. Scott Fitzgerald: The Last Laocoön
    (New York: Oxford Univ. Press, 1967), 242–244.

"The Ordeal"
    Sklar, Robert. F. Scott Fitzgerald: The Last Laocoön
    (New York: Oxford Univ. Press, 1967), 12–13.

"Outside the Cabinet-Maker's"
    Mizener, Arthur, Ed. Afternoon of an Author: A Se-
    lection of Uncollected Stories and Essays by F. Scott
    Fitzgerald (Princeton: Princeton Univ. Press, 1957),
    137; reprinted, with changes, in his "The Maturity
    of F. Scott Fitzgerald," Sewanee R, LXVII (1959),
    662–663; reprinted, with additions, in his The Sense
    of Life in the Modern Novel (Boston: Houghton Mif-
    flin, 1963), 187–190.

"The Pierian Springs and the Last Straw"
    Sklar, Robert. F. Scott Fitzgerald: The Last Laocoön
    (New York: Oxford Univ. Press, 1967), 21–23.

"The Rich Boy"
   Hindus, Milton. F. Scott Fitzgerald: An Introduction
      and Interpretation (New York: Holt, Rinehart & Win-
      ston, 1968), 96–102.
   Katz, Joseph. "The Narrator and 'The Rich Boy,'"
      Fitzgerald Newsletter, No. 32 (Winter, 1966), 2–3.
   Rees, Robert A., and Barry Menikoff. A Manual to
      Accompany "The Short Story: An Introductory An-
      thology" (Boston: Little, Brown, 1969), 8–9.
   Sklar, Robert. F. Scott Fitzgerald: The Last Laocoön
      (New York: Oxford Univ. Press, 1967), 210–212.

"Six of One —"
   Sklar, Robert. F. Scott Fitzgerald: The Last Laocoön
      (New York: Oxford Univ. Press, 1967), 246–247.

"The Swimmers"
   Sklar, Robert. F. Scott Fitzgerald: The Last Laocoön
      (New York: Oxford Univ. Press, 1967), 236–239.

"Winter Dreams"
   Burhans, Clinton S., Jr. "'Magnificently Attune to
      Life': The Value of 'Winter Dreams,'" Stud Short
      Fiction, VI (1969), 401–412.
   Sklar, Robert. F. Scott Fitzgerald: The Last Laocoön
      (New York: Oxford Univ. Press, 1967), 158–159.

GUSTAVE FLAUBERT

"Bouvard and Pécuchet"
   Bart, Benjamin F. Flaubert (Syracuse: Syracuse Univ.
      Press, 1967), 592–620.
   Brombert, Victor. The Novels of Flaubert: A Study of
      Themes and Techniques (Princeton: Princeton Univ.
      Press, 1966), 258–281.

"Hérodias"
   Bart, Benjamin F. Flaubert (Syracuse: Syracuse Univ.
      Press, 1967), 698–704.

Brombert, Victor. The Novels of Flaubert: A Study of
   Themes and Techniques (Princeton: Princeton Univ.
   Press, 1966), 246–257.
Tillett, M. G. "An Approach to 'Hérodias,'" French
   Stud, XXI (1967), 24–31.

"St. Julien"
   Bart, Benjamin F. Flaubert (Syracuse: Syracuse Univ.
      Press, 1967), 677–686.
   Bart, Heidi C., and Benjamin F. Bart. "Space, Time,
      and Reality in Flaubert's 'Saint Julien,'" Romanic
      R, LIX (1968), 30–39.
   Brombert, Victor. The Novels of Flaubert: A Study
      of Themes and Techniques (Princeton: Princeton
      Univ. Press, 1966), 217–232.

"A Simple Heart"
   Bart, Benjamin F. Flaubert (Syracuse: Syracuse Univ.
      Press, 1967), 686–697.
   Böker, Uwe. "Die Zeit in Flauberts 'Un coeur simple,"
      Neuphilologische Mitteilungen, LXIX (1968), 129–
      148.
   Brombert, Victor. The Novels of Flaubert: A Study of
      Themes and Techniques (Princeton: Princeton Univ.
      Press, 1966), 233–245.
   Howe, Irving, Ed. Classics of Modern Fiction (New
      York: Harcourt, Brace & World, 1968), 179–184.
   Laubenthal, Wilhelm. "Gustave Flaubert: 'Un coeur
      simple,'" Die Neueren Sprachen, XVII (1968), 438–
      443.
   Showalter, English. "'Un coeur simple' as an Ironic
      Reply to Bernardin de Saint-Pierre," French R, XL
      (1966), 47–55.

E. M. FORSTER

"Albergo Empedocle"
   Kelvin, Norman. E. M. Forster (Carbondale: Southern
      Illinois Univ. Press, 1967), 36–37.

Stone, Wilfred. The Cave and the Mountain: A Study of
E. M. Forster (Stanford: Stanford Univ. Press, 1966),
144–145.

Thomson, George H. The Fiction of E. M. Forster (Detroit: Wayne State Univ. Press, 1967), 72–74.

"The Celestial Omnibus"
Dietrich, R. F., and Roger H. Sundell. Instructor's
Manual for "The Art of Fiction" (New York: Holt,
Rinehart & Winston, 1967), 16–20.

Stone, Wilfred. The Cave and the Mountain: A Study of
E. M. Forster (Stanford: Stanford Univ. Press, 1966),
148–152.

Thomson, George H. The Fiction of E. M. Forster (Detroit: Wayne State Univ. Press, 1967), 68–71.

"Co-ordination"
Stone, Wilfred. The Cave and the Mountain: A Study of
E. M. Forster (Stanford: Stanford Univ. Press, 1966),
158–159.

"The Curate's Friend"
Stone, Wilfred. The Cave and the Mountain: A Study of
E. M. Forster (Stanford: Stanford Univ. Press, 1966),
156–157.

"The Eternal Moment"
Godfrey, Denis. E. M. Forster's Other Kingdom (New
York: Barnes & Noble, 1968), 17–19.

Kelvin, Norman. E. M. Forster (Carbondale: Southern
Illinois Univ. Press, 1967), 24–27.

Stone, Wilfred. The Cave and the Mountain: A Study of
E. M. Forster (Stanford: Stanford Univ. Press, 1966),
137–144.

"The Machine Stops"
Godfrey, Denis. E. M. Forster's Other Kingdom (New
York: Barnes & Noble, 1968), 15–16.

Kelvin, Norman. E. M. Forster (Carbondale: Southern
Illinois Univ. Press, 1967), 32–33.

Stone, Wilfred. The Cave and the Mountain: A Study of
E. M. Forster (Stanford: Stanford Univ. Press, 1966),
152–155.

"Other Kingdom"
Godfrey, Denis. E. M. Forster's Other Kingdom (New
York: Barnes & Noble, 1968), 11–12.
Kelvin, Norman. E. M. Forster (Carbondale: Southern
Illinois Univ. Press, 1967), 28–30.
Stone, Wilfred. The Cave and the Mountain: A Study of
E. M. Forster (Stanford: Stanford Univ. Press, 1966),
157–158.

"The Other Side of the Hedge"
Stone, Wilfred. The Cave and the Mountain: A Study of
E. M. Forster (Stanford: Stanford Univ. Press, 1966),
147–148.

"The Point of It"
Kelvin, Norman. E. M. Forster (Carbondale: Southern
Illinois Univ. Press, 1967), 34–35.
Stone, Wilfred. The Cave and the Mountain: A Study of
E. M. Forster (Stanford: Stanford Univ. Press, 1966),
159.
Thomson, George H. The Fiction of E. M. Forster (De-
troit: Wayne State Univ. Press, 1967), 63–68.

"The Road from Colonus"
Godfrey, Denis. E. M. Forster's Other Kingdom (New
York: Barnes & Noble, 1968), 16–17.
Kelvin, Norman. E. M. Forster (Carbondale: Southern
Illinois Univ. Press, 1967), 30–32.
Stone, Wilfred. The Cave and the Mountain: A Study of
E. M. Forster (Stanford: Stanford Univ. Press, 1966),
145–147.
Thomson, George H. The Fiction of E. M. Forster
(Detroit: Wayne State Univ. Press, 1967), 75–77.
Trilling, Lionel. The Experience of Literature (New
York: Holt, Rinehart & Winston, 1967), 683–684.

"The Story of a Panic"
    Kelvin, Norman. E. M. Forster (Carbondale: Southern
        Illinois Univ. Press, 1967), 21–24.
    Stone, Wilfred. The Cave and the Mountain: A Study of
        E. M. Forster (Stanford: Stanford Univ. Press, 1966),
        130–137.
    Thomson, George H. The Fiction of E. M. Forster
        (Detroit: Wayne State Univ. Press, 1967), 74–75.

"The Story of the Siren"
    Godfrey, Denis. E. M. Forster's Other Kingdom (New
        York: Barnes & Noble, 1968), 14–15.
    Kelvin, Norman. E. M. Forster (Carbondale: Southern
        Illinois Univ. Press, 1967), 35–36.
    Thomson, George H. The Fiction of E. M. Forster
        (Detroit: Wayne State Univ. Press, 1967), 84–88.

MARY E. WILKINS FREEMAN

"The Balking of Christopher"
    Westbrook, Perry D. Mary Wilkins Freeman (New
        York: Twayne, 1967), 169–170.

"A Conflict Ended"
    Westbrook, Perry D. Mary Wilkins Freeman (New
        York: Twayne, 1967), 81–83.

"Evelina's Garden"
    Westbrook, Perry D. Mary Wilkins Freeman (New
        York: Twayne, 1967), 141–142.

"The Great Pine"
    Westbrook, Perry D. Mary Wilkins Freeman (New
        York: Twayne, 1967), 151–152.

"A New England Prophet"
    Westbrook, Perry D. Mary Wilkins Freeman (New
        York: Twayne, 1967), 140–141.

CARLOS FUENTES

"Chac Mool"
  Harss, Luis, and Barbara Dohmann. Into the Main-
  stream (New York: Harper & Row, 1967), 285-286.

GABRIEL GARCÍA MÁRQUEZ

"The Day After Saturday"
  Harss, Luis, and Barbara Dohmann. Into the Main-
  stream (New York: Harper & Row, 1967), 333-334.

"Tuesday Nap"
  Harss, Luis, and Barbara Dohmann. Into the Main-
  stream (New York: Harper & Row, 1967), 328-329.

VSEVOLOD M. GARSHIN

"The Incident"
  Lejins, Hamilkars. "Suicide in Garshin's Life and
  Stories," So-Central Bull, XXVII (Winter, 1967),
  42-43.

"The Red Flower"
  Proffer, Carl R., Ed. From Karamzin to Bunin: An
  Anthology of Russian Short Stories (Bloomington:
  Indiana Univ. Press, 1969), 31-32.

THÉOPHILE GAUTIER

"Arria Marcella"
  Smith, Albert B. Ideal and Reality in the Fictional
  Narratives of Theophile Gautier (Gainesville: Univ.
  of Florida Press, 1969), 22-26.

"Jettatura"
  Smith, Albert B. Ideal and Reality in the Fictional
    Narratives of Theophile Gautier (Gainesville: Univ.
    of Florida Press, 1969), 30–32.

"La Morte amoureuse"
  Smith, Albert B. Ideal and Reality in the Fictional
    Narratives of Theophile Gautier (Gainesville: Univ.
    of Florida Press, 1969), 38–39.

ANDRÉ GIDE

"Genevieve"
  Guerard, Albert. André Gide (Cambridge: Harvard
    Univ. Press, 1951), 146–148; Second edition (1969),
    146–148.
  Painter, George D. André Gide, A Critical Biography
    (New York: Atheneum, 1968), 105–107.

"The Immoralist"
  Goodhand, Robert. "The Religious Leitmotif in 'L'Im-
    moraliste,'" Romanic R, LVII (1966), 263–276.
  Guerard, Albert. André Gide (Cambridge: Harvard
    Univ. Press, 1951), 99–118; Second edition (1969),
    99–118.
  Painter, George D. André Gide, A Critical Biography
    (New York: Atheneum, 1968), 40–44.
  Savage, Catharine H. "'L'Immoraliste': Psychology
    and Rhetoric," Xavier Univ Stud, VI (1967), 43–62.

"Isabelle"
  Guerard, Albert. André Gide (Cambridge: Harvard
    Univ. Press, 1951), 124–128; Second edition (1969),
    124–128.
  Painter, George D. André Gide, A Critical Biography
    (New York: Atheneum, 1968), 59–62.

"Marshlands"
>   Guerard, Albert. André Gide (Cambridge: Harvard
>   Univ. Press, 1951), 69–71; Second edition (1969),
>   69–71.
>   Painter, George D. André Gide, A Critical Biography
>   (New York: Atheneum, 1968), 23–25.

"The Pastoral Symphony"
>   Falk, Eugene H. Types of Thematic Structure: The
>   Nature and Function of Motifs in Gide, Camus, and
>   Sartre (Chicago: Univ. of Chicago Press, 1967), 30–
>   51.
>   Guerard, Albert. André Gide (Cambridge: Harvard
>   Univ. Press, 1951), 139–144; Second edition (1969),
>   139–144.
>   Painter, George D. André Gide, A Critical Biography
>   (New York: Atheneum, 1968), 80–84.

"The Return of the Prodigal Son"
>   Guerard, Albert. André Gide (Cambridge: Harvard
>   Univ. Press, 1951), 82; Second edition (1969), 82.
>   Painter, George D. André Gide, A Critical Biography
>   (New York: Atheneum, 1968), 53–55.

"Robert"
>   Painter, George D. André Gide, A Critical Biography
>   (New York: Atheneum, 1968), 104–105.

"School for Wives"
>   Guerard, Albert. André Gide (Cambridge: Harvard
>   Univ. Press, 1951), 145–146; Second edition (1969),
>   145–146.
>   Painter, George D. André Gide, A Critical Biography
>   (New York: Atheneum, 1968), 103–104.

"Strait Is the Gate"
>   Guerard, Albert. André Gide (Cambridge: Harvard
>   Univ. Press, 1951), 118–124; Second edition (1969),
>   118–124.

Knecht, Loring D. "A New Reading of Gide's 'La Porte
étroite,'" PMLA, LXXXII (1967), 640–648.
Painter, George D. André Gide, A Critical Biography
(New York: Atheneum, 1968), 55–59.
Sonnenfield, Albert. "'Strait Is the Gate': Byroads in
Gide's Labyrinth," Novel, I (1968), 118–132.

"Theseus"
Guerard, Albert. André Gide (Cambridge: Harvard
Univ. Press, 1951), 90–92; Second edition (1969),
90–92.
Painter, George D. André Gide, A Critical Biography
(New York: Atheneum, 1968), 127–129.

NIKOLAI GOGOL

"The Nevsky Prospect"
Holquist, James M. "The Devil in Mufti: The 'Märchenwelt' in Gogol's Short Stories," PMLA, LXXXII (1967)
358–360.

"The Nose"
Hollander, Robert, and Sidney E. Lind, Eds. The Art
of the Story: An Introduction (New York: American
Book, 1968), 61–63.
Holquist, James M. "The Devil in Mufti: The 'Märchen-
welt' in Gogol's Short Stories," PMLA, LXXXII (1967)
360.
Oulianoff, Micholas I. "Arabesque or Apocalypse? On
the Fundamental Idea of Gogol's Story 'The Nose,'"
Canadian Slavic Stud, I (1967), 158–171.

"Old World Landowners"
Holquist, James M. "The Devil in Mufti: The 'Märchenwelt' in Gogol's Short Stories," PMLA, LXXXII (1967)
357.

"The Overcoat"

Eichenbaum, B. "The Structure of Gogol's 'The Overcoat,'" Russian R, XXII (1963), 377–399.

Holquist, James M. The Devil in Mufti: The 'Märchenwelt' in Gogol's Short Stories," PMLA, LXXXII (1967), 358–360.

Proffer, Carl R., Ed. From Karamzin to Bunin: An Anthology of Russian Short Stories (Bloomington: Indiana Univ. Press, 1969), 12–17.

Woodward, James B. "The Threadbare Fabric of Gogol's 'Overcoat,'" Canadian Slavic Stud, I (1967), 95–104.

"The Quarrel Between Ivan Ivanovich and Ivan Nikiforovich"

Holquist, James M. "The Devil in Mufti: The 'Märchenwelt' in Gogol's Short Stories," PMLA, LXXXII (1967), 356–357.

"The Sorochinsty Fair"

Holquist, James M. "The Devil in Mufti: The 'Märchenwelt' in Gogol's Short Stories," PMLA, LXXXII (1967), 355.

HERBERT GOLD

"The Witch"

Krupp, Kathleen M. "Psychological Tripling in 'The Witch,'" in McKenzie, Barbara, Ed. The Process of Fiction (New York: Harcourt, Brace & World, 1969), 161–167.

PAUL GOODMAN

"The Architect from New York"

Smith, Hadley A. "The Measure of Harry Hodges," in McKenzie, Barbara, Ed. The Process of Fiction (New York: Harcourt, Brace & World, 1969), 280–285.

CAROLINE GORDON

"The Brilliant Leaves"
> Fletcher, Marie. "The Fate of Women in a Changing
> South: A Persistent Theme in the Fiction of Caroline
> Gordon," Mississippi Q, XXI (1968), 20–21.

"The Captive"
> Lynskey, Winifred, Ed. Reading Modern Fiction, Sec-
> ond edition (New York: Scribner, 1957), 239–240;
> Fourth edition (1968), 237–238.
> Rubin, Larry. "Christian Allegory in Caroline Gordon's
> 'The Captive,'" Stud Short Fiction, V (1968), 283–289.

"Old Red"
> Huck, Wilbur, and William Shanahan, Eds. The Modern
> Short Story (New York: American Book, 1968), 55–57.
> Mizener, Arthur. A Handbook for Use with "Modern
> Short Stories: The Uses of Imagination, Revised Edi-
> tion" (New York: Norton, 1966), 158–161.

MAXIM GORKI

"At the Salt Marsh"
> Borras, F. M. Maxim Gorky the Writer (London: Ox-
> ford Univ. Press, 1967), 79.

"Boles"
> Borras, F. M. Maxim Gorky the Writer (London: Ox-
> ford Univ. Press, 1967), 86.

"Chelkash"
> Borras, F. M. Maxim Gorky the Writer (London, Ox-
> ford Univ. Press, 1967), 66–72.
> Proffer, Carl R., Ed. From Karamzin to Bunin: An
> Anthology of Russian Short Stories (Bloomington:
> Indiana Univ. Press, 1969), 41–43.

Weil, Irwin. <u>Gorky: His Literary Development and Influence on Soviet Intellectual Life</u> (New York: Random House, 1966), 33–34.

"The Coachman"
Borras, F. M. <u>Maxim Gorky the Writer</u> (London: Oxford Univ. Press, 1967), 91–93.

"Creatures That Once Were Men"
Borras, F. M. <u>Maxim Gorky the Writer</u> (London: Oxford Univ. Press, 1967), 77–78.

"He Ran Off"
Borras, F. M. <u>Maxim Gorky the Writer</u> (London: Oxford Univ. Press, 1967), 85–86.

"Kain and Artyom"
Borras, F. M. <u>Maxim Gorky the Writer</u> (London: Oxford Univ. Press, 1967), 82–83.

"Karamora"
Borras, F. M. <u>Maxim Gorky the Writer</u> (London: Oxford Univ. Press, 1967), 90–91.

"Konovalov"
Borras, F. M. <u>Maxim Gorky the Writer</u> (London: Oxford Univ. Press, 1967), 72–75.

"Makar Chudra"
Borras, F. M. <u>Maxim Gorky the Writer</u> (London: Oxford Univ. Press, 1967), 59–61.

"The Mistake"
Borras, F. M. <u>Maxim Gorky the Writer</u> (London: Oxford Univ. Press, 1967), 84.

"My Fellow Traveller"
Borras, F. M. <u>Maxim Gorky the Writer</u> (London: Oxford Univ. Press, 1967), 79–81.

"Old Izergil"
  Borras, F. M. Maxim Gorky the Writer (London: Ox-
    ford Univ. Press, 1967), 61–63.

"On a Raft"
  Borras, F. M. Maxim Gorky the Writer (London: Ox-
    ford Univ. Press, 1967), 83–84.

"One Autumn Evening"
  Borras, F. M. Maxim Gorky the Writer (London: Ox-
    ford Univ. Press, 1967), 89–90.

"The Orlovs"
  Borras, F. M. Maxim Gorky the Writer (London: Ox-
    ford Univ. Press, 1967), 76–77.
  Weil, Irwin. Gorky: His Literary Development and In-
    fluence on Soviet Intellectual Life (New York: Ran-
    dom House, 1966), 34–35.

"Out of Boredom"
  Borras, F. M. Maxim Gorky the Writer (London: Ox-
    ford Univ. Press, 1967), 85–86.

"A Rolling Stone"
  Borras, F. M. Maxim Gorky the Writer (London: Ox-
    ford Univ. Press, 1967), 72–75.

"A Tale of Unrequited Love"
  Borras, F. M. Maxim Gorky the Writer (London: Ox-
    ford Univ. Press, 1967), 93–94.

"Twenty-Six Men and a Girl"
  Borras, F. M. Maxim Gorky the Writer (London: Ox-
    ford Univ. Press, 1967), 86–87.
  Weil, Irwin. Gorky: His Literary Development and In-
    fluence on Soviet Intellectual Life (New York: Ran-
    dom House, 1966), 35–37.

"Vanka Mazin"
  Borras, F. M. Maxim Gorky the Writer (London: Ox-
    ford Univ. Press, 1967), 88–89.

WILLIAM GOYEN

"The White Rooster"
Phillips, Robert. "Samuels and Samson: Theme and
Legend in 'The White Rooster,'" Stud Short Fiction,
VI (1969), 331–333.

GÜNTER GRASS

"The Left-Handers"
Hollander, Robert, and Sidney E. Lind, Eds. The Art
of the Story: An Introduction (New York: American
Book, 1968), 396–397.

GRAHAM GREENE

"The Basement Room"
Schorer, Mark, Ed. The Story: A Critical Anthology
(New York: Prentice-Hall, 1950), 183–185; Second
edition (Englewood Cliffs: Prentice-Hall, 1967), 157–
159.

"The Destructors"
Rees, Robert A., and Barry Menikoff. A Manual to Ac-
company "The Short Story: An Introductory Anthology" (Boston: Little, Brown, 1969), 1–2.

"The Second Death"
Lynskey, Winifred, Ed. Reading Modern Fiction, Sec-
ond edition (New York: Scribner, 1957), 245–246;
Fourth edition (1968), 243–244.

DMITRI V. GRIGOROVICH

"Karelin's Dream"
Struve, Gleb. "On Chekhov's Craftmanship: The Anatomy of a Story," Slavic R, XX (1961), 466–468.

"The Village"
    Strong, Robert L. "Grigorovich's 'The Village': An
        Etude in Sentimental Naturalism," Slavic & East
        European J, XII (1968), 169–175.

FRANZ GRILLPARZER

"The Poor Player"
    Gutmann, Anna. "Grillparzers 'Der arme Spielmann':
        Erlebtes und Erdichtetes," J International Arthur
        Schnitzler Research Assoc, VI, i (1967), 14–44.
    Ivask, Ivar. "Introduction," in Grillparzer, Franz.
        The Poor Fiddler, trans. Alexander and Elizabeth
        Henderson (New York: Ungar, 1967), 15–25.
    Straubinger, O. Paul. "'Der arme Spielmann,'" Grill-
        parzer Forum Forchtenstein 1966 (1967), 97–102.
    Swales, M. W. "The Narrative Perspective in Grill-
        parzer's 'Der Arme Spielmann,'" Germ Life & Let-
        ters, XX (1967), 107–116.

WILL N. HARBEN

"The Heresy of Abner Calihan"
    Bush, Robert. "Will N. Harben's Northern Georgia Fic-
        tion," Mississippi Q, XX (1967), 107.

"The Whipping of Uncle Henry"
    Bush, Robert. "Will N. Harben's Northern Georgia Fic-
        tion," Mississippi Q, XX (1967), 106–107.

THOMAS HARDY

"A Few Crusted Characters"
    Howe, Irving. "A Note on Hardy's Stories," Hudson R,
        XIX (1966), 261–262.

"The Fiddler of the Reels"
    Howe, Irving. "A Note on Hardy's Stories," Hudson R,
       XIX (1966), 265–266.

"The Waiting Supper"
    Howe, Irving. "A Note on Hardy's Stories," Hudson R,
       XIX (1966), 265.

BRET HARTE

"The Passing of Enríquez"
    Robinson, Cecil. With the Ears of Strangers: The Mexi-
      can in American Literature (Tucson: Univ. of Arizona
      Press, 1963), 154–155.

NATHANIEL HAWTHORNE

"Alice Doane's Appeal"
    Fossum, Robert H. "The Summer of the Past: Hawthorne's
      'Alice Doane's Appeal,'" Nineteenth-Century Fiction,
      XXIII (1968), 294–303.

"The Ambitious Guest"
    Moss, Sidney P. "The Mountain God of Hawthorne's 'The
      Ambitious Guest,'" Emerson Soc Q, No. 47 (Second
      Quarter, 1967), 74–75.

"The Artist of the Beautiful"
    Bell, Millicent. Hawthorne's View of the Artist (New
      York: State Univ. of New York, 1962), 94–111.
    Curran, Ronald T. "Irony: Another Thematic Dimen-
      sion to 'The Artist of the Beautiful,'" Stud Romanti-
      cism, VI (1966), 34–45.
    Fairbanks, Henry G. "Hawthorne Amid the Alien Corn,"
      Coll Engl, XVII (1956), 266; reprinted in his The
      Lasting Loneliness of Nathaniel Hawthorne (Albany:
      Magi, 1965), 150–151.

Rees, Robert A., and Barry Menikoff. A Manual to Ac-
company "The Short Story: An Introductory Anthology" (Boston: Little, Brown, 1969), 15.
Yoder, R. A. "Hawthorne and His Artist," Stud Romanticism, VII (1968), 193–206.

"The Birthmark"
Dahl, Curtis. "The Devil Is a Wise One," Cithara, VI
(May, 1967), 52–58.
Fairbanks, Henry G. The Lasting Loneliness of
Nathaniel Hawthorne (Albany: Magi, 1965), 100–
105.
Miller, James E. "Hawthorne and Melville: The Un-
pardonable Sin," PMLA, LXX (1955), 92–93, 101–
102; reprinted in his Quests Surd and Absurd (Chi-
cago: Univ. of Chicago Press, 1967), 211, 222–223.
Shrodes, Caroline, Justine Van Gundy, and Joel Dorius.
Instructor's Manual for "Reading for Understanding"
(New York: Macmillan, 1968), 3–5.

"The Celestial Railroad"
Pattison, Joseph C. "'The Celestial Railroad' as
Dream-Tale," Am Q, XX (1968), 224–236.

"David Swann: A Fantasy"
Tharpe, Jac. Nathaniel Hawthorne: Identity and Knowledge (Carbondale: Southern Illinois Univ. Press,
1967), 106–107.

"Dr. Heidegger's Experiment"
Fairbanks, Henry G. "Man's Separation from Nature:
Hawthorne's Philosophy of Suffering and Death,"
Christian Scholar, XLII (1959), 61; reprinted in his
The Lasting Loneliness of Nathaniel Hawthorne
(Albany: Magi, 1965), 92–93.

"Drowne's Wooden Image"
Bell, Millicent. Hawthorne's View of the Artist (New
York: State Univ. of New York, 1962), 127–134.

"Egotism; or, The Bosom Serpent"
   Miller, James E. "Hawthorne and Melville: The Un-
      pardonable Sin," PMLA, LXX (1955), 94; reprinted
      in his Quests Surd and Absurd (Chicago: Univ. of
      Chicago Press, 1967), 212–213.

"Endicott and the Red Cross"
   Bercovitch, Sacvan. "Endicott's Breastplate: Symbolism
      and Typology in 'Endicott and the Red Cross,'" Stud
      Short Fiction, IV (1967), 289–299.
   Gallagher, Edward J. "History in 'Endicott and the
      Red Cross,'" Emerson Soc Q, L, Suppl. (1968),
      62–65.

"Ethan Brand"
   Baym, Nina. "The Head, the Heart, and the Unpardon-
      able Sin," New England Q, XL (1967), 41–47.
   Dahl, Curtis. "The Devil Is a Wise One," Cithara, VI
      (May, 1967), 52–58.
   Davison, Richard A. "The Villagers and 'Ethan Brand,'"
      Stud Short Fiction, IV (1967), 260–262.
   Dusenbery, Robert. "Hawthorne's Merry Company:
      The Anatomy of Laughter in the Tales and Short
      Stories," PMLA, LXXXII (1967), 286–287.
   Miller, James E. "Hawthorne and Melville: The Un-
      pardonable Sin," PMLA, LXX (1955), 95–96, 98; re-
      printed in his Quests Surd and Absurd (Chicago:
      Univ. of Chicago Press, 1967), 214–215, 218.
   White, William M. "Hawthorne's Eighteen-Year Cycle:
      Ethan Brand and Reuben Bourne," Stud Short Fic-
      tion, VI (1969), 215–218.

"Feathertop"
   Tharpe, Jac. Nathaniel Hawthorne: Identity and Know-
      ledge (Carbondale: Southern Illinois Univ. Press,
      1967), 84–85.

"The Great Carbuncle"
   Levy, Leo B. "Hawthorne and the Sublime," Am Lit,
      XXXVII (1966), 392–395.

Morrow, Patrick. "A Writer's Workshop: Hawthorne's
'The Great Carbuncle,'" Stud Short Fiction, VI (1969),
157–164.

"The Great Stone Face"
Levy, Leo B. "Hawthorne and the Sublime," Am Lit,
XXXVII (1966), 395–397.
Miller, James E. "Hawthorne and Melville: The Un-
pardonable Sin," PMLA, LXX (1955), 104–105; re-
printed in his Quests Surd and Absurd (Chicago:
Univ. of Chicago Press, 1967), 225–226.

"The Intelligence Office"
Tharpe, Jac. Nathaniel Hawthorne: Identity and Knowledge (Carbondale: Southern Illinois Univ. Press,
1967), 56–57.

"Lady Eleanore's Mantle"
Miller, James E. "Hawthorne and Melville: The Un-
pardonable Sin," PMLA, LXX (1955), 97–99; reprinted in his Quests Surd and Absurd (Chicago:
Univ. of Chicago Press, 1967), 216–217.

"The Minister's Black Veil"
Allen, M. L. "The Black Veil: Three Versions of a
Symbol," Engl Stud, XLVII (1966), 286–289.
Canaday, Nicholas. "Hawthorne's Minister and the
Veiling Deceptions of Self," Stud Short Fiction, IV
(1967), 135–142.
Carnochan, W. B. "'The Minister's Black Veil': Sym-
bol, Meaning, and Context of Hawthorne's Art,"
Nineteenth-Century Fiction, XXIV (1969), 182–192.
Cochran, Robert W. "Hawthorne's Choice: The Veil
or the Jaundiced Eye," Coll Engl, XXIII (1962), 342–
346; reprinted in Freedman, Morris, and Paul B.
Davis, Eds. Controversy in Literature (New York:
Scribner, 1968), 41–46.
Crie, Robert D. "'The Minister's Black Veil': Mr.
Hooper's Symbolic Leaf," Lit & Psych, XVII (1967),
211–217.

Fogle, Richard H. "An Ambiguity of Sin and Sorrow,"
New England Q, XXI (1948), 342–349; reprinted in
his Hawthorne's Fiction: The Light and the Dark
(Norman: Univ. of Oklahoma Press, 1952), 33–40;
Freedman, Morris, and Paul B. Davis, Eds. Controversy in Literature (New York: Scribner, 1968),
36–40.

Stibitz, E. E. "Ironic Unity in Hawthorne's 'The Minister's Black Veil,'" Am Lit, XXXIV (1962), 182–190;
reprinted in Clifton, Lucile, and Alexander MacGibbon, Eds. Composition: An Approach Through Reading (New York: Harcourt, Brace & World, 1968), 441–
448.

Tharpe, Jac. Nathaniel Hawthorne: Identity and Knowledge (Carbondale: Southern Illinois Univ. Press,
1967), 77–80.

Turner, Frederick W. "Hawthorne's Black Veil," Stud
Short Fiction, V (1968), 186–187.

"My Kinsman, Major Molineux"
Allison, Alexander. "The Literary Contexts of 'My
Kinsman, Major Molineux,'" Nineteenth-Century
Fiction, XXIII (1968), 304–311.

Carpenter, Richard C. "Hawthorne's Polar Explorations:
'Young Goodman Brown' and 'My Kinsman, Major
Molineux,'" Nineteenth-Century Fiction, XXIV (1969),
45–56.

Dusenbery, Robert. "Hawthorne's Merry Company:
The Anatomy of Laughter in the Tales and Short
Stories," PMLA, LXXXII (1967), 287–288.

Gross, Seymour L. "Hawthorne's 'My Kinsman, Major
Molineux': History as Moral Adventure," Nineteenth-
Century Fiction, XII (1957), 97–109; reprinted in
Donohue, Agnes, Ed. A Casebook on the Hawthorne
Question (New York: Crowell, 1963), 51–63; Browne,
Ray B., and Martin Light, Eds. Critical Approaches
to American Literature, I (New York: Crowell, 1965),
212–222; Timko, Michael, and Clinton F. Oliver, Eds.
Thirty-Eight Short Stories (New York: Knopf, 1968),
58–69.

Hollander, Robert, and Sidney E. Lind, Eds. The Art
of the Story: An Introduction (New York: American
Book, 1968), 41–42.
Rose, Marilyn G. "Theseus Motif in 'My Kinsman,
Major Molineux,'" Emerson Soc Q, No. 47 (Second
Quarter, 1967), 21–23.
Russell, John. "Allegory and 'My Kinsman, Major
Molineux,'" New England Q, XL (1967), 432–440.
Tharpe, Jac. Nathaniel Hawthorne: Identity and Know-
ledge (Carbondale: Southern Illinois Univ. Press,
1967), 80–82.
Trilling, Lionel. The Experience of Literature (New
York: Holt, Rinehart & Winston, 1967), 438–440.
Waggoner, Hyatt H. Hawthorne: A Critical Study (Cam-
bridge: Harvard Univ. Press, 1955), 46–53; Second
edition (1963), 56–64; reprinted in Locke, Louis G.,
William M. Gibson, and George Arms, Eds. Intro-
duction to Literature, Fifth edition (New York: Holt,
Rinehart & Winston, 1967), 257–262.

"The Old Apple Dealer"
Fairbanks, Henry G. The Lasting Loneliness of Nathaniel Hawthorne: A Study of the Sources of Alienation in Modern Man (Albany: Magi, 1965), 112–113.

"Rappaccini's Daughter"
Anderson, Norman A. "'Rappaccini's Daughter': A
Keatsian Analogue?" PMLA, LXXXIII (1968), 271–
283.
Dahl, Curtis. "The Devil Is a Wise One," Cithara, VI
(May, 1967), 52–58.
Fairbanks, Henry G. The Lasting Loneliness of Na-
thaniel Hawthorne: A Study of the Sources of Alien-
ation in Modern Man (Albany: Magi, 1965), 105–108.
Kloeckner, Alfred J. "The Flower and the Fountain:
Hawthorne's Chief Symbols in 'Rappaccini's Daughter"
Am Lit, XXXVIII (1966), 323–336.
Miller, James E. "Hawthorne and Melville: The Un-
pardonable Sin," PMLA, LXX (1955), 93–94; reprinte
in his Quests Surd and Absurd (Chicago: Univ. of Chi
cago Press, 1967), 212.

Smith, Julian. "Keats and Hawthorne: A Romantic
Bloom in Rappaccini's Garden," Emerson Soc Q,
No. 42 (First Quarter, 1966), 8–12.
Tharpe, Jac. Nathaniel Hawthorne: Identity and Know-
ledge (Carbondale: Southern Illinois Univ. Press,
1967), 89–94.

"Roger Malvin's Burial"
Donohue, Agnes M. "'From Whose Bourn No Traveller
Returns': A Reading of 'Roger Malvin's Burial,'"
Nineteenth-Century Fiction, XVIII (1963), 1–19;
reprinted in Levin, Gerald, Ed. The Short Story:
An Inductive Approach (New York: Harcourt, Brace
& World, 1967), 502–511.
Robillard, Douglas. "Hawthorne's 'Roger Malvin's
Burial,'" Explicator, XXVI (1968), Item 56.
Stock, Ely. "History and the Bible in Hawthorne's
'Roger Malvin's Burial,'" Essex Institute Historical
Collections, C (October, 1964), 279–296.
White, William M. "Hawthorne's Eighteen-Year Cycle:
Ethan Brand and Reuben Bourne," Stud Short Fiction,
VI (1969), 215–218.

"A Virtuoso's Collection"
Fairbanks, Henry G. The Lasting Loneliness of Nathaniel Hawthorne (Albany: Magi, 1965), 90–92.

"Wakefield"
Tharpe, Jac. Nathaniel Hawthorne: Identity and Knowledge (Carbondale: Southern Illinois Univ. Press,
1967), 82–83.

"The Wedding Knell"
Homan, John. "Hawthorne's 'The Wedding Knell' and
Cotton Mather," Emerson Soc Q, No. 43 (1966), 66–
67.

"The Wives of the Dead"
Stephenson, Edward R. "Hawthorne's 'The Wives of
the Dead,'" Explicator, XXV (1967), Item 63.

"Young Goodman Brown"

Abel, Darrel. "Black Glove and Pink Ribbon: Hawthorne's Metonymic Symbols," New England Q, XLII
(1969), 168–180.

Adams, Richard P. "Hawthorne's Provincial Tales,"
New England Q, XXX (1957), 41–44, 56–57; reprinted
in Connolly, Thomas E., Ed. Nathaniel Hawthorne:
"Young Goodman Brown" (Columbus: Merrill, 1968),
54–62.

Carpenter, Richard C. "Hawthorne's Polar Explorations:
'Young Goodman Brown' and 'My Kinsman, Major
Molineux,'" Nineteenth-Century Fiction, XXIV (1969),
45–56.

Cherry, Fannye N. "The Sources of Hawthorne's 'Young
Goodman Brown,'" Am Lit, V (1934), 342–349.

Connolly, Thomas E. "Hawthorne's 'Young Goodman
Brown': An Attack on Puritan Calvinism," Am Lit,
XXVIII (1956), 370–375; reprinted in Connolly,
Thomas E., Ed. Nathaniel Hawthorne: "Young
Goodman Brown" (Columbus: Merrill, 1968), 49–53;
reprinted in part in Beebe, Maurice, Ed. Literary
Symbolism (San Francisco: Wadsworth, 1960), 107–111.

――――――. "How Young Goodman Brown Became Old
Badman Brown," Coll Engl, XXIV (1962), 153.

Crews, Frederick C. The Sins of the Fathers: Hawthorne's Psychological Themes (New York: Oxford
Univ. Press, 1966), 98–106; reprinted in Connolly,
Thomas E., Ed. Nathaniel Hawthorne: "Young Goodman Brown" (Columbus: Merrill, 1968), 125–139.

Ferguson, J. M. "Hawthorne's 'Young Goodman Brown,'"
Explicator, XXVIII (1969), Item 32.

Fogle, Richard H. "Ambiguity and Clarity in Hawthorne's
'Young Goodman Brown,'" New England Q, XVIII
(1945), 448–465; reprinted in his Hawthorne's Fiction: The Light and the Dark (Norman: Univ. of Oklahoma Press, 1952), 15–32; Locke, Louis, William
Gibson, and George Arms, Eds. Introduction to
Literature, Third edition (New York: Rinehart,
1957), 280–290; Donohue, Agnes, Ed. A Casebook
on the Hawthorne Question (New York: Crowell,

1963), 207–221; Connolly, Thomas E., Ed. Nathaniel
Hawthorne: "Young Goodman Brown" (Columbus: Merrill, 1968), 80–95; reprinted in part in Beebe, Maurice, Ed. Literary Symbolism (San Francisco: Wadsworth, 1960), 102–103.
Guerin, Wilfred L., Earle G. Labor, Lee Morgan, and
John R. Willingham. A Handbook of Critical Approaches to Literature (New York: Harper & Row,
1966), 57–65.
Hoffman, Daniel G. Form and Fable in American Fic-
tion (New York: Oxford Univ. Press, 1961), 149–168;
reprinted in Donohue, Agnes, Ed. A Casebook on the
Hawthorne Question (New York: Crowell, 1963), 222–
237; Connolly, Thomas E., Ed. Nathaniel Hawthorne:
"Young Goodman Brown" (Columbus: Merrill, 1968),
80–95.
Hurley, Paul J. "Young Goodman Brown's 'Heart of
Darkness,'" Am Lit, XXXVII (1966), 410–419; re-
printed in Connolly, Thomas E., Ed. Nathaniel
Hawthorne: "Young Goodman Brown" (Columbus:
Merrill, 1968), 116–124.
Klammer, Enno. "The Fatal Flaw in 'Young Goodman
Brown,'" Cresset, XXVIII (February, 1965), 8–10.
Levin, David. "Shadows of Doubt: Specter Evidence in
Hawthorne's 'Young Goodman Brown,'" Am Lit,
XXXIV (1962), 344–352; reprinted in Browne, Ray B.,
and Martin Light, Eds. Critical Approaches to
American Literature, I (New York: Crowell, 1965),
239–247; Connolly, Thomas E., Ed. Nathaniel Haw-
thorne: "Young Goodman Brown" (Columbus: Mer-
rill, 1968), 96–104.
McKeithan, Daniel M. "Hawthorne's 'Young Goodman
Brown': An Interpretation," Mod Lang Notes, LXVII
(1952), 93–96; reprinted in Connolly, Thomas E.,
Ed. Nathaniel Hawthorne: "Young Goodman Brown"
(Columbus: Merrill, 1968), 45–48; reprinted in part
in Beebe, Maurice, Ed. Literary Symbolism (San
Francisco: Wadsworth, 1960), 104.
Mathews, James W. "Antinomianism in 'Young Goodman
Brown,'" Stud Short Fiction, III (1965), 73–75; re-

printed in Connolly, Thomas E., Ed. Nathaniel
    Hawthorne: "Young Goodman Brown" (Columbus:
    Merrill, 1968), 113–115.
Miller, Paul W. "Hawthorne's 'Young Goodman Brown':
    Cynicism or Meliorism?" Nineteenth-Century Fic-
    tion, XIV (1959), 255–264; reprinted in Connolly,
    Thomas E., Ed. Nathaniel Hawthorne: "Young Good-
    man Brown" (Columbus: Merrill, 1968), 70–79.
Robinson, E. Arthur. "The Vision of Goodman Brown:
    A Source and Interpretation," Am Lit, XXXV (1963),
    218–225; reprinted in Connolly, Thomas E., Ed.
    Nathaniel Hawthorne: "Young Goodman Brown"
    (Columbus: Merrill, 1968), 105–112.
Steinmann, Martin, and Gerald Willen, Eds. Literature
    for Writing (Belmont: Wadsworth, 1962), 139–140;
    Second edition (1967), 130–132.
Tharpe, Jac. Nathaniel Hawthorne: Identity and Know-
    ledge (Carbondale: Southern Illinois Univ. Press,
    1967), 74–77.
Van Doren, Mark, Ed. The Best of Hawthorne (New
    York: Ronald, 1951), 416–417.
————. Nathaniel Hawthorne (New York: William
    Sloane, 1949), 76–79; reprinted in part in Frakes,
    James R., and Isadore Traschen, Eds. Short Fic-
    tion: A Critical Collection, Second edition (Engle-
    wood Cliffs: Prentice-Hall, 1969), 233–234.
Walsh, Thomas F. "The Bedeviling of Young Goodman
    Brown," Mod Lang Q, XIX (1958), 331–336; reprinted
    in Connolly, Thomas E., Ed. Nathaniel Hawthorne:
    "Young Goodman Brown" (Columbus: Merrill, 1968),
    63–69.

                    HAIYIM HAZAZ

"A Flowing River"
    Rabinovich, Isaiah. Major Trends in Modern Hebrew
        Fiction, trans. M. Roston (Chicago: Univ. of Chicago
        Press, 1968), 175–176.

"The Sermon"
  Rabinovich, Isaiah. Major Trends in Modern Hebrew
  Fiction, trans. M. Roston (Chicago: Univ. of Chicago
  Press, 1968), 173–174.

ROBERT HEINLEIN

"All You Zombies"
  Panshin, Alexei. "Heinlein in Dimension, Part II: The
  Period of Alienation," Riverside Q, II (1966), 37–39.

"Life-Line"
  Panshin, Alexei. "Heinlein in Dimension, Part I: The
  Period of Influence," Riverside Q, I (1965), 140–142.

"Misfit"
  Panshin, Alexei. "Heinlein in Dimension, Part I: The
  Period of Influence," Riverside Q, I (1965), 142.

"They"
  Panshin, Alexei. "Heinlein in Dimension, Part I: The
  Period of Influence," Riverside Q, I (1965), 152–153.

"Universe"
  Panshin, Alexei. "Heinlein in Dimension, Part I: The
  Period of Influence," Riverside Q, I (1965), 153.

ERNEST HEMINGWAY

"After the Storm"
  Atkins, Anselm. "Ironic Action in 'After the Storm,'"
  Stud Short Fiction, V (1968), 189–192.
  Gurko, Leo. Ernest Hemingway and the Pursuit of
  Heroism (New York: Crowell, 1968), 180; Apollo
  edition (1969), 180.

"An Alpine Idyll"
  Hovey, Richard B. Hemingway: The Inward Terrain
  (Seattle: Univ. of Washington Press, 1968), 9–10.

Young, Philip. Ernest Hemingway (New York: Rinehart, 1952), 31–32; Second edition (University Park: Pennsylvania State Univ. Press, 1966), 59–60; reprinted in Browne, Ray B., and Martin Light, Eds. Critical Approaches to American Literature, II (New York: Crowell, 1965), 278.

"The Battler"
Gurko, Leo. Ernest Hemingway and the Pursuit of Heroism (New York: Crowell, 1968), 185–186; Apollo edition (1969), 185–186.
Young, Philip. Ernest Hemingway (New York: Rinehart, 1952), 8–11; Second edition (University Park: Pennsylvania State Univ. Press, 1966), 36–40; reprinted in Weeks, Robert P., Ed. Hemingway: A Collection of Critical Essays (Englewood Cliffs: Prentice-Hall, 1962), 99–103.

"Big Two-Hearted River"
Baker, Sheridan. Ernest Hemingway: An Introduction and Interpretation (New York: Holt, Rinehart & Winston, 1967), 31–32.
Benson, Jackson J. Hemingway: The Writer's Art of Self-Defense (Minneapolis: Univ. of Minnesota Press, 1969), 137–140.
Green, James L. "Symbolic Sentences in 'Big Two-Hearted River,'" Mod Fiction Stud, XIV (1968), 307–312.
Gurko, Leo. Ernest Hemingway and the Pursuit of Heroism (New York: Crowell, 1968), 201–203; Apollo edition (1969), 201–203.
Hovey, Richard B. Hemingway: The Inward Terrain (Seattle: Univ. of Washington Press, 1968), 32–36.
Korn, Barbara. "Form and Idea in Hemingway's 'Big Two-Hearted River,'" Engl J, LVI (1967), 979–981.
Stewart, Randall. American Literature and Christian Doctrine (Baton Rouge: Louisiana State Univ. Press, 1958), 135–137; reprinted in his Regionalism and Beyond: Essays of Randall Stewart, ed. George Core (Nashville: Vanderbilt Univ. Press, 1968), 204–205.

Young, Philip. Ernest Hemingway (New York: Rinehart,
1952), 15–20; Second edition (University Park: Pennsylvania State Univ. Press, 1966), 43–48; reprinted
in Weeks, Robert P., Ed. Hemingway: A Collection
of Critical Essays (Englewood Cliffs: Prentice-Hall,
1962), 104–107.

"A Canary for One"
Hovey, Richard B. Hemingway: The Inward Terrain
(Seattle: Univ. of Washington Press, 1968), 42–43.
Smith, Julian. "'A Canary for One': Hemingway in the
Wasteland," Stud Short Fiction, V (1968), 355–361.

"The Capital of the World"
Grebstein, Sheldon N. "Hemingway's Dark and Bloody
Capital," in French, Warren, Ed. The Thirties: Fic-
tion, Poetry, Drama (Deland: Everett Edwards, 1967),
21–30.
Gurko, Leo. Ernest Hemingway and the Pursuit of
Heroism (New York: Crowell, 1968), 193–194; Apollo
edition (1969), 193–194.
Hovey, Richard B. Hemingway: The Inward Terrain
(Seattle: Univ. of Washington Press, 1968), 119–123.

"Cat in the Rain"
Hovey, Richard B. Hemingway: The Inward Terrain
(Seattle: Univ. of Washington Press, 1968), 10–11.
Magee, John D. "Hemingway's 'Cat in the Rain,'" Ex-
plicator, XXVI (1967), Item 8.

"A Clean, Well-Lighted Place"
Baker, Sheridan. Ernest Hemingway: An Introduction
and Interpretation (New York: Holt, Rinehart & Win-
ston, 1967), 86–87.
Barnes, Daniel R. "Ritual and Parody in 'A Clean,
Well-Lighted Place," Cithara, V (May, 1966), 15–25.
Benson, Jackson J. Hemingway: The Writer's Art of
Self-Defense (Minneapolis: Univ. of Minnesota Press,
1969), 116–118.

Gabriel, Joseph F. "The Logic of Confusion in Heming-
    way's 'A Clean, Well-Lighted Place,'" Coll Engl,
    XXII (1961), 539–546; reprinted in Freedman, Morris,
    and Paul B. Davis, Eds. Controversy in Literature
    (New York: Scribner, 1968), 126–135.
Gurko, Leo. Ernest Hemingway and the Pursuit of
    Heroism (New York: Crowell, 1968), 186–187; Apollo
    edition (1969), 186–187.
Hagopian, John V. "Tidying Up Hemingway's Clean,
    Well-Lighted Place," Stud Short Fiction, I (1964),
    140–146; reprinted in Freedman, Morris, and Paul
    B. Davis, Eds. Controversy in Literature (New
    York: Scribner, 1968), 135–141.
Henss, Hubert. "Edgar Allan Poe, 'The Masque of the
    Red Death'; Ernest Hemingway,'A Clean, Well-
    Lighted Place,'" Die Neueren Sprachen, N. S. XVI
    (1967), 327–338.
Hovey, Richard B. Hemingway: The Inward Terrain
    (Seattle: Univ. of Washington Press, 1968), 24–25.
Schorer, Mark, Ed. The Story: A Critical Anthology
    (New York: Prentice-Hall, 1950), 425–428; Second
    edition (Englewood Cliffs: Prentice-Hall, 1967),
    323–325.
Stewart, Randall. American Literature and Christian
    Doctrine (Baton Rouge: Louisiana State Univ. Press,
    1958), 134–135; reprinted in his Regionalism and
    Beyond: Essays of Randall Stewart, ed. George Core
    (Nashville: Vanderbilt Univ. Press, 1968), 203–204.
Young, Philip. Ernest Hemingway (New York: Rinehart,
    1952), 165–166; Second edition (University Park:
    Pennsylvania State Univ. Press, 1966), 195–196.

"Cross-Country Snow"
    Young, Philip. Ernest Hemingway (New York: Rinehart,
        1952), 14–15; Second edition (University Park: Penn-
        sylvania State Univ. Press, 1966), 42–43; reprinted
        in Weeks, Robert P., Ed. Hemingway: A Collection
        of Critical Essays (Englewood Cliffs: Prentice-Hall,
        1962), 103.

"A Day's Wait"
Hovey, Richard B. Hemingway: The Inward Terrain
(Seattle: Univ. of Washington Press, 1968), 43–44.
Mahony, Patrick J. "Hemingway's 'A Day's Wait,'"
Explicator, XXVII (1968), Item 18.

"The Doctor and the Doctor's Wife"
Hovey, Richard B. Hemingway: The Inward Terrain
(Seattle: Univ. of Washington Press, 1968), 38–39.
Young, Philip. Ernest Hemingway (New York: Rinehart,
1952), 336; Second edition (University Park: Pennsylvania State Univ. Press, 1966), 32–33; reprinted
in Weeks, Robert P., Ed. Hemingway: A Collection
of Critical Essays (Englewood Cliffs: Prentice-Hall,
1962), 97–98.

"The End of Something"
Gurko, Leo. Ernest Hemingway and the Pursuit of
Heroism (New York: Crowell, 1968), 183–184; Apollo
edition (1969), 183–184.
Kruse, Horst H. "Ernest Hemingway's 'The End of
Something': Its Independence as a Short Story and
Its Place in the 'Education of Nick Adams,'" Stud
Short Fiction, IV (1967), 152–166.
Young, Philip. Ernest Hemingway (New York: Rinehart,
1952), 5–6; Second edition (University Park: Penn-
sylvania State Univ. Press, 1966), 32–35; reprinted
in Weeks, Robert P., Ed. Hemingway: A Collection
of Critical Essays (Englewood Cliffs: Prentice-Hall,
1962), 98.

"Fathers and Sons"
Hovey, Richard B. Hemingway: The Inward Terrain
(Seattle: Univ. of Washington Press, 1968), 44–47.
Young, Philip. Ernest Hemingway (New York: Rinehart,
1952), 36–37; Second edition (University Park: Penn-
sylvania State Univ. Press, 1966), 60–62; reprinted
in Browne, Ray B., and Martin Light, Eds. Critical
Approaches to American Literature, II (New York:
Crowell, 1965), 279–280.

"Fifty Grand"
 Gurko, Leo. Ernest Hemingway and the Pursuit of
   Heroism (New York: Crowell, 1968), 178–179;
   Apollo edition (1969), 178–179.
 Young, Philip. Ernest Hemingway (New York: Rinehart,
   1952), 36–37; Second edition (University Park: Penn-
   sylvania State Univ. Press, 1966), 64–65; reprinted
   in Browne, Ray B., and Martin Light, Eds. Critical
   Approaches to American Literature, II (New York:
   Crowell, 1965), 281.

"The Gambler, the Nun, and the Radio"
 Hovey, Richard B. Hemingway: The Inward Terrain
   (Seattle: Univ. of Washington Press, 1968), 27–28.
 Mizener, Arthur. A Handbook for Use with "Modern
   Short Stories: The Uses of Imagination, Revised
   Edition" (New York: Norton, 1966), 68–73.
 Young, Philip. Ernest Hemingway (New York: Rinehart,
   1952), 38–41; Second edition (University Park: Penn-
   sylvania State Univ. Press, 1966), 66–68; reprinted
   in Browne, Ray B., and Martin Light, Eds. Critical
   Approaches to American Literature, II (New York:
   Crowell, 1965), 282–284.

"God Rest You Merry, Gentlemen"
 Hovey, Richard B. Hemingway: The Inward Terrain
   (Seattle: Univ. of Washington Press, 1968), 22–24.

"Hills Like White Elephants"
 Gurko, Leo. Ernest Hemingway and the Pursuit of
   Heroism (New York: Crowell, 1968), 191–193; Apollo
   edition (1969), 191–193.
 Hovey, Richard B. Hemingway: The Inward Terrain
   (Seattle: Univ. of Washington Press, 1968), 14.
 Trilling, Lionel. The Experience of Literature (New
   York: Holt, Rinehart & Winston, 1967), 729–732.

"Homage to Switzerland"
 Hovey, Richard B. Hemingway: The Inward Terrain
   (Seattle: Univ. of Washington Press, 1968), 11–12.

"In Another Country"
Benson, Jackson J. Hemingway: The Writer's Art of
Self-Defense (Minneapolis: Univ. of Minnesota Press,
1969), 144–145.
Gurko, Leo. Ernest Hemingway and the Pursuit of
Heroism (New York: Crowell, 1968), 180–181; Apollo
edition (1969), 180–181.
Irwin, Richard. "'Of War, Wounds, and Silly Machines':
An Examination of Hemingway's 'In Another Country,'"
Serif, V, ii (1968), 21–29.
Shrodes, Caroline, Justine Van Gundy, and Joel Dorius.
Instructor's Manual for "Reading for Understanding"
(New York: Macmillan, 1968), 27–28.
Steinmann, Martin, and Gerald Willen, Eds. Literature
for Writing (Belmont: Wadsworth, 1962), 175–176;
Second edition (1967), 168–169.
Stephens, Rosemary. "'In Another Country': Three as
Symbol," Univ Mississippi Stud Engl, VII (1966), 77–
83.
Young, Philip. Ernest Hemingway (New York: Rinehart,
1952), 30–31; Second edition (University Park: Penn-
sylvania State Univ. Press, 1966), 58–59; reprinted
in Browne, Ray B., and Martin Light, Eds. Critical
Approaches to American Literature, II (New York:
Crowell, 1965), 277.

"Indian Camp"
Hovey, Richard B. Hemingway: The Inward Terrain
(Seattle: Univ. of Washington Press, 1968), 15–16.
Young, Philip. Ernest Hemingway (New York: Rinehart,
1952), 3–4; Second edition (University Park: Pennsylvania State Univ. Press, 1966), 31–32; reprinted
in Weeks, Robert P., Ed. Hemingway: A Collection
of Critical Essays (Englewood Cliffs: Prentice-Hall,
1962), 96–97.

"The Killers"
Benson, Jackson J. Hemingway: The Writer's Art of
Self-Defense (Minneapolis: Univ. of Minnesota Press,
1969), 142–144.

Gurko, Leo. <u>Ernest Hemingway and the Pursuit of</u>
  <u>Heroism</u> (New York: Crowell, 1968), 188–191; Apollo
  edition (1969), 188–191.
Oliver, Clinton F. "Hemingway's 'The Killers' and
  Mann's 'Disorder and Early Sorrow,'" in Timko,
  Michael, and Clinton F. Oliver, Eds. <u>Thirty-Eight</u>
  <u>Short Stories</u> (New York: Knopf, 1968), 69–86.
Stone, Edward. "Some Questions About Hemingway's
  'The Killers,'" <u>Stud Short Fiction</u>, V (1967), 12–17.
Walz, Lawrence A. "Hemingway's 'The Killers,'"
  <u>Explicator</u>, XXV (1967), Item 38.
Young, Philip. <u>Ernest Hemingway</u> (New York: Rinehart,
  1952), 20–22; Second edition (University Park: Pennsylvania State Univ. Press, 1966), 48–49; reprinted
  in Weeks, Robert P., Ed. <u>Hemingway: A Collection</u>
  <u>of Critical Essays</u> (Englewood Cliffs: Prentice-Hall,
  1962), 107–108.

"The Light of the World"
  Benson, Jackson J. <u>Hemingway: The Writer's Art of</u>
    <u>Self-Defense</u> (Minneapolis: Univ. of Minnesota Press,
    1969), 57–60.
  Hovey, Richard B. <u>Hemingway: The Inward Terrain</u>
    (Seattle: Univ. of Washington Press, 1968), 18–20.
  Stavrou, C. N. "Nada, Religion, & Hemingway," <u>Topic</u>,
    VI (Fall, 1966), 5–20.

"The Mother of a Queen"
  Hovey, Richard B. <u>Hemingway: The Inward Terrain</u>
    (Seattle: Univ. of Washington Press, 1968), 21–22.

"Mr. and Mrs. Elliot"
  Hovey, Richard B. <u>Hemingway: The Inward Terrain</u>
    (Seattle: Univ. of Washington Press, 1968), 13.

"My Old Man"
  Hovey, Richard B. <u>Hemingway: The Inward Terrain</u>
    (Seattle: Univ. of Washington Press, 1968), 39–41.

"A Natural History of the Dead"
  Hovey, Richard B. Hemingway: The Inward Terrain
  (Seattle: Univ. of Washington Press, 1968), 105–107.

"Now I Lay Me"
  Baker, Sheridan. Ernest Hemingway: An Introduction
  and Interpretation (New York: Holt, Rinehart & Win-
  ston, 1967), 33–34.
  Hovey, Richard B. Hemingway: The Inward Terrain
  (Seattle: Univ. of Washington Press, 1968), 47–53.
  Young, Philip. Ernest Hemingway (New York: Rinehart,
  1952), 29–30; Second edition (University Park: Penn-
  sylvania State Univ. Press, 1966), 57–58; reprinted
  in Browne, Ray B., and Martin Light, Eds. Critical
  Approaches to American Literature, II (New York:
  Crowell, 1965), 276–277.

"The Old Man and the Sea"
  Baker, Carlos. Hemingway: The Writer as Artist,
  Second edition (Princeton: Princeton Univ. Press,
  1956), 289–328; Third edition (1963), 289–328; re-
  printed as "Hemingway's Ancient Mariner," in Baker,
  Carlos, Ed. Ernest Hemingway: Critiques of Four
  Major Novels (New York: Scribner, 1962), 156–172;
  reprinted in part in Jobes, Katharine T., Ed. Twen-
  tieth Century Interpretations of "The Old Man and
  the Sea" (Englewood Cliffs: Prentice-Hall, 1968),
  27–33.
  ――――. "Marvel Who Must Die," Sat R, XXXV
  (September 6, 1952), 10–11; reprinted in Wagen-
  knecht, Edward, Ed. A Preface to Literature (New
  York: Holt, 1954), 341–344.
  Benson, Jackson J. Hemingway: The Writer's Art of
  Self-Defense (Minneapolis: Univ. of Minnesota Press,
  1969), 123–126.
  Burhans, Clinton S. "'The Old Man and the Sea': Hemingway's Tragic Vision of Man," Am Lit, XXXI (1960),
  446–455; reprinted in Baker, Carlos, Ed. Hemingway
  and His Critics: An International Anthology (New
  York: Hill & Wang, 1961), 259–268; Baker, Carlos, Ed.

Ernest Hemingway: Critiques of Four Major Novels
(New York: Scribner, 1962), 150–155; Westbrook,
Max, Ed. The Modern American Novel: Essays in
Criticism (New York: Random House, 1966), 118–130;
Jobes, Katharine T., Ed. Twentieth Century Inter-
pretations of "The Old Man and the Sea" (Englewood
Cliffs: Prentice-Hall, 1968), 72–80.

Cowley, Malcolm. "Hemingway's Novel Has the Rich
Simplicity of a Classic," N Y Herald Tribune Bks
(September 7, 1952), 1, 17; reprinted in part in Jobes,
Katharine T., Ed. Twentieth Century Interpretations
of "The Old Man and the Sea" (Englewood Cliffs:
Prentice-Hall, 1968), 106–108.

D'Agostino, Nemi. "The Later Hemingway," Sewanee R,
LXVIII (1960), 491–492; reprinted from Belfagor, XI
(1956), as translated by Barbara M. Arnett; reprinted
in part in Jobes, Katharine T., Ed. Twentieth Century
Interpretations of "The Old Man and the Sea" (Englewood Cliffs: Prentice-Hall, 1968), 108–109.

Gurko, Leo. Ernest Hemingway and the Pursuit of
Heroism (New York: Crowell, 1968), 159–174; Apollo
edition (1969), 159–174.

————. "'The Old Man and the Sea,'" Coll Engl,
XVII (1955), 11–15; also in Engl J, XLIV (1955), 377–
382; reprinted in Jobes, Katharine T., Ed. Twentieth Century Interpretations of "The Old Man and
the Sea" (Englewood Cliffs: Prentice-Hall, 1968),
64–71.

Harlow, Benjamin C. "Some Archetypal Motifs in 'The
Old Man and the Sea,'" McNeese R, XVII (1966), 74–
79.

Hovey, Richard B. Hemingway: The Inward Terrain
(Seattle: Univ. of Washington Press, 1968), 191–203.

Rosenfield, Claire. "New World, Old Myths," in Jobes,
Katharine T., Ed. Twentieth Century Interpretations
of "The Old Man and the Sea" (Englewood Cliffs:
Prentice-Hall, 1968), 41–55.

Rovit, Earl. Ernest Hemingway (New York: Twayne,
1963), 85–94; reprinted in part in Jobes, Katharine T.,

Ed. Twentieth Century Interpretations of "The Old Man and the Sea" (Englewood Cliffs: Prentice-Hall, 1968), 103–106.

Schwartz, Delmore. "The Fiction of Ernest Hemingway," Perspectives USA, No. 13 (Autumn, 1955), 82–88; reprinted in Jobes, Katharine T., Ed. Twentieth Century Interpretations of "The Old Man and the Sea" (Englewood Cliffs: Prentice-Hall, 1968), 97–102.

Scoville, Samuel. "The Weltanschauung of Steinbeck and Hemingway: An Analysis of Themes," Engl J, LVI (1967), 60–63, 66.

Sylvester, Bickford. "Hemingway's Extended Vision: 'The Old Man and the Sea,'" PMLA, LXXXI (1966), 130–138; reprinted in Jobes, Katharine T., Ed. Twentieth Century Interpretations of "The Old Man and the Sea" (Englewood Cliffs: Prentice-Hall, 1968), 81–96.

————. "'They Went Through This Fiction Every Day': Informed Illusion in 'The Old Man and the Sea,'" Mod Fiction Stud, XII (1966), 473–477.

Ueno, Naozo. "An Oriental View of 'The Old Man and the Sea,'" East-West R, II (1965), 67–76.

Weeks, Robert P. "Fakery in 'The Old Man and the Sea,'" Coll Engl, XXIV (1962), 188–192; reprinted in Jobes, Katharine T., Ed. Twentieth Century Interpretations of "The Old Man and the Sea" (Englewood Cliffs: Prentice-Hall, 1968), 34–40.

Wells, Arvin R. "The Old Man and the Sea," in Hagopian, John V., and Martin Dolch, Eds. Insight I: Analyses of American Literature (Frankfurt: Hirschgraben, 1962), 112–122; reprinted, with new title, "A Ritual of Transfiguration: 'The Old Man and the Sea,'" Univ R, XXX (1963), 95–101; Jobes, Katharine T., Ed. Twentieth Century Interpretations of "The Old Man and the Sea" (Englewood Cliffs: Prentice-Hall, 1968), 56–63.

Wylder, Delbert E. Hemingway's Heroes (Albuquerque: Univ. of New Mexico Press, 1969), 199–222.

Young, Philip. Ernest Hemingway (New York: Rinehart,
1952), 93–105; Second edition (University Park: Pennsylvania State Univ. Press, 1966), 121–133; Jobes,
Katharine T., Ed. Twentieth Century Interpretations
of "The Old Man and the Sea" (Englewood Cliffs:
Prentice-Hall, 1968), 18–25.

"Old Man at the Bridge"
Hovey, Richard B. Hemingway: The Inward Terrain
(Seattle: Univ. of Washington Press, 1968), 150–151.

"On the Quai at Smyrna"
Leiter, Louis H. "Neural Projections in Hemingway's
'On the Quai at Smyrna,'" Stud Short Fiction, V
(1968), 384–386.

"Out of Season"
Young, Philip. Ernest Hemingway (New York: Rinehart,
1952), 149–150; Second edition (University Park:
Pennsylvania State Univ. Press, 1966), 178.

"The Short Happy Life of Francis Macomber"
Beck, Warren. "The Shorter Happy Life of Mrs. Mac-
omber," Mod Fiction Stud, I (1955), 28–37; reprinted
in Howell, John M., Ed. Hemingway's African
Stories (New York: Scribner, 1969), 119–128.
Benson, Jackson J. Hemingway: The Writer's Art of
Self-Defense (Minneapolis: Univ. of Minnesota Press,
1969), 146–148.
Crane, Ronald S. "On 'The Short Happy Life of Francis
Macomber,'" English "A" Analyst, No. 16 (published
by Northwestern University Department of English);
reprinted in his The Idea of the Humanities and
Other Essays (Chicago: Univ. of Chicago Press,
1967), 315–326; Locke, Louis G., William M. Gibson,
and George Arms, Eds. Introduction to Literature,
Third edition (New York: Rinehart, 1957), 470–479;
Fifth edition (New York: Holt, Rinehart & Winston,
1967), 409–417; Howell, John M., Ed. Hemingway's
African Stories (New York: Scribner, 1969), 129–136.

Gurko, Leo. Ernest Hemingway and the Pursuit of
   Heroism (New York: Crowell, 1968), 196–198;
   Apollo edition (1969), 196–198.
Holland, Robert B. "Macomber and the Critics,"
   Stud Short Fiction, V (1968), 171–178; reprinted in
   Howell, John M., Ed. Hemingway's African Stories
   (New York: Scribner, 1969), 137–141.
Hovey, Richard B. Hemingway: The Inward Terrain
   (Seattle: Univ. of Washington Press, 1968), 123–127.
Howell, John M. "The Macomber Case," Stud Short
   Fiction, IV (1967), 171–172.
Rogers, Katharine M. The Troublesome Helpmate: A
   History of Misogyny in Literature (Seattle: Univ. of
   Washington Press, 1966), 250–251.
Young, Philip. Ernest Hemingway (New York: Rinehart,
   1952), 41–46; Second edition (University Park: Penn-
   sylvania State Univ. Press, 1966), 69–74; reprinted
   in Browne, Ray B., and Martin Light, Eds. Critical
   Approaches to American Literature, II (New York:
   Crowell, 1965), 284–288.

"The Snows of Kilimanjaro"
Baker, Carlos. Hemingway: The Writer as Artist
   (Princeton: Princeton Univ. Press, 1952), 191–196;
   Second edition (1956), 191–196; Third edition (1963),
   191–196; reprinted in Weeks, Robert P., Ed. Hem-
   ingway: A Collection of Critical Essays (Englewood
   Cliffs: Prentice-Hall, 1962), 122–126; reprinted in
   part in Howell, John M., Ed. Hemingway's African
   Stories (New York: Scribner, 1969), 113–115.
————. "The Slopes of Kilimanjaro," Novel: Forum
   on Fiction, I (1967), 19–23; reprinted, with changes,
   in Am Heritage, XIX, v (August, 1968), 40–43, 90–91.
Benson, Jackson J. Hemingway: The Writer's Art of
   Self-Defense (Minneapolis: Univ. of Minnesota Press,
   1969), 130–134.
Bevis, R. W., and M. A. J. Smith. "Leopard Tracks in
   'The Snows . . . ,'" Am Notes & Queries, VI (1968), 115.

Crane, John Kenny. "Crossing the Bar Twice: Post-
Mortem Consciousness in Bierce, Hemingway, and
Golding," Stud Short Fiction, VI (1969), 361–376.
Dussinger, Gloria R. "Hemingway's 'The Snows of
Kilimanjaro,'" Explicator, XXVI (1968), Item 67.
————. "'The Snows of Kilimanjaro': Harry's Sec-
ond Chance," Stud Short Fiction, V (1967), 54–59;
reprinted in Howell, John M., Ed. Hemingway's
African Stories (New York: Scribner, 1969), 158–
161.
Evans, Oliver. "'The Snows of Kilimanjaro': A Re-
valuation," PMLA, LXXVI (1961), 601–607; re-
printed in Howell, John M., Ed. Hemingway's Afri-
can Stories (New York: Scribner, 1969), 150–157.
Gordon, Caroline, and Allen Tate. The House of Fic-
tion (New York: Scribner, 1950), 419–423; reprinted
in Howell, John M., Ed. Hemingway's African
Stories (New York: Scribner, 1969), 142–144.
Gurko, Leo. Ernest Hemingway and the Pursuit of
Heroism (New York: Crowell, 1968), 198–201;
Apollo edition (1969), 198–201.
Hovey, Richard B. Hemingway: The Inward Terrain
(Seattle: Univ. of Washington Press, 1968), 127–131.
Lynskey, Winifred, Ed. Reading Modern Fiction (New
York: Scribner, 1952), 266–268; Second edition (1957),
266–268; Third edition (1962), 266–268; Fourth edi-
tion (1968), 264–266.
Maynard, Reid. "The Decay Motif in 'The Snows of
Kilimanjaro,'" Discourse, X (1967), 436–439.
Montgomery, Marion. "The Leopard and the Hyena in
'The Snows of Kilimanjaro,'" Univ Kansas City R,
XXVII (1961), 277–282; reprinted in Howell, John M.,
Ed. Hemingway's African Stories (New York: Scrib-
ner, 1969), 145–149.
Stephen, Robert O. "Hemingway's Riddle of Kiliman-
jaro: Idea and Image," Am Lit, XXXII (1960), 84–87;
reprinted in Howell, John M., Ed. Hemingway's
African Stories (New York: Scribner, 1969), 93–94.
Young, Philip. Ernest Hemingway (New York: Rinehart,
1952), 46–50; Second edition (University Park: Penn-

sylvania State Univ. Press, 1966), 74–78; reprinted
in Browne, Ray B., and Martin Light, Eds. Critical
Approaches to American Literature, II (New York:
Crowell, 1965), 288–291; reprinted in part in Howell,
John M., Ed. Hemingway's African Stories (New
York: Scribner, 1969), 116–118.

"Soldier's Home"
    Gurko, Leo. Ernest Hemingway and the Pursuit of Hero-
       ism (New York: Crowell, 1968), 181–183; Apollo edi-
       tion (1969), 181–183.
    Hovey, Richard B. Hemingway: The Inward Terrain
       (Seattle: Univ. of Washington Press, 1968), 41–42.
    Petrarea, Anthony J. "Irony of Situation in Ernest
       Hemingway's 'Soldier's Home,'" Engl J, LVIII (1969),
       664–667.

"Ten Indians"
    Aiken, William. "Hemingway's 'Ten Indians,'" Expli-
       cator, XXVIII (1969), Item 31.
    Hovey, Richard B. Hemingway: The Inward Terrain
       (Seattle: Univ. of Washington Press, 1968), 6–7.

"The Three-Day Blow"
    Hovey, Richard B. Hemingway: The Inward Terrain
       (Seattle: Univ. of Washington Press, 1968), 7–8.

"The Undefeated"
    Gurko, Leo. Ernest Hemingway and the Pursuit of
       Heroism (New York: Crowell, 1968), 194–196;
       Apollo edition (1969), 194–196.
    Hovey, Richard B. Hemingway: The Inward Terrain
       (Seattle: Univ. of Washington Press, 1968), 26–27.

"Up in Michigan"
    Young, Philip. Ernest Hemingway (New York: Rinehart,
       1952), 150; Second edition (University Park: Pennsyl-
       vania State Univ. Press, 1966), 179–180.

"A Way You'll Never Be"
   Hovey, Richard B. Hemingway: The Inward Terrain
   (Seattle: Univ. of Washington Press, 1968), 29–32.
   Young, Philip. Ernest Hemingway (New York: Rinehart,
   1952), 23–26; Second edition (University Park: Penn-
   sylvania State Univ. Press, 1966), 50–54.

HERMANN HESSE

"A Child's Soul"
   Boulby, Mark. Hermann Hesse: His Mind and Art
   (Ithaca: Cornell Univ. Press, 1967), 95–96.

"Iris"
   Boulby, Mark. Hermann Hesse: His Mind and Art
   (Ithaca: Cornell Univ. Press, 1967), 124–127.

"Journey to the East"
   Boulby, Mark. Hermann Hesse: His Mind and Art
   (Ithaca: Cornell Univ. Press, 1967), 245–261.

"Klein and Wagner"
   Boulby, Mark. Hermann Hesse: His Mind and Art
   (Ithaca: Cornell Univ. Press, 1967), 130–131.

"Klingsor's Last Summer"
   Boulby, Mark. Hermann Hesse: His Mind and Art
   (Ithaca: Cornell Univ. Press, 1967), 128–130.

"Siddhartha"
   Boulby, Mark. Hermann Hesse: His Mind and Art
   (Ithaca: Cornell Univ. Press, 1967), 132–157.
   Misra, Bhabagrahi. "An Analysis of Indic Tradition
   in Hermann Hesse's 'Siddharta,'" Indian Lit, XI,
   ii (1968), 111–123.

"The Steep Road"
   Boulby, Mark. Hermann Hesse: His Mind and Art
   (Ithaca: Cornell Univ. Press, 1967), 154–155.

"The Trip to Nuremberg"
  Boulby, Mark. Hermann Hesse: His Mind and Art
  (Ithaca: Cornell Univ. Press, 1967), 166–167.

"Youth, Beautiful Youth"
  Boulby, Mark. Hermann Hesse: His Mind and Art
  (Ithaca: Cornell Univ. Press, 1967), 92–93.

E. T. A. HOFFMANN

"The Sandman"
  Lawson, Ursula D. "Pathological Time in E. T. A. Hoffmann's 'Der Sandmann,'" Monatshefte, LX (1968),
  51–61.

LANGSTON HUGHES

"Slave on the Block"
  Turpin, Waters E. "Four Short Fiction Writers of the
  Harlem Renaissance: Their Legacy of Achievement,"
  Coll Lang Assoc J, XI (1967), 64–67.

WASHINGTON IRVING

"Rip Van Winkle"
  Hollander, Robert, and Sidney E. Lind, Eds. The Art
  of the Story: An Introduction (New York: American
  Book, 1968), 7–9.
  Le Fevre, Louis. "Paul Bunyan and Rip Van Winkle,"
  Yale R, XXXVI (1946), 66–76; reprinted in Baskett,
  Sam S., and Theodore B. Strandness, Eds. The Ameri-
  can Identity (Boston: Heath, 1962), 275–281; Clifton,
  Lucile, and Alexander MacGibbon, Eds. Composition:
  An Approach Through Reading (New York: Harcourt,
  Brace & World, 1968), 313–321.

Mengeling, Marvin E. "Structure and Tone in 'Rip Van
    Winkle': The Irony of Silence," Discourse, IX (1966),
    457–463.
Sugiyama, Yoko. "Time and Folk Literature: A Com-
    parative Study," East-West R, I (1964), 28–31.
Young, Philip. "Fallen from Time: The Mythic Rip
    Van Winkle," Kenyon R, XXII (1960), 547–573; re-
    printed in Oldsey, Bernard S., and Arthur O. Lewis,
    Eds. Visions and Revisions in Modern American
    Literary Criticism (New York: Dutton, 1962), 284–
    308; Miller, James E., and Bernice Slote, Eds. The
    Dimensions of the Short Story (New York: Dodd,
    Mead, 1964), 545–554; Malin, Irving, Ed. Psycho-
    analysis and American Fiction (New York: Dutton,
    1965), 23–45; Goldhurst, William, Ed. Contours of
    Experience (Englewood Cliffs: Prentice-Hall, 1967),
    189–209; reprinted in part in Waldhorn, Arthur, and
    Hilda Waldhorn, Eds. The Rite of Becoming: Stories
    and Studies of Adolescence (Cleveland: World, 1966),
    287–292.

DAN JACOBSON

"Beggar My Neighbor"
    Mizener, Arthur. A Handbook for Use with "Modern
    Short Stories: The Uses of Imagination, Revised Edi-
    tion" (New York: Norton, 1966), 83–86.

HENRY JAMES

"The Abasement of the Northmores"
    Putt, S. Gorley. Henry James: A Reader's Guide
    (Ithaca: Cornell Univ. Press, 1966), 234–235.

"Adina"
    Putt, S. Gorley. Henry James: A Reader's Guide
    (Ithaca: Cornell Univ. Press, 1966), 78–79.

"The Altar of the Dead"
Putt, S. Gorley. Henry James: A Reader's Guide
(Ithaca: Cornell Univ. Press, 1966), 392–394.

"The Aspern Papers"
Hartsock, Mildred. "Unweeded Garden: A View of 'The
Aspern Papers,'" Stud Short Fiction, V (1967), 60–68.
McLean, Robert C. "Poetic Justice in James's 'Aspern
Papers,'" Papers Lang & Lit, III (1967), 260–266.
Putt, S. Gorley. Henry James: A Reader's Guide
(Ithaca: Cornell Univ. Press, 1966), 221–222.

"The Author of Beltraffio"
Putt, S. Gorley. Henry James: A Reader's Guide
(Ithaca: Cornell Univ. Press, 1966), 215–218.
Shine, Muriel G. The Fictional Children of Henry James
(Chapel Hill: Univ. of North Carolina Press, 1968),
72–75.
Winner, Viola H. "The Artist and the Man in 'The Author
of Beltraffio,'" PMLA, LXXXIII (1968), 102–108.

"The Beast in the Jungle"
Johnson, Courtney. "John Marcher and the Paradox of
the 'Unfortunate' Fall," Stud Short Fiction, VI (1969),
121–135.
Jost, Edward F. "Love and Two Kinds of Existentialism,"
Engl Record, XVI (February, 1966), 14–18.
Mays, Milton A. "Henry James, or, The Beast in the
Palace of Art," Am Lit, XXXIX (1968), 467–487.
Putt, S. Gorley. Henry James: A Reader's Guide
(Ithaca: Cornell Univ. Press, 1966), 297.
Shrodes, Caroline, Justine Van Gundy, and Joel Dorius.
Instructor's Manual for "Reading for Understanding"
(New York: Macmillan, 1968), 6–9.
Thorberg, Raymond. "Terror Made Relevant: James's
Ghost Stories," Dalhousie R, XLVII (1967), 187–188.
Van Kaam, Adrian, and Kathleen Healy. The Demon
and the Dove (Pittsburgh: Duquesne Univ. Press, 1967),
197–224.

"The Beldonald Holbein"
 Putt, S. Gorley. Henry James: A Reader's Guide
   (Ithaca: Cornell Univ. Press, 1966), 236–237.
 Thorberg, Raymond. "Henry James and the Real
   Thing: 'The Beldonald Holbein,'" Southern Hum R,
   III (1968), 78–85.

"The Bench of Desolation"
 Lynskey, Winifred, Ed. Reading Modern Fiction, Sec-
   ond edition (New York: Scribner, 1957), 306–310;
   Third edition (1962), 306–310; Fourth edition (1968),
   304–308.
 Putt, S. Gorley. Henry James: A Reader's Guide
   (Ithaca: Cornell Univ. Press, 1966), 297–298.

"Benvolio"
 Putt, S. Gorley. Henry James: A Reader's Guide
   (Ithaca: Cornell Univ. Press, 1966), 87–91.

"Brooksmith"
 Dow, Eddy. "James' 'Brooksmith,'" Explicator, XXVII
   (1969), Item 35.
 Putt, S. Gorley. Henry James: A Reader's Guide
   (Ithaca: Cornell Univ. Press, 1966), 279–281.

"A Bundle of Letters"
 Putt, S. Gorley. Henry James: A Reader's Guide
   (Ithaca: Cornell Univ. Press, 1966), 124–125.

"The Chaperon"
 Clair, John A. The Ironic Dimension in the Fiction of
   Henry James (Pittsburgh: Duquesne Univ. Press,
   1965), 103–109.
 Putt, S. Gorley. Henry James: A Reader's Guide
   (Ithaca: Cornell Univ. Press, 1966), 281–283.

"Collaboration"
 Putt, S. Gorley. Henry James: A Reader's Guide
   (Ithaca: Cornell Univ. Press, 1966), 223–224.

"Covering End"
Putt, S. Gorley. Henry James: A Reader's Guide
(Ithaca: Cornell Univ. Press, 1966), 246-247.

"The Coxon Fund"
Putt, S. Gorley. Henry James: A Reader's Guide
(Ithaca: Cornell Univ. Press, 1966), 228-230.

"Crapy Cornelia"
Purdy, Strother B. "Language as Art: The Ways of
Knowing in Henry James's 'Crapy Cornelia,'" Style,
I (1967), 139-149.
Putt, S. Gorley. Henry James: A Reader's Guide
(Ithaca: Cornell Univ. Press, 1966), 301-304.

"Crawford's Consistency"
Putt, S. Gorley. Henry James: A Reader's Guide
(Ithaca: Cornell Univ. Press, 1966), 267-268.

"Daisy Miller"
Baxter, Annette K. "Archetypes of American Innocence:
Lydia Blood and Daisy Miller," Am Q, V (1953), 31-
38; reprinted in Cohen, Hennig, Ed. The American
Experience (Boston: Houghton Mifflin, 1968), 148-167.
Davis, O. B. Introduction to the Novel (New York: Hayden,
1969), 137-141.
Deakin, Motley F. "Daisy Miller, Tradition, and the
European Heroine," Comp Lit Stud, VI (1969), 45-59.
Draper, R. P. "Death of a Hero? Winterbourne and
Daisy Miller," Stud Short Fiction, VI (1969), 601-
608.
Houghton, Donald E. "Attitude and Illness in James's
'Daisy Miller,'" Lit & Psych, XIX (1969), 51-60.
Leyburn, Ellen D. Strange Alloy: The Relation of
Comedy to Tragedy in the Fiction of Henry James
(Chapel Hill: Univ. of North Carolina Press, 1968),
24-28.
Putt, S. Gorley. Henry James: A Reader's Guide
(Ithaca: Cornell Univ. Press, 1966), 122-123.

"The Death of the Lion"
   Putt, S. Gorley. Henry James: A Reader's Guide
   (Ithaca: Cornell Univ. Press, 1966), 227–229.

"Eugene Pickering"
   Putt, S. Gorley. Henry James: A Reader's Guide
   (Ithaca: Cornell Univ. Press, 1966), 91–93.

"The Figure in the Carpet"
   Finch, G. A. "A Retreading of James' Carpet," Twen-
   tieth-Century Lit, XIV (1968), 98–101.
   Putt, S. Gorley. Henry James: A Reader's Guide
   (Ithaca: Cornell Univ. Press, 1966), 232–233.
   Van Cromphout, G. "Artist and Society in Henry
   James," Engl Stud, XLIX (1968), 139–140.

"Flickerbridge"
   Putt, S. Gorley. Henry James: A Reader's Guide
   (Ithaca: Cornell Univ. Press, 1966), 65–66.

"Four Meetings"
   Aziz, Maqbool. "'Four Meetings': A Caveat for James
   Critics," Essays in Criticism, XVIII (1968), 258–274.
   Clair, John A. The Ironic Dimension in the Fiction of
   Henry James (Pittsburgh: Duquesne Univ. Press,
   1965), 1–16.
   Putt, S. Gorley. Henry James: A Reader's Guide
   (Ithaca: Cornell Univ. Press, 1966), 119–120.

"Gabrielle de Bergerac"
   Putt, S. Gorley. Henry James: A Reader's Guide
   (Ithaca: Cornell Univ. Press, 1966), 37–38.

"Georgina's Reasons"
   Putt, S. Gorley. Henry James: A Reader's Guide
   (Ithaca: Cornell Univ. Press, 1966), 270–271.

"The Ghostly Rental"
   Andreach, Robert J. "Literary Allusions as a Clue to
   Meaning: James's 'The Ghostly Rental' and Pascal's
   Pensées," Comp Lit Stud, IV (1967), 299–306.

"Glasses"
> Putt, S. Gorley. Henry James: A Reader's Guide
> (Ithaca: Cornell Univ. Press, 1966), 285–286.

"The Great Condition"
> Putt, S. Gorley. Henry James: A Reader's Guide
> (Ithaca: Cornell Univ. Press, 1966), 289–290.

"The Great Good Place"
> Fadiman, Clifton, Ed. The Short Stories of Henry
> James (New York: Random House, 1945), 413–415;
> reprinted in Locke, Louis G., William M. Gibson,
> and George Arms, Eds. Introduction to Literature,
> Fifth edition (New York: Holt, Rinehart & Winston,
> 1967), 298–299.
> Putt, S. Gorley. Henry James: A Reader's Guide
> (Ithaca: Cornell Univ. Press, 1966), 93–94.

"Greville Fane"
> Putt, S. Gorley. Henry James: A Reader's Guide
> (Ithaca: Cornell Univ. Press, 1966), 225–226.
> Shine, Muriel G. The Fictional Children of Henry
> James (Chapel Hill: Univ. of North Carolina Press,
> 1968), 57–61.

"An International Episode"
> Daniels, Howell. "Henry James and 'An International
> Episode,'" Bull Brit Assoc Am Stud [Manchester],
> I N. S. (1960), 3–35.
> Leyburn, Ellen D. Strange Alloy: The Relation of
> Comedy to Tragedy in the Fiction of Henry James
> (Chapel Hill: Univ. of North Carolina Press, 1968),
> 54–56.
> Putt, S. Gorley. Henry James: A Reader's Guide
> (Ithaca: Cornell Univ. Press, 1966), 120–122.

"In the Cage"
> Aswell, E. Duncan. "James's 'In the Cage': The Tele-
> graphist as Artist," Texas Stud Lit & Lang, VIII
> (1966), 375–384.

Füger, Wilhelm. "'In the Cage': Versuche zur Deutung
    einer umstrittenen Henry James Novelle," Die
    Neueren Sprachen, XV (1966), 506–513.
Putt, S. Gorley. Henry James: A Reader's Guide
    (Ithaca: Cornell Univ. Press, 1966), 287–289.
Shine, Muriel G. The Fictional Children of Henry
    James (Chapel Hill: Univ. of North Carolina Press,
    1968), 139–145.

"The Jolly Corner"
    Clair, John A. The Ironic Dimension in the Fiction of
        Henry James (Pittsburgh: Duquesne Univ. Press,
        1965), 17–36.
    Mays, Milton A. "Henry James, or, The Beast in the
        Palace of Art," Am Lit, XXXIX (1968), 467–487.
    Mizener, Arthur. A Handbook for Use with "Modern
        Short Stories: The Uses of Imagination, Revised Edi-
        tion" (New York: Norton, 1966), 51–55.
    Putt, S. Gorley. Henry James: A Reader's Guide
        (Ithaca: Cornell Univ. Press, 1966), 51–54.
    Thorberg, Raymond. "Terror Made Relevant: James's
        Ghost Stories," Dalhousie R, XLVII (1967), 188–189.

"Julia Bride"
    Putt, S. Gorley. Henry James: A Reader's Guide
        (Ithaca: Cornell Univ. Press, 1966), 299–300.

"Lady Barberina"
    Putt, S. Gorley. Henry James: A Reader's Guide
        (Ithaca: Cornell Univ. Press, 1966), 128–131.

"The Last of the Valerii"
    Putt, S. Gorley. Henry James: A Reader's Guide
        (Ithaca: Cornell Univ. Press, 1966), 77–78.

"The Lesson of the Master"
    Mizener, Arthur. A Handbook for Use with "Modern
        Short Stories: The Uses of Imagination, Revised
        Edition" (New York: Norton, 1966), 57–59.

Putt, S. Gorley. Henry James: A Reader's Guide
(Ithaca: Cornell Univ. Press, 1966), 218–220.
Smith, Charles R. "'The Lesson of the Master': An
Interpretive Note," Stud Short Fiction, 654–658.
Van Cromphout, G. "Artist and Society in Henry
James," Engl Stud, XLIX (1968), 134–135.

"The Liar"
Putt, S. Gorley. Henry James: A Reader's Guide
(Ithaca: Cornell Univ. Press, 1966), 274–275.

"A London Life"
Clair, John A. The Ironic Dimension in the Fiction of
Henry James (Pittsburgh: Duquesne Univ. Press,
1965), 111–127.
Putt, S. Gorley. Henry James: A Reader's Guide
(Ithaca: Cornell Univ. Press, 1966), 275–277.
Shine, Muriel G. The Fictional Children of Henry
James (Chapel Hill: Univ. of North Carolina Press,
1968), 53–57.

"Lord Beaupré"
Putt, S. Gorley. Henry James: A Reader's Guide
(Ithaca: Cornell Univ. Press, 1966), 283–284.

"Louisa Pallant"
Putt, S. Gorley. Henry James: A Reader's Guide
(Ithaca: Cornell Univ. Press, 1966), 273–274.

"Madame de Mauves"
Putt, S. Gorley. Henry James: A Reader's Guide
(Ithaca: Cornell Univ. Press, 1966), 69–73.

"The Madonna of the Future"
Putt, S. Gorley. Henry James: A Reader's Guide
(Ithaca: Cornell Univ. Press, 1966), 214–215.

"The Marriages"
Putt, S. Gorley. Henry James: A Reader's Guide
(Ithaca: Cornell Univ. Press, 1966), 279–280.

"Master Eustace"
> Shine, Muriel G. The Fictional Children of Henry
> James (Chapel Hill: Univ. of North Carolina Press,
> 1968), 35–41.

"Maud-Evelyn"
> Putt, S. Gorley. Henry James: A Reader's Guide
> (Ithaca: Cornell Univ. Press, 1966), 291–292.

"The Middle Years"
> Putt, S. Gorley. Henry James: A Reader's Guide
> (Ithaca: Cornell Univ. Press, 1966), 244–245.

"The Modern Warning"
> Putt, S. Gorley. Henry James: A Reader's Guide
> (Ithaca: Cornell Univ. Press, 1966), 132–134.

"Mora Montravers"
> Putt, S. Gorley. Henry James: A Reader's Guide
> (Ithaca: Cornell Univ. Press, 1966), 300–301.

"Mrs. Medwin"
> Putt, S. Gorley. Henry James: A Reader's Guide
> (Ithaca: Cornell Univ. Press, 1966), 293–294.

"A New England Winter"
> Putt, S. Gorley. Henry James: A Reader's Guide
> (Ithaca: Cornell Univ. Press, 1966), 271–272.

"The Next Time"
> Putt, S. Gorley. Henry James: A Reader's Guide
> (Ithaca: Cornell Univ. Press, 1966), 230–232.

"Osborne's Revenge"
> Shine, Muriel G. The Fictional Children of Henry
> James (Chapel Hill: Univ. of North Carolina Press,
> 1968), 30–32.

"Pandora"
> Putt, S. Gorley. Henry James: A Reader's Guide
> (Ithaca: Cornell Univ. Press, 1966), 131–132.

Shine, Muriel G. The Fictional Children of Henry
James (Chapel Hill: Univ. of North Carolina Press,
1968), 49–52.
Vandersee, Charles. "James's 'Pandora': The Mixed
Consequences of Revision," Stud Bibliog, XXI (1968),
93–108.

"The Papers"
Putt, S. Gorley. Henry James: A Reader's Guide
(Ithaca: Cornell Univ. Press, 1966), 294–296.

"A Passionate Pilgrim"
Putt, S. Gorley. Henry James: A Reader's Guide
(Ithaca: Cornell Univ. Press, 1966), 61–64.

"Paste"
Putt, S. Gorley. Henry James: A Reader's Guide
(Ithaca: Cornell Univ. Press, 1966), 290–291.

"The Patagonia"
Putt, S. Gorley. Henry James: A Reader's Guide
(Ithaca: Cornell Univ. Press, 1966), 277–279.

"The Path of Duty"
Levy, Leo B. Versions of Melodrama: A Study of the
Fiction and Drama of Henry James, 1865–1897
(Berkeley: Univ. of California Press, 1957), 52–55.

"The Pension Beaurepas"
Leyburn, Ellen D. Strange Alloy: The Relation of
Comedy to Tragedy in the Fiction of Henry James
(Chapel Hill: Univ. of North Carolina Press, 1968),
51–54.
Putt, S. Gorley. Henry James: A Reader's Guide
(Ithaca: Cornell Univ. Press, 1966), 123–124.

"The Point of View"
Putt, S. Gorley. Henry James: A Reader's Guide
(Ithaca: Cornell Univ. Press, 1966), 45–46.

"The Private Life"
   Putt, S. Gorley. Henry James: A Reader's Guide
      (Ithaca: Cornell Univ. Press, 1966), 391–392.

"Professor Fargo"
   Putt, S. Gorley. Henry James: A Reader's Guide
      (Ithaca: Cornell Univ. Press, 1966), 43–45.

"The Pupil"
   Howe, Irving, Ed. Classics of Modern Fiction (New
      York: Harcourt, Brace & World, 1968), 217–225.
   Putt, S. Gorley. Henry James: A Reader's Guide
      (Ithaca: Cornell Univ. Press, 1966), 390–391.
   Shine, Muriel G. The Fictional Children of Henry
      James (Chapel Hill: Univ. of North Carolina Press,
      1968), 84–90.
   Trilling, Lionel. The Experience of Literature (New
      York: Holt, Rinehart & Winston, 1967), 591–593.

"The Real Thing"
   Dietrich, R. F., and Roger H. Sundell. Instructor's
      Manual for "The Art of Fiction" (New York: Holt,
      Rinehart & Winston, 1967), 9–15.
   Kehler, Harold. "James's 'The Real Thing,'" Expli-
      cator, XXV (1967), Item 79.
   Mueller, Lavonne. "Henry James: The Phenomenal
      Self in 'The Real Thing,'" Forum, VI, ii (Spring,
      1968), 46–50.
   Putt, S. Gorley. Henry James: A Reader's Guide
      (Ithaca: Cornell Univ. Press, 1966), 222–223.
   Toor, David. "Narrative Irony in Henry James' 'The
      Real Thing,'" Univ R, XXXIV (1967), 95–99.

"A Round of Visits"
   Purdy, Strother B. "Conversation and Awareness in
      Henry James's 'A Round of Visits,'" Stud Short Fic-
      tion, VI (1969), 421–432.

"The Siege of London"
   Putt, S. Gorley. Henry James: A Reader's Guide
      (Ithaca: Cornell Univ. Press, 1966), 125–128.

"The Solution"
    Putt, S. Gorley. Henry James: A Reader's Guide
        (Ithaca: Cornell Univ. Press, 1966), 278-279.

"The Special Type"
    Putt, S. Gorley. Henry James: A Reader's Guide
        (Ithaca: Cornell Univ. Press, 1966), 291-292.

"The Story in It"
    Putt, S. Gorley. Henry James: A Reader's Guide
        (Ithaca: Cornell Univ. Press, 1966), 296-297.

"The Third Person"
    Putt, S. Gorley. Henry James: A Reader's Guide
        (Ithaca: Cornell Univ. Press, 1966), 395-396.

"The Tone of Time"
    Mizener, Arthur. A Handbook for Use with "Modern
        Short Stories: The Uses of Imagination, Revised
        Edition" (New York: Norton, 1966), 47-50.
    Putt, S. Gorley. Henry James: A Reader's Guide
        (Ithaca: Cornell Univ. Press, 1966), 233-234.

"A Tragedy of Error"
    Putt, S. Gorley. Henry James: A Reader's Guide
        (Ithaca: Cornell Univ. Press, 1966), 33-34.
    Shine, Muriel G. The Fictional Children of Henry
        James (Chapel Hill: Univ. of North Carolina Press,
        1968), 26-29.

"The Tree of Knowledge"
    Frakes, James, and Isadore Traschen, Eds. Short
        Stories: A Critical Collection, Second edition (Engle-
        wood Cliffs: Prentice-Hall, 1969), 102-105.

"The Turn of the Screw"
    Aldrich, C. Knight. "Another Twist to 'The Turn of the
        Screw,'" Mod Fiction Stud, XIII (1967), 167-178; re-
        printed in Willen, Gerald, Ed. A Casebook on Henry
        James's "The Turn of the Screw," Second edition
        (New York: Crowell, 1969), 367-378.

Aswell, E. Duncan. "Reflections of a Governess: Image
and Distortion in 'The Turn of the Screw,'" Nineteenth-Century Fiction, XXIII (1968), 49–63.

Berner, R. L. "Douglas in 'The Turn of the Screw,'"
Engl Notes, III (Winter, 1968), 3–7.

Cargill, Oscar. "Henry James as Freudian Pioneer,"
Chicago R, X (Summer, 1956), 13–29; reprinted in
Ray, David, Ed. Chicago Review Anthology (Chicago:
Univ. of Chicago Press, 1959), 17–31; Willen, Gerald,
Ed. A Casebook on Henry James's "The Turn of the
Screw" (New York: Crowell, 1960), 223–238; Second
edition (1969), 223–238.

Clair, John A. The Ironic Dimension in the Fiction of
Henry James (Pittsburgh: Duquesne Univ. Press, 1965)
37–58.

Domaniecki, Hildegard. "Complementary Terms in
'The Turn of the Screw': The Straight Turning,"
Jarbuch für Amerikastudien, No. 10 (1965), 206–214.

Evans, Oliver. "James' Air of Evil: 'The Turn of the
Screw,'" Partisan R, XVI (1949), 175–187; reprinted
in Willen, Gerald, Ed. A Casebook on Henry James's
"The Turn of the Screw" (New York: Crowell, 1960),
200–211; Second edition (1969), 200–211.

Fagin, Nathan B. "Another Reading of 'The Turn of the
Screw,'" Mod Lang Notes, LVI (1941), 196–202; reprinted in Willen, Gerald, Ed. A Casebook on Henry
James's "The Turn of the Screw" (New York: Crowell,
1960), 154–159; Second edition (1969), 154–159.

Firebaugh, Joseph. "Inadequacy in Eden: Knowledge
and 'The Turn of the Screw,'" Mod Fiction Stud, III
(1957), 57–63; reprinted in Willen, Gerald, Ed. A
Casebook on Henry James's "The Turn of the Screw"
(New York: Crowell, 1960), 291–297; Second edition
(1969), 291–297.

Fraser, John. "The Turn of the Screw Again," Midwest Q, VII (1966), 327–336.

Girling, H. K. "The Strange Case of Dr. James and Mr.
Stevenson," Wascana R, III (1968), 65–79.

Goddard, Harold C. "A Pre-Freudian Reading of 'The
Turn of the Screw,'" Nineteenth-Century Fiction, XII

(1957), 1–36; reprinted in Willen, Gerald, Ed. A
Casebook on Henry James's "The Turn of the Screw"
(New York: Crowell, 1960), 244–272; Kimbrough,
Robert, Ed. The Turn of the Screw (New York:
Norton, 1966), 181–209; Willen, Gerald, Ed. A
Casebook on Henry James's "The Turn of the Screw,"
Second edition (New York: Crowell, 1969), 244–272.
Heilman, Robert B. "The Freudian Reading of 'The
Turn of the Screw,'" Mod Lang Notes, LXIII (1947),
433–445.
————. "The Lure of the Demonic: James and Dür-
renmatt," Comparative Lit, XIII (1961), 346–357.
————. "'The Turn of the Screw' as Poem," Univ
Kansas City R, XIV (1948), 272–289; reprinted in
O'Connor, William V., Ed. Forms of Modern Fic-
tion (Minneapolis: Univ. of Minnesota Press, 1948),
211–228; Schorer, Mark, Ed. The Story: A Critical
Anthology (New York: Prentice-Hall, 1950), 586–606;
Willen, Gerald, Ed. A Casebook on Henry James's
"The Turn of the Screw" (New York: Crowell, 1960),
174–188; Kimbrough, Robert, Ed. The Turn of the
Screw (New York: Norton, 1966), 214–228; Willen,
Gerald, Ed. A Casebook on Henry James's "The
Turn of the Screw," Second edition (New York:
Crowell, 1969), 174–188.
Hoffmann, Charles G. "Innocence and Evil in James's
'The Turn of the Screw,'" Univ Kansas City R, XX
(1953), 97–105; reprinted, revised, in his The Short
Novels of Henry James (New York: Bookman Asso-
ciates, 1957), 70–96; reprinted in Willen, Gerald,
Ed. A Casebook on Henry James's "The Turn of
the Screw," Second edition (New York: Crowell,
1969), 212–222.
Jones, Alexander E. "Point of View in 'The Turn of the
Screw,'" PMLA, LXXIV (1959), 112–122; reprinted
in Willen, Gerald, Ed. A Casebook on Henry James's
"The Turn of the Screw" (New York: Crowell, 1960),
298–318; Second edition (1969), 298–318.
Katan, M. "A Causerie on Henry James's 'The Turn
of the Screw,'" The Psychoanalytic Study of the Child,

XVII (1962), 473–493; reprinted in Willen, Gerald,
Ed. A Casebook on Henry James's "The Turn of
the Screw," Second edition (New York: Crowell,
1969), 319–337.
Kenton, Edna. "Henry James to the Ruminant Reader:
'The Turn of the Screw,'" Arts, VI (1924), 245–255;
reprinted in Willen, Gerald, Ed. A Casebook on
Henry James's "The Turn of the Screw" (New York:
Crowell, 1960), 102–114; Second edition (1969),
102–114; reprinted in part in Kimbrough, Robert,
Ed. The Turn of the Screw (New York: Norton, 1966),
209–211.
Lydenberg, John. "Comment on Mr. Spilka's Paper,"
Lit & Psych, XIV (1964), 6–8, 34.
————. "The Governess Turns the Screws," Nine-
teenth-Century Fiction, XII (1957), 37–58; reprinted
in Willen, Gerald, Ed. A Casebook on Henry James's
"The Turn of the Screw" (New York: Crowell, 1960),
273–290; Second edition (1969), 273–290.
McMaster, Juliet. "'The Full Image of a Repetition'
in 'The Turn of the Screw,'" Stud Short Fiction, VI
(1969), 377–382.
Porter, Katherine A., Allen Tate, and Mark Van Doren,
Eds. The New Invitation to Learning (New York: New
Home Library, 1942), 221–235; reprinted in Willen,
Gerald, Ed. A Casebook on Henry James's "The
Turn of the Screw" (New York: Crowell, 1960), 160–
170; Second edition (1969), 160–170.
Putt, S. Gorley. Henry James: A Reader's Guide
(Ithaca: Cornell Univ. Press, 1966), 396–399.
Reed, Glenn. "Another Turn on James's 'The Turn of
the Screw,'" Am Lit, XX (1949), 413–423; reprinted
in Willen, Gerald, Ed. A Casebook on Henry James's
"The Turn of the Screw" (New York: Crowell, 1960),
189–199; Second edition (1969), 189–199.
Rubin, Louis D. "One More Turn of the Screw," Mod
Fiction Stud, IX (1963), 314–328; reprinted in Willen,
Gerald, Ed. A Casebook on Henry James's "The
Turn of the Screw," Second edition (New York:
Crowell, 1969), 350–366.

Shine, Muriel G. The Fictional Children of Henry
James (Chapel Hill: Univ. of North Carolina Press,
1968), 131-139.
Siegel, Paul N. "'Miss Jessel': Mirror Image of the
Governess," Lit & Psych, XVIII (1968), 30-38.
Silver, John. "A Note on the Freudian Ending of 'The
Turn of the Screw,'" Am Lit, XXIX (1957), 207-211;
reprinted in Willen, Gerald, Ed. A Casebook on
Henry James's "The Turn of the Screw" (New York:
Crowell, 1960), 239-243; Second edition (1969), 239-
243.
Waldock, A. J. "Mr. Edmund Wilson and 'The Turn of
the Screw,'" Mod Lang Notes, LXII (1947), 331-334;
reprinted in Willen, Gerald, Ed. A Casebook on
Henry James's "The Turn of the Screw" (New York:
Crowell, 1960), 171-173; Second edition (1969), 171-
173.
West, Muriel. "The Death of Miles in 'The Turn of
the Screw,'" PMLA, LXXIX (1964), 283-288; re-
printed in Willen, Gerald, Ed. A Casebook on Henry
James's "The Turn of the Screw," Second edition
(New York: Crowell, 1969), 338-349.
Wilson, Edmund. "The Ambiguity of Henry James,"
Hound & Horn, VII (1934), 385-391; revised and ex-
panded in his The Triple Thinkers, Revised edition
(New York: Oxford Univ. Press, 1948), 124-132;
reprinted in Dupee, F. W., Ed. The Question of
Henry James (New York: Holt, 1945), 160-168; Wil-
len, Gerald, Ed. A Casebook on Henry James's "The
Turn of the Screw" (New York: Crowell, 1960), 115-
122; plus Postscript (1959), 153; Malin, Irving, Ed.
Psychoanalysis and American Fiction (New York:
Dutton, 1965), 143-150; Willen, Gerald, Ed. A Casebook on Henry James's "The Turn of the Screw,"
Second edition (1969), 115-122; plus Postscript
(1959), 153.

"The Two Faces"
Putt, S. Gorley. Henry James: A Reader's Guide
(Ithaca: Cornell Univ. Press, 1966), 292-293.

"The Velvet Glove"
Putt, S. Gorley. Henry James: A Reader's Guide
(Ithaca: Cornell Univ. Press, 1966), 236–238.

"Washington Square"
Levy, Leo B. Versions of Melodrama: A Study of the
Fiction and Drama of Henry James, 1865–1897
(Berkeley: Univ. of California Press, 1957), 38–40.
Leyburn, Ellen D. Strange Alloy: The Relation of
Comedy to Tragedy in the Fiction of Henry James
(Chapel Hill: Univ. of North Carolina Press, 1968),
28–30.
Poirier, Richard. The Comic Sense of Henry James:
A Study of the Early Novels (London: Chatto & Windus
1960), 165–182.
Shine, Muriel G. The Fictional Children of Henry
James (Chapel Hill: Univ. of North Carolina Press,
1968), 43–46.

SARAH ORNE JEWETT

"A Foreigner"
Thorp, Margaret F. Sarah Orne Jewett (Minneapolis:
Univ. of Minnesota Press, 1966), 40–41.

"The Landscape Chamber"
Thorp, Margaret F. Sarah Orne Jewett (Minneapolis:
(Univ. of Minnesota Press, 1966), 38–39.

"Law Lane"
Thorp, Margaret F. Sarah Orne Jewett (Minneapolis:
Univ. of Minnesota Press, 1966), 36–37.

"A Lost Lover"
Thorp, Margaret F. Sarah Orne Jewett (Minneapolis:
Univ. of Minnesota Press, 1966), 23.

"The Only Rose"
Thorp, Margaret F. Sarah Orne Jewett (Minneapolis:
Univ. of Minnesota Press, 1966), 37–38.

"A White Heron"
Thorp, Margaret F. Sarah Orne Jewett (Minneapolis:
Univ. of Minnesota Press, 1966), 39–40.

UWE JOHNSON

"Eine Kneipe Geht Verloren"
Lepper, K. H. "Dichter im Geteilten Deutschland: Be-
merkungen zu Uwe Johnsons Erzählung 'Eine Kneipe
Geht Verloren,'" Monatshefte, LX (1968), 23–34.

RICHARD MALCOLM JOHNSTON

"Mr. Fortner's Marital Claims"
Bush, Robert. "Richard Malcolm Johnston's Marriage
Group," Georgia R, XVIII (1964), 433–435.

JAMES JOYCE

"After the Race"
Adams, Robert M. James Joyce: Common Sense and
Beyond (New York: Random House, 1966), 64–68.
Beck, Warren. Joyce's "Dubliners": Substance, Vision,
and Art (Durham: Duke Univ. Press, 1969), 123–132.
Bowen, Zack. "'After the Race,'" in Hart, Clive, Ed.
James Joyce's "Dubliners": Critical Essays (London:
Faber and Faber, 1969), 53–61.
Ghiselin, Brewster. "The Unity of Joyce's 'Dubliners,'"
Accent, XVI (1956), 200; reprinted in Garrett, Peter
K., Ed. Twentieth Century Interpretations of "Dub-
liners" (Englewood Cliffs: Prentice-Hall, 1968), 73.

"Araby"
apRoberts, Robert P. "'Araby' and the Palimpsest of
Criticism or, Through a Glass Eye Darkly," Antioch
R, XXVI (1967), 469–489.

Atherton, J. S. "'Araby,'" in Hart, Clive, Ed. James Joyce's "Dubliners": Critical Essays (London: Faber and Faber, 1969), 39–47.

Beck, Warren. Joyce's "Dubliners": Substance, Vision, and Art (Durham: Duke Univ. Press, 1969), 96–109.

Benstock, Bernard. "Arabesques: Third Position of Concord," James Joyce Q, V (1967), 30–39.

Burto, William. "Joyce's 'Araby,'" Explicator, XXV (1967), Item 67.

Collins, Ben L. "Joyce's 'Araby' and the 'Extended Simile,'" James Joyce Q, IV (1967), 84–90; reprinted in Garrett, Peter K., Ed. Twentieth Century Interpretations of "Dubliners" (Englewood Cliffs: Prentice-Hall, 1968), 93–99.

Friedman, Stanley. "Joyce's 'Araby,'" Explicator, XXIV (1966), Item 43.

Ghiselin, Brewster. "The Unity of Joyce's 'Dubliners,'" Accent, XVI (1956), 199; reprinted in Garrett, Peter K., Ed. Twentieth Century Interpretations of "Dubliners" (Englewood Cliffs: Prentice-Hall, 1968), 72.

Going, William T. "Joyce's 'Araby,'" Explicator, XXVI (1968), Item 39.

LaHood, Marvin J. "A Note on the Priest in Joyce's 'Araby,'" Revue des Langues Vivantes, XXXIV (1968), 24–25.

Levin, Richard, and Charles Shattuck. "First Flight to Ithaca: A New Reading of Joyce's 'Dubliners,'" Accent, IV (1944), 82; reprinted in Givens, Seon, Ed. James Joyce: Two Decades of Criticism (New York: Vanguard, 1948), 58–60; Freedman, Morris, and Paul B. Davis, Eds. Controversy in Literature (New York: Scribner, 1968), 112–114.

Lyons, John O. "James Joyce and Chaucer's Prioress," Engl Lang Notes, II (1964), 127–132.

Mizener, Arthur. A Handbook for Use with "Modern Short Stories: The Uses of Imagination, Revised Edition" (New York: Norton, 1966), 118–119.

Stein, William B. "Joyce's 'Araby': Paradise Lost," Perspective, XII (1962), 215–222; reprinted in Freed-

man, Morris, and Paul B. Davis, Eds. Controversy
   in Literature (New York: Scribner, 1968), 114–120.
Stone, Harry. "'Araby' and the Writings of James
   Joyce," Antioch R, XXV (1965), 375–410; reprinted
   in Scholes, Robert, and A. Walton Litz, Eds. "Dub-
   liners": Text, Criticism, and Notes (New York:
   Viking, 1969), 344–367.
West, Ray B. The Art of Writing Fiction (New York:
   Crowell, 1968), 241–246.

"The Boarding House"
   Adams, Robert M. James Joyce: Common Sense and
      Beyond (New York: Random House, 1966), 74–75.
   Beck, Warren. Joyce's "Dubliners": Substance, Vision,
      and Art (Durham: Duke Univ. Press, 1969), 147–159.
   Ghiselin, Brewster. "The Unity of Joyce's 'Dubliners,'"
      Accent, XVI (1956), 201–202; reprinted in Garrett,
      Peter K., Ed. Twentieth Century Interpretations of
      "Dubliners" (Englewood-Cliffs: Prentice-Hall, 1968),
      74–75.
   Halper, Nathan. "'The Boarding House,'" in Hart,
      Clive, Ed. James Joyce's "Dubliners": Critical
      Essays (London: Faber and Faber, 1969), 72–83.
   Kenner, Hugh. Dublin's Joyce (Bloomington: Indiana
      Univ. Press, 1956), 49–50; reprinted in Garrett,
      Peter K., Ed. Twentieth Century Interpretations of
      "Dubliners" (Englewood Cliffs: Prentice-Hall, 1968),
      44–45.
   ————, Ed. Studies in Change: A Book of the Short
      Story (Englewood Cliffs: Prentice-Hall, 1965), vii–x.
   Rosenberg, Bruce A. "The Crucifixion in 'The Board-
      ing House,'" Stud Short Fiction, V (1967), 44–53.
   San Juan, E. "Joyce's 'The Boarding House': The Plot
      of Character," Univ R, XXXV (1969), 229–236.

"Clay"
   Adams, Robert M. James Joyce: Common Sense and
      Beyond (New York: Random House, 1966), 75–76.
   Beck, Warren. Joyce's "Dubliners": Substance, Vision,
      and Art (Durham: Duke Univ. Press, 1969), 199–218.

Cowan, S. A. "Celtic Folklore in 'Clay': Maria and the
    Irish Washerwoman," Stud Short Fiction, VI (1969),
    213-215.
Dietrich, R. F., and Roger H. Sundell. Instructor's
    Manual for "The Art of Fiction" (New York: Holt,
    Rinehart & Winston, 1967), 58-64.
Ghiselin, Brewster. "The Unity of Joyce's 'Dubliners,'"
    Accent, XVI (1956), 203-204; reprinted in Garrett,
    Peter K., Ed. Twentieth Century Interpretations of
    "Dubliners" (Englewood Cliffs: Prentice-Hall, 1968),
    76-77.
Glasheen, Adaline. "'Clay,'" in Hart, Clive, Ed.
    James Joyce's "Dubliners": Critical Essays (London:
    Faber and Faber, 1969), 100-106.
Goldman, Arnold. The Joyce Paradox: Form and Free-
    dom in His Fiction (Evanston: Northwestern Univ.
    Press, 1966), 120-123.
Madden, David. "James Joyce's 'Clay,'" Univ R, XXXIII
    (1967), 229-233.
Mathews, F. X. "Punchestime: A New Look at 'Clay,'"
    James Joyce Q, IV (1967), 102-106.
Scholes, Robert. Elements of Fiction (New York: Ox-
    ford Univ. Press, 1958), 66-77.
Walzl, Florence L. "Joyce's 'Clay,'" Explicator, XX
    (1962), Item 46; reprinted in Garrett, Peter K., Ed.
    Twentieth Century Explications of 'Dubliners" (Engle-
    wood Cliffs: Prentice-Hall, 1968), 107-109.
————. "The Liturgy of the Epiphany Season and the
    Epiphanies of Joyce," PMLA, LXXX (1965), 447-448.
————. "Pattern of Paralysis in Joyce's Dubliners:
    A Study of the Original Framework," Coll Engl,
    XXII (1961), 226.

"Counterparts"
    Beck, Warren. Joyce's "Dubliners": Substance, Vision,
        and Art (Durham: Duke Univ. Press, 1969), 186-198.
    Ghiselin, Brewster. "The Unity of Joyce's 'Dubliners,'"
        Accent, XVI (1956), 202-203; reprinted in Garrett,
        Peter K., Ed. Twentieth Century Interpretations of

"Dubliners" (Englewood Cliffs: Prentice-Hall, 1968),
75–76.

Rees, Robert A., and Barry Menikoff. A Manual to Ac-
company "The Short Story: An Introductory Anthology"
(Boston: Little, Brown, 1969), 18–19.

Scholes, Robert. "'Counterparts,'" in Hart, Clive, Ed.
James Joyce's "Dubliners": Critical Essays (London:
Faber and Faber, 1969), 93–99; reprinted in Scholes,
Robert, and A. Walton Litz, Eds. "Dubliners": Text,
Criticism, and Notes (New York: Viking, 1969), 379–
387.

"The Dead"

Adams, Robert M. James Joyce: Common Sense and
Beyond (New York: Random House, 1966), 83–86.

Beck, Warren. Joyce's "Dubliners": Substance, Vision,
and Art (Durham: Duke Univ. Press, 1969), 303–360.

Benstock, Bernard. "'The Dead,'" in Hart, Clive, Ed.
James Joyce's "Dubliners": Critical Essays (London:
Faber and Faber, 1969), 153–169.

Burke, Kenneth. "Three Definitions," Kenyon R, XIII
(1951), 186–197; reprinted in Scholes, Robert, and
A. Walton Litz, Eds. "Dubliners": Text, Criticism,
and Notes (New York: Viking, 1969), 410–416; reprinted in part in Moynihan, William T., Ed. Joyce's
"The Dead" (Boston: Allyn & Bacon, 1965), 95–99.

Daiches, David. The Novel and the Modern World (Chi-
cago: Univ. of Chicago Press, 1939), 91–100; Second
edition (1960), 73–82; reprinted in Schorer, Mark,
Ed. Modern British Fiction: Essays in Criticism
(New York: Oxford Univ. Press, 1961), 315–321; Sum-
mers, Hollis, Ed. Discussions of the Short Story
(Boston: Heath, 1963), 84–88; Garrett, Peter K., Ed.
Twentieth Century Interpretations of "Dubliners"
(Englewood Cliffs: Prentice-Hall, 1968), 32–37.

Ellmann, Richard. "The Backgrounds of 'The Dead,'"
Kenyon R, XX (1958), 507–528; reprinted with
changes in his James Joyce (New York: Oxford Univ.
Press, 1959), 254–263; Albrecht, Robert C., Ed.
The World of Short Fiction (New York: Free Press,

1969), 459–465; Scholes, Robert, and A. Walton Litz,
Eds. "Dubliners": Text, Criticism, and Notes (New
York: Viking, 1969), 388–403.
————————. "The Limits of Joyce's Naturalism," Sewanee
R, LXIII (1955), 570–571.
Ghiselin, Brewster. "The Unity of Joyce's 'Dubliners,'"
Accent, XVI (1956), 207–212; reprinted in Garrett,
Peter K., Ed. Twentieth Century Interpretations of
"Dubliners" (Englewood Cliffs: Prentice-Hall, 1968),
80–84.
Goldberg, S. L. James Joyce (New York: Grove Press,
1962), 41–45; reprinted in Garrett, Peter K., Ed.
Twentieth Century Interpretations of "Dubliners"
(Englewood Cliffs: Prentice-Hall, 1968), 90–92.
Goldman, Arnold. The Joyce Paradox: Form and Free-
dom in His Fiction (Evanston: Northwestern Univ.
Press, 1966), 123–125.
Hutton, Virgil. "James Joyce's 'The Dead,'" East-
West R, II (1966), 124–139.
Kenner, Hugh. Dublin's Joyce (Bloomington: Indiana
Univ. Press, 1956), 62–68; reprinted in Garrett,
Peter K., Ed. Twentieth Century Interpretations of
"Dubliners" (Englewood Cliffs: Prentice-Hall, 1968),
51–56.
Kopper, Edward A. "Joyce's 'The Dead,'" Explicator,
XXVI (1968), Item 46.
Loomis, C. C. "Structure and Sympathy in Joyce's 'The
Dead,'" PMLA, LXXV (1960), 149–151; reprinted in
Moynihan, William T., Ed. Joyce's "The Dead" (Bos-
ton: Allyn & Bacon, 1965), 100–104; Garrett, Peter K.,
Ed. Twentieth Century Interpretations of "Dubliners"
(Englewood Cliffs: Prentice-Hall, 1968), 110–114;
Scholes, Robert, and A. Walton Litz, Eds. "Dubliners'
Text, Criticism, and Notes (New York: Viking, 1969),
417–422.
Lytle, Andrew. "A Reading of Joyce's 'The Dead,'"
Sewanee R, LXXVII (1969), 193–216.
O'Brien, Darcy. The Conscience of James Joyce
(Princeton: Princeton Univ. Press, 1968), 16–21.

O'Connor, Frank. "And It's a Lonely, Personal Art,"
in Brown, Francis, Ed. Highlights of Modern Literature (New York: New American Library, 1954),
78.
————. The Lonely Voice: A Study of The Short
Story (Cleveland: World, 1963), 123–126; reprinted
in Garrett, Peter K., Ed. Twentieth Century Inter-
pretations of "Dubliners" (Englewood Cliffs: Prentice-Hall, 1968), 24–26.
————. The Mirror in the Roadway: A Study of the
Modern Novel (New York: Knopf, 1956), 299–301.
Steinmann, Martin, and Gerald Willen, Eds. Literature
for Writing (Belmont: Wadsworth, 1962), 310–311;
Second edition (1967), 313–314.
Tate, Allen. "Three Commentaries: Poe, James, and
Joyce," Sewanee R, LVIII (1950), 10–15; reprinted
in Gordon, Caroline, and Allen Tate. The House of
Fiction (New York: Scribner, 1950), 279–282; Second
edition (1960), 183–186; Scholes, Robert, and A. Wal-
ton Litz, Eds. "Dubliners": Text, Criticism, and
Notes (New York: Viking, 1969), 404–409.
Trilling, Lionel. The Experience of Literature (New
York: Holt, Rinehart & Winston, 1967), 652–655.
Walzl, Florence L. "Ambiguity in the Structural Sym-
bols of Gabriel's Vision in Joyce's 'The Dead,'" Wis-
consin Stud Lit, No. 2 (1965), 60–69.
————. "Gabriel and Michael: The Conclusion of
'The Dead,'" James Joyce Q, IV (1966), 17–31; re-
printed in Scholes, Robert, and A. Walton Litz, Eds.
"Dubliners": Text, Criticism, and Notes (New York:
Viking, 1969), 423–443.
————. "The Liturgy of the Epiphany Season and the
Epiphanies of Joyce," PMLA, LXXX (1965), 449.

"An Encounter"
Beck, Warren. Joyce's "Dubliners": Substance, Vision,
and Art (Durham: Duke Univ. Press, 1969), 79–95.
Degnan, James P. "The Reluctant Indian in Joyce's 'An
Encounter,'" Stud Short Fiction, VI (1969), 152–156.

Ghiselin, Brewster. "The Unity of Joyce's 'Dubliners,'"
    Accent, XVI (1956), 198; reprinted in Garrett, Peter
    K., Ed. Twentieth Century Interpretations of "Dub-
    liners" (Englewood Cliffs: Prentice-Hall, 1968), 71–
    72.
Senn, Fritz. "'An Encounter,'" in Hart, Clive, Ed.
    James Joyce's "Dubliners": Critical Essays (London:
    Faber and Faber, 1969), 26–38.

"Eveline"
    Adams, Robert M. James Joyce: Common Sense and
        Beyond (New York: Random House, 1966), 68–70.
    Beck, Warren. Joyce's "Dubliners": Substance, Vision,
        and Art (Durham: Duke Univ. Press, 1969), 110–122.
    Ghiselin, Brewster. "The Unity of Joyce's 'Dubliners,'"
        Accent, XVI (1956), 199–200; reprinted in Garrett,
        Peter K., Ed. Twentieth Century Interpretations of
        "Dubliners" (Englewood Cliffs: Prentice-Hall, 1968),
        72–73.
    Goldman, Arnold. The Joyce Paradox: Form and Free-
        dom in His Fiction (Evanston: Northwestern Univ.
        Press, 1966), 18–21.
    Hart, Clive. "'Eveline,'" in Hart, Clive, Ed. James
        Joyce's "Dubliners": Critical Essays (London: Faber
        and Faber, 1969), 48–52.
    Pira, Gisela. "James Joyce: 'Eveline,'" Die Neueren
        Sprachen, N. S. XVI (1967), 552–554.
    Shrodes, Caroline, Justine Van Gundy, and Joel Dorius.
        Instructor's Manual for "Reading for Understanding"
        (New York: Macmillan, 1968), 13–14.
    Torchiana, Donald T. "Joyce's 'Eveline' and the Blessed
        Margaret Mary Alacoque," James Joyce Q, VI (Fall,
        1968), 22–28.

"Grace"
    Abbott, H. Porter. "The Importance of Martin Cunning-
        ham," James Joyce Q, V (Fall, 1967), 47–52.
    Adams, Robert M. James Joyce: Common Sense and
        Beyond (New York: Random House, 1966), 80–83.

Beck, Warren. Joyce's "Dubliners": Substance, Vision, and Art (Durham: Duke Univ. Press, 1969), 277–302.

Cunningham, Frank R. "Joyce's 'Grace': Gracelessness in a Lost Paradise," James Joyce Q, VI (1968), 219–223.

Ghiselin, Brewster. "The Unity of Joyce's 'Dubliners,'" Accent, XVI (1956), 206–207; reprinted in Garrett, Peter K., Ed. Twentieth Century Interpretations of "Dubliners" (Englewood Cliffs: Prentice-Hall, 1968), 79–80.

Kain, Richard M. "'Grace,'" in Hart, Clive, Ed. James Joyce's "Dubliners": Critical Essays (London: Faber and Faber, 1969), 134–152.

Kauvar, Elaine M. "Swift's Clothing Philosophy in A Tale of a Tub and Joyce's 'Grace,'" James Joyce Q, V (1968), 162–165.

Moseley, Virginia. "The 'Coincidence' of 'Contrarieties' in 'Grace,'" James Joyce Q, VI (Fall, 1968), 3–21.

O'Connor, Frank. The Lonely Voice: A Study of the Short Story (Cleveland: World, 1963), 121–123; reprinted in Garrett, Peter K., Ed. Twentieth Century Interpretations of "Dubliners" (Englewood Cliffs: Prentice-Hall, 1968), 23–24.

————. The Mirror in the Roadway: A Study of the Modern Novel (New York: Knopf, 1956), 298–299.

"Ivy Day in the Committee Room"

Adams, Robert M. James Joyce: Common Sense and Beyond (New York: Random House, 1966), 77–80.

Beck, Warren. Joyce's "Dubliners": Substance, Vision, and Art (Durham: Duke Univ. Press, 1969), 237–258.

Boyle, Robert. "'Two Gallants' and 'Ivy Day in the Committee Room,'" James Joyce Q, I (1963), 3–9; reprinted in Garrett, Peter K., Ed. Twentieth Century Explications of "Dubliners" (Englewood Cliffs: Prentice-Hall, 1968), 100–106.

Daiches, David. The Novel and the Modern World (Chicago: Univ. of Chicago Press, 1939), 89–90; Second edition (1960), 71–72; reprinted in Summers, Hollis,

Ed. Discussions of the Short Story (Boston: Heath,
1963), 83–84; Garrett, Peter K., Ed. Twentieth
Century Interpretations of "Dubliners" (Englewood
Cliffs: Prentice-Hall, 1968), 30–31.

Ghiselin, Brewster. "The Unity of Joyce's 'Dubliners,'"
Accent, XVI (1956), 205–206; reprinted in Garrett,
Peter K., Ed. Twentieth Century Interpretations of
"Dubliners" (Englewood Cliffs: Prentice-Hall, 1968),
77–78.

Hodgart, M. J. C. "'Ivy Day in the Committee Room,'"
in Hart, Clive, Ed. James Joyce's "Dubliners":
Critical Essays (London: Faber and Faber, 1969),
115–121.

"A Little Cloud"

Beck, Warren. Joyce's "Dubliners": Substance, Vision,
and Art (Durham: Duke Univ. Press, 1969), 160–185.

Boyle, Robert. "'A Little Cloud,'" in Hart, Clive, Ed.
James Joyce's "Dubliners": Critical Essays (London:
Faber and Faber, 1969), 84–92.

Ghiselin, Brewster. "The Unity of Joyce's 'Dubliners,'"
Accent, XVI (1956), 202; reprinted in Garrett, Peter
K., Ed. Twentieth Century Interpretations of "Dub-
liners" (Englewood Cliffs: Prentice-Hall, 1968), 75.

Kenner, Hugh. Dublin's Joyce (Bloomington: Indiana
Univ. Press, 1956), 56–57; reprinted in Garrett,
Peter K., Ed. Twentieth Century Interpretations of
"Dubliners" (Englewood Cliffs: Prentice-Hall, 1968),
45–47.

Rees, Robert A., and Barry Menikoff. A Manual to Ac-
company "The Short Story: An Introductory Anthology"
(Boston: Little, Brown, 1969), 17–18.

"A Mother"

Beck, Warren. Joyce's "Dubliners": Substance, Vision,
and Art (Durham: Duke Univ. Press, 1969), 259–276.

Ghiselin, Brewster. "The Unity of Joyce's 'Dubliners,'"
Accent, XVI (1956), 206; reprinted in Garrett, Peter
K., Ed. Twentieth Century Interpretations of "Dub-
liners" (Englewood Cliffs: Prentice-Hall, 1968), 78–79.

Hayman, David. "'A Mother,'" in Hart, Clive, Ed.
James Joyce's "Dubliners": Critical Essays (London: Faber and Faber, 1969), 122–133.

"A Painful Case"
Beck, Warren. Joyce's "Dubliners": Substance, Vision,
and Art (Durham: Duke Univ. Press, 1969), 219–236.
Connolly, Thomas E. "'A Painful Case,'" in Hart, Clive,
Ed. James Joyce's "Dubliners": Critical Essays
(London: Faber and Faber, 1969), 107–114.
Ghiselin, Brewster. "The Unity of Joyce's 'Dubliners,'"
Accent, XVI (1956), 204; reprinted in Garrett, Peter
K., Ed. Twentieth Century Interpretations of "Dub-
liners" (Englewood Cliffs: Prentice-Hall, 1968), 77.
Goldberg, S. L. James Joyce (New York: Grove Press,
1962), 40–41; reprinted in Garrett, Peter K., Ed.
Twentieth Century Interpretations of "Dubliners"
(Englewood Cliffs: Prentice-Hall, 1968), 88–90.
Kenner, Hugh. Dublin's Joyce (Bloomington: Indiana
Univ. Press, 1956), 58–61; reprinted in Garrett,
Peter K., Ed. Twentieth Century Interpretations of
"Dubliners" (Englewood Cliffs: Prentice-Hall, 1968),
47–49.

"The Sisters"
Adams, Robert M. James Joyce: Common Sense and
Beyond (New York: Random House, 1966), 70–72.
Beck, Warren. Joyce's "Dubliners": Substance, Vision,
and Art (Durham: Duke Univ. Press, 1969), 42–78.
Brandabur, Edward. "The Sisters," in Scholes, Robert,
and A. Walton Litz, Eds. "Dubliners": Text, Criti-
cism, and Notes (New York: Viking, 1969), 333–343.
Corrington, John W. "'The Sisters,'" in Hart, Clive,
Ed. James Joyce's "Dubliners": Critical Essays
(London: Faber and Faber, 1969), 13–25.
Doherty, Paul C. "Words as Idols: The Epiphany in
James Joyce's 'The Sisters,'" Coll Engl Assoc
Critic, XXXII (October, 1969), 10–11.
Fabian, David R. "Joyce's 'The Sisters': Gnomon,
Gnomic, Gnome," Stud Short Fiction, V (1968), 187–189.

Ghiselin, Brewster. "The Unity of Joyce's 'Dubliners,'"
Accent, XVI (1956), 196–198; reprinted in Garrett,
Peter K., Ed. Twentieth Century Interpretations of
"Dubliners" (Englewood Cliffs: Prentice-Hall, 1968),
69–71.

Goldman, Arnold. The Joyce Paradox: Form and Freedom in His Fiction (Evanston: Northwestern Univ.
Press, 1966), 12–16.

Kenner, Hugh. Dublin's Joyce (Bloomington: Indiana
Univ. Press, 1956), 50–53; reprinted in Garrett,
Peter K., Ed. Twentieth Century Interpretations of
"Dubliners" (Englewood Cliffs: Prentice-Hall, 1968),
40–42.

Reynolds, Michael S. "The Feast of the Most Precious
Blood and Joyce's 'The Sisters,'" Stud Short Fiction,
VI (1969), 336.

"Two Gallants"

Adams, Robert M. James Joyce: Common Sense and
Beyond (New York: Random House, 1966), 72–74.

Beck, Warren. Joyce's "Dubliners": Substance, Vision,
and Art (Durham: Duke Univ. Press, 1969), 133–146.

Boyle, Robert. "'Two Gallants' and 'Ivy Day in the
Committee Room,'" James Joyce Q, I (1963), 3–9;
reprinted in Garrett, Peter K., Ed. Twentieth Century Interpretations of "Dubliners" (Englewood
Cliffs: Prentice-Hall, 1968), 100–106.

Ghiselin, Brewster. "The Unity of Joyce's 'Dubliners,'"
Accent, XVI (1956), 200–201; reprinted in Garrett,
Peter K., Ed. Twentieth Century Interpretations of
"Dubliners" (Englewood Cliffs: Prentice-Hall, 1968),
73–74.

Litz, A. Walton. "'Two Gallants,'" in Hart, Clive, Ed.
James Joyce's "Dubliners": Critical Essays (London:
Faber and Faber, 1969), 62–71; reprinted in Scholes,
Robert, and A. Walton Litz, Eds. "Dubliners": Text,
Criticism, and Notes (New York: Viking, 1969), 368–
378.

Torchiana, Donald T. "Joyce's 'Two Gallants': A Walk
Through the Ascendancy," James Joyce Q, VI (1968),
115–127.

FRANZ KAFKA

"Blumfeld, an Elderly Bachelor"
Emrich, Wilhelm. Franz Kafka: A Critical Study of His
Writings, trans. Sheema Z. Buehne (New York: Ungar,
1968), 116-124.

"The Burrow"
Emrich, Wilhelm. Franz Kafka: A Critical Study of His
Writings, trans. Sheema Z. Buehne (New York: Ungar,
1968), 206-224.
Friedman, Maurice. Problematic Rebel: An Image of
Modern Man (New York: Random House, 1963), 138-
140.
Osborne, Charles. Kafka (New York: Barnes & Noble,
1967), 53-54.

"The Cares of a Family Man"
Stahl, August. "'Konfusion ohne Absicht'? Zur Inter-
pretation von Kafkas Erzählung 'Die Sorge des Haus-
vaters,'" in Malter, Rudolf, and Alois Brandstetter,
Eds. Saarbrücker Beiträge zur Ästhetik (Saarbrücken:
Saarbrücker Zeitung, 1966), 67-78.

"The Conscription of Troops"
Emrich, Wilhelm. Franz Kafka: A Critical Study of His
Writings, trans. Sheema Z. Buehne (New York: Ungar,
1968), 257-268.

"A Country Doctor"
Church, Margaret. "Kafka's 'A Country Doctor,'" Ex-
plicator, XVI (1958), Item 45; reprinted in Beebe,
Maurice. Literary Symbolism (San Francisco: Wads-
worth, 1960), 138-139; Locke, Louis G., William M.
Gibson, and George Arms, Eds. Introduction to Lit-
erature, Fifth edition (New York: Holt, Rinehart &
Winston, 1967), 344-345.
————. Time and Reality: Studies in Contemporary
Fiction (Chapel Hill: Univ. of North Carolina Press,
1963), 187-189.

Emrich, Wilhelm. Franz Kafka: A Critical Study of His Writings, trans. Sheema Z. Buehne (New York: Ungar, 1968), 151–161.

Guth, Hans P. "Symbol and Contextual Restraint: Kafka's 'Country Doctor,'" PMLA, LXXX (1965), 427–431; reprinted in Guth, Hans P., Ed. Literature, Second edition (Belmont: Wadsworth, 1968), 283–291.

Kurkiala, Juhani. "'Kafkamainen' elämänkatsomus kertomuksessa 'Ein Landarzt,'" Valvoja, LXXXVII (1967), 309–315.

Servotte, Hermann. "Franz Kafka: Der Landarzt," Deutschunterricht für Ausländer, VIII (1958), 33–38.

Shrodes, Caroline, Justine Van Gundy, and Joel Dorius. Instructor's Manual for "Reading for Understanding" (New York: Macmillan, 1968), 15–16.

Timko, Michael. "Kafka's 'A Country Doctor,' Williams' 'The Use of Force,' and White's 'The Second Tree from the Corner,'" in Timko, Michael, and Clinton F. Oliver, Eds. Thirty-Eight Short Stories (New York: Knopf, 1968), 86–101.

"The Giant Mole"

Emrich, Wilhelm. Franz Kafka: A Critical Study of His Writings, trans. Sheema Z. Buehne (New York: Ungar, 1968), 172–178.

"The Great Wall of China"

Friedman, Maurice. Problematic Rebel: An Image of Modern Man (New York: Random House, 1963), 154–157.

"A Hunger Artist"

Flores, Kate. "The Judgment," in Flores, Angel, and Homer Swander, Eds. Franz Kafka Today (Madison: Univ. of Wisconsin Press, 1958), 19–20; paperback editions (1962, 1964), 19–20.

Friedman, Maurice. Problematic Rebel: An Image of Modern Man (New York: Random House, 1963), 150–152, 163–167.

"The Hunter Gracchus"
  Friedman, Maurice. Problematic Rebel: An Image of
    Modern Man (New York: Random House, 1963), 145–
    149.
  Trilling, Lionel. The Experience of Literature (New
    York: Holt, Rinehart & Winston, 1967), 659–662.

"A Hybrid"
  Emrich, Wilhelm. Franz Kafka: A Critical Study of His
    Writings, trans. Sheema Z. Buehne (New York: Ungar,
    1968), 161–164.

"In Our Synagogue"
  Emrich, Wilhelm. Franz Kafka: A Critical Study of His
    Writings, trans. Sheema Z. Buehne (New York: Ungar,
    1968), 168–172.

"In the Penal Colony"
  Emrich, Wilhelm. Franz Kafka: A Critical Study of His
    Writings, trans. Sheema Z. Buehne (New York: Ungar,
    1968), 268–275.
  Kramer, Dale. "The Aesthetics of Theme: Kafka's 'In
    the Penal Colony,'" Stud Short Fiction, V (1968),
    362–367.
  Osborne, Charles. Kafka (New York: Barnes & Noble,
    1967), 41–43.

"Investigations of a Dog"
  Emrich, Wilhelm. Franz Kafka: A Critical Study of His
    Writings, trans. Sheema Z. Buehne (New York: Ungar,
    1968), 180–200.
  Friedman, Maurice. Problematic Rebel: An Image of
    Modern Man (New York: Random House, 1963), 152–
    154.
  Osborne, Charles. Kafka (New York: Barnes & Noble,
    1967), 52–53.
  Winkelman, John. "Kafka's 'Forschungen eines Hundes,'"
    Monatshefte, LIX (1967), 204–216.

"Jackals and Arabs"
  Rubinstein, William C. "Kafka's 'Jackals and Arabs,'"
    Monatshefte, LIX (1967), 13–18.

"Josephine, the Singer"
  Emrich, Wilhelm. Franz Kafka: A Critical Study of
    His Writings, trans. Sheema Z. Buehne (New York:
    Ungar, 1968), 200–206.

"The Judgment"
  Flores, Kate. "Franz Kafka and the Nameless Guilt:
    An Analysis of 'The Judgment,'" Quarterly R Lit,
    III (1947), 382–405; reprinted in Flores, Angel, and
    Homer Swander, Eds. Franz Kafka Today (Madison:
    Univ. of Wisconsin Press, 1958), 5–24; paperback
    editions (1962, 1964), 5–24.
  Osborne, Charles. Kafka (New York: Barnes & Noble,
    1967), 35–37.
  Tauber, Herbert. Franz Kafka (New Haven: Yale Univ.
    Press, 1948), 15–17; reprinted in Frakes, James,
    and Isadore Traschen. Short Fiction: A Critical Col-
    lection (Englewood Cliffs: Prentice-Hall, 1959), 457–
    458; Second edition (1969), 394–395.

"Metamorphosis"
  Emrich, Wilhelm. Franz Kafka: A Critical Study of His
    Writings, trans. Sheema Z. Buehne (New York: Ungar,
    1968), 136–148.
  Friedman, Maurice. Problematic Rebel: An Image of
    Modern Man (New York: Random House, 1963), 141–
    145.
  Friedman, Norman. "The Struggle of Vermin: Parasit-
    ism and Family Love in Kafka's 'Metamorphosis,'"
    Ball State Univ Forum, IX, i (1968), 23–32.
  Howe, Irving, Ed. Classics of Modern Fiction (New
    York: Harcourt, Brace & World, 1968), 399–407.
  Osborne, Charles. Kafka (New York: Barnes & Noble,
    1967), 38–41.

Van Duyn, J. "The Metaphysical Aspects of Kafka's
'The Metamorphosis,'" Descant (Fall, 1967), 41–46.

"The New Advocate"
Friedman, Maurice. Problematic Rebel: An Image of
Modern Man (New York: Random House, 1963), 149–
150.

"An Old Page [Manuscript]"
Lynskey, Winifred, Ed. Reading Modern Fiction, Second edition (New York: Scribner, 1957), 320–321;
Third edition (1962), 320–321; Fourth edition (1968),
314–316.

"A Report to an Academy"
Emrich, Wilhelm. Franz Kafka: A Critical Study of His
Writings, trans. Sheema Z. Buehne (New York: Ungar,
1968), 148–151.
Friedman, Maurice. Problematic Rebel: An Image of
Modern Man (New York: Random House, 1963), 137–
138.
Stuart, Dabney. "Kafka's 'A Report to an Academy':
An Exercise in Method," Stud Short Fiction, VI (1969),
413–420.

NIKOLAI KARAMZIN

"Poor Liza"
Proffer, Carl R., Ed. From Karamzin to Bunin: An
Anthology of Russian Short Stories (Bloomington:
Indiana Univ. Press, 1969), 1–4.

GOTTFRIED KELLER

"Clothes Make the Man"
Friedrichsmeyer, Erhard. "Strapinskis Krise in Kellers
'Kleider machen Leute': Eine Komplementärperspektive,"
Germ Q, XL (1967), 1–13.

"A Village Romeo and Juliet"
Fuerst, Norbert. The Victorian Age of German Literature (University Park: Pennsylvania State Univ. Press, 1966), 105–108.

RUDYARD KIPLING

"Beauty Spots"
Dobrée, Bonamy. Rudyard Kipling, Realist and Fabulist (London: Oxford Univ. Press, 1967), 141–143.

"Bread Upon the Waters"
Dobrée, Bonamy. Rudyard Kipling, Realist and Fabulist (London: Oxford Univ. Press, 1967), 139–140.

"The Bull That Thought"
Dobrée, Bonamy. Rudyard Kipling, Realist and Fabulist (London: Oxford Univ. Press, 1967), 163–164.

"Children of the Zodiac"
Dobrée, Bonamy. Rudyard Kipling, Realist and Fabulist (London: Oxford Univ. Press, 1967), 147–148.

"The Church That Was at Antioch"
Dobrée, Bonamy. Rudyard Kipling, Realist and Fabulist (London: Oxford Univ. Press, 1967), 160–161.

"Dayspring Mishandled"
Dobrée, Bonamy. Rudyard Kipling, Realist and Fabulist (London: Oxford Univ. Press, 1967), 143–144.

"The Enlightenments of Pagett, M. P."
Rao, K. Bhaskara. Rudyard Kipling's India (Norman: Univ. of Oklahoma Press, 1967), 77–86.

"The Eye of Allah"
Dobrée, Bonamy. Rudyard Kipling, Realist and Fabulist (London: Oxford Univ. Press, 1967), 159–160.

"The Gardener"
  Mizener, Arthur. A Handbook for Use with "Modern
    Short Stories: The Uses of Imagination, Revised Edi-
    tion" (New York: Norton, 1966), 129–132.

"The Head of the District"
  Rao, K. Bhaskara. Rudyard Kipling's India (Norman:
    Univ. of Oklahoma Press, 1967), 87–90.

"The Knife and the Naked Chalk"
  Dobrée, Bonamy. Rudyard Kipling, Realist and Fabu-
    list (London: Oxford Univ. Press, 1967), 157–158.

"The Maltese Cat"
  Dobrée, Bonamy. Rudyard Kipling, Realist and Fabu-
    list (London: Oxford Univ. Press, 1967), 151–152.

"The Man Who Would Be King"
  Dobrée, Bonamy. Rudyard Kipling, Realist and Fabu-
    list (London: Oxford Univ. Press, 1967), 156.
  Meyers, Jeffrey. "The Idea of Moral Authority in 'The
    Man Who Would Be King,'" Stud Engl Lit, VIII (1968),
    711–723.
  Rees, Robert A., and Barry Menikoff. A Manual to Ac-
    company "The Short Story: An Introductory Anthology"
    (Boston: Little, Brown, 1969), 1.

"The Mark of the Beast"
  Dobrée, Bonamy. Rudyard Kipling, Realist and Fabu-
    list (London: Oxford Univ. Press, 1967), 128–129.

"Mary Postgate"
  Dobrée, Bonamy. Rudyard Kipling, Realist and Fabu-
    list (London: Oxford Univ. Press, 1967), 130–133.

"The Moral Reformers"
  Dobrée, Bonamy. Rudyard Kipling, Realist and Fabu-
    list (London: Oxford Univ. Press, 1967), 128.

"Pig"
  Dobrée, Bonamy. Rudyard Kipling, Realist and Fabu-
    list (London: Oxford Univ. Press, 1967), 139.

"Sea Constables"
  Dobrée, Bonamy. Rudyard Kipling, Realist and Fabu-
    list (London: Oxford Univ. Press, 1967), 133–135.

"The Ship That Found Herself"
  Dobrée, Bonamy. Rudyard Kipling, Realist and Fabu-
    list (London: Oxford Univ. Press, 1967), 149–150.

"Teem"
  Dobrée, Bonamy. Rudyard Kipling, Realist and Fabu-
    list (London: Oxford Univ. Press, 1967), 165–167.

"They"
  Dobrée, Bonamy. Rudyard Kipling, Realist and Fabu-
    list (London: Oxford Univ. Press, 1967), 158–159.
  Scott-Giles, C. W., and Mrs. Scott-Giles. "A Note on
    'They,'" Kipling J, XXXV, No. 167 (September, 1968),
    18–20.

"The Village That Voted the Earth Was Flat"
  Dobrée, Bonamy. Rudyard Kipling, Realist and Fabu-
    list (London: Oxford Univ. Press, 1967), 140–141.

"A Wayside Comedy"
  Adams, Elsie B. "No Exit: An Explication of Kipling's
    'A Wayside Comedy,'" Engl Lit in Transition, XI
    (1968), 180–183.

"With the Night Mail"
  Dobrée, Bonamy. Rudyard Kipling, Realist and Fabu-
    list (London: Oxford Univ. Press, 1967), 150–151.

HEINRICH VON KLEIST

"The Earthquake in Chile"
Gearey, John. Heinrich von Kleist: A Study in Tragedy
and Anxiety (Philadelphia: Univ. of Pennsylvania Press,
1968), 43-48.

"The Foundling"
Gearey, John. Heinrich von Kleist: A Study in Tragedy
and Anxiety (Philadelphia: Univ. of Pennsylvania Press,
1968), 76-79.

"Die Heilige Cäcilie oder die Gewalt der Musik"
Gearey, John. Heinrich von Kleist: A Study in Tragedy
and Anxiety (Philadelphia: Univ. of Pennsylvania Press,
1968), 56-58.
Hoffmeister, Werner. "Die Doppeldeutigkeit der Erzähl-
weise in Heinrich von Kleists 'Die heilige Cäcilie
oder die Gewalt der Musik," in Lederer, Herbert,
and Joachim Seyppel, Eds. Festschrift für Werner
Neuse fides anlässlich des vierzigjährigen Bestehens
der Deutschen Sommerschule am Middlebury College
und der Emeritierung ihres Leiters (Berlin: Die
Diagonale, 1967), 44-56.

"The Marquise of O—"
Crosby, Donald H. "Psychological Realism in the Works
of Kleist: Penthesilea and 'Die Marquise von O—,'"
Lit & Psych, XIX (1969), 9-16.
Gearey, John. Heinrich von Kleist: A Study in Tragedy
and Anxiety (Philadelphia: Univ. of Pennsylvania Press,
1968), 60-70.
Müller-Seidel, Walter. "Die Struktur des Widerspruchs
in Kleists 'Marquise von O,' in Müller-Seidel, Walter,
Ed. Heinrich von Kleist: Aufsätze und Essays (Darm-
stadt: Wissenschaftl, Buchgesellschaft, 1967), 244-
268.
Sokel, Walter H. "Kleist's Marquise of O., Kierkegaard's
Abraham, and Musil's Tonka: Three Stages of the Ab-

surd as the Touchstone of Faith," Wisconsin Stud
Contemporary Lit, VIII (1967), 505–516.

"Michael Kohlhaas"
   Bernd, Clifford A. "Der Lutherbrief in Kleists 'Michael
      Kohlhaas,'" Zeitschrift für Deutsche Philologie, LXXX
      (1967), 627–633.
   ————————. "On the Two Divergent Parts of Kleist's
      'Michael Kohlhaas,'" in Fowkes, Robert A., and Volk-
      mar Sander, Eds. New York University Department
      of German Studies in Germanic Languages and Lit-
      erature (Reutlingen: Hutzler, 1967), 47–56.
   Büttner, Ludwig. "'Michael Kohlhaas' — eine paranoische
      oder heroische Gestalt," Seminar, IV (1968), 26–41.
   Dechert, Hans-Wilhelm. "'Indem er ans Fenster trat
      ...': Zur Funktion einer Gebärde in Kleists 'Michael
      Kohlhaas," Euphorion, LXII (1968), 77–84.
   Ellis, John M. "Der Herr lässt regnen über Gerechte
      und Ungerechte: Kleists 'Michael Kohlhaas,'" Monat-
      shefte, LIX (1967), 35–40.
   Gearey, John. Heinrich von Kleist: A Study in Tragedy
      and Anxiety (Philadelphia: Univ. of Pennsylvania Press,
      1968), 103–119.
   Hertling, Gunter H. "Kleists 'Michael Kohlhaas' und
      Fontanes 'Grete Minde': Freiheit und Fügung," Germ
      Q, XL (1967), 24–40.
   Schlütter, Hans-Jürgen. "Kohlhaas, Ide und die Welt,"
      Zeitschrift für Deutsche Philologie, LXXXVI (1967),
      634.

"Die Verlobung in St. Domingo"
   Gearey, John. Heinrich von Kleist: A Study in Tragedy
      and Anxiety (Philadelphia: Univ. of Pennsylvania
      Press, 1968), 70–76.

"Der Zweikampf"
   Gearey, John. Heinrich von Kleist: A Study in Tragedy
      and Anxiety (Philadelphia: Univ. of Pennsylvania
      Press, 1968), 48–56.

A. KOLLONTAY

"The Love of Three Generations"
Gasiorowska, Xenia. Women in Soviet Fiction, 1917–
1964 (Madison: Univ. of Wisconsin Press, 1968),
118–119.

VLADIMIR KOROLENKO

"Makar's Dream"
Proffer, Carl R., Ed. From Karamzin to Bunin: An
Anthology of Russian Short Stories (Bloomington:
Indiana Univ. Press, 1969), 32–34.

ALEXANDER KUPRIN

"The Garnet Bracelet"
Proffer, Carl R., Ed. From Karamzin to Bunin: An
Anthology of Russian Short Stories (Bloomington:
Indiana Univ. Press, 1969), 43–44.

RING LARDNER

"Golden Honeymoon"
Frakes, James, and Isadore Traschen, Eds. Short Fiction: A Critical Collection (Englewood Cliffs: Prentice-Hall, 1959), 88–90; Second edition (1969), 87–89.

D. H. LAWRENCE

"The Blind Man"
Frakes, James R., and Isadore Traschen, Eds. Short
Fiction: A Critical Collection, Second edition (Engle-
wood Cliffs: Prentice-Hall, 1969), 163–166.
Marks, W. S. "The Psychology of Regression in D. H.
Lawrence's 'The Blind Man,'" Lit & Psych, XVII
(1967), 177–192.

"The Captain's Doll"
    Howarth, Herbert. "D. H. Lawrence from Island to Gla-
        cier," Univ Toronto Q, XXXVII (1968), 225–226.

"Fanny and Annie"
    Secor, Robert. "Language and Movement in 'Fanny
        and Annie,'" Stud Short Fiction, VI (1969), 395–400.

"The Fox"
    Fulmer, O. Bryan. "The Significance of the Death of the
        Fox in D. H. Lawrence's 'The Fox,'" Stud Short Fic-
        tion, V (1968), 275–282.
    Levin, Gerald. "The Symbolism of Lawrence's 'The
        Fox,'" Coll Lang Assoc J, XI (1967), 135–141.

"The Horse Dealer's Daughter"
    Junkins, Donald. "D. H. Lawrence's 'The Horse Dealer's
        Daughter,'" Stud Short Fiction, VI (1969), 210–212.
    Lerner, Laurence. The Truthtellers: Jane Austen,
        George Eliot, D. H. Lawrence (New York: Schocken,
        1967), 208–209.
    Schorer, Mark, Ed. The Story: A Critical Anthology
        (New York: Prentice-Hall, 1950), 326–329; Second
        edition (Englewood Cliffs: Prentice-Hall, 1967), 264–
        266.
    Shrodes, Caroline, Justine Van Gundy, and Joel Dorius.
        Instructor's Manual for "Reading for Understanding"
        (New York: Macmillan, 1968), 17–18.

"The Last Laugh"
    Baim, Joseph. "The Second Coming of Pan: A Note on
        D. H. Lawrence's 'The Last Laugh,'" Stud Short Fic-
        tion, VI (1968), 98–100.

"The Man Who Died"
    Fiderer, Gerald. "D. H. Lawrence's 'The Man Who
        Died': The Phallic Christ," Am Imago, XXV (1968),
        91–96.

"A Modern Lover"
  Sagar, Keith. "'The Best I Have Known': D. H. Law-
    rence's 'A Modern Lover' and 'The Shades of Spring,'"
    Stud Short Fiction, IV (1967), 144–146.

"Odour of Chrysanthemums"
  Hudspeth, Robert N. "Lawrence's 'Odour of Chrysan-
    themums': Isolation and Paradox," Stud Short Fic-
    tion, VI (1969), 630–636.
  Mizener, Arthur. A Handbook for Use with "Modern
    Short Stories: The Uses of Imagination, Revised Edi-
    tion" (New York: Norton, 1966), 93–94.

"The Princess"
  Cowan, James C. "D. H. Lawrence's 'The Princess' as
    Ironic Romance," Stud Short Fiction, IV (1967), 245–
    251.

"The Prussian Officer"
  Rees, Robert A., and Barry Menikoff. A Manual to Ac-
    company "The Short Story: An Introductory Anthology"
    (Boston: Little, Brown, 1969), 20–21.

"The Rocking-Horse Winner"
  Cowan, S. A. "Lawrence's 'The Rocking-Horse Winner,'"
    Explicator, XXVII (1968), Item 9.
  Goldberg, Michael. "Lawrence's 'The Rocking Horse
    Winner': A Dickensian Fable?" Mod Fiction Stud,
    XV (1969), 525–536.
  Snodgrass, W. D. "A Rocking-Horse: The Symbol, the
    Pattern, the Way to Live," Hudson R, XI (1958), 191–
    200; reprinted in Spilka, Mark, Ed. D. H. Lawrence:
    A Collection of Critical Essays (Englewood Cliffs:
    Prentice-Hall, 1963), 117–126; Albrecht, Robert C.,
    Ed. The World of Short Fiction (New York: Free
    Press, 1969), 539–548.
  Steinmann, Martin, and Gerald Willen, Eds. Literature
    for Writing (Belmont: Wadsworth, 1962), 192–193;
    Second edition (1967), 185–186.

"St. Mawr"
  Halperin, Irving. "Unity in 'St. Mawr,'" So Dakota R,
    IV (Summer, 1966), 58–60.
  Lerner, Laurence. The Truthtellers: Jane Austen,
    George Eliot, D. H. Lawrence (New York: Schocken,
    1967), 185–191.
  Smith, Bob L. "D. H. Lawrence's 'St. Mawr': Trans-
    position of Myth," Arizona Q, XXIV (1968), 197–208.

"The Shades of Spring"
  Sagar, Keith. "'The Best I Have Known': D. H. Law-
    rence's 'A Modern Lover' and 'The Shades of Spring,'
    Stud Short Fiction, IV (1967), 146–151.
  Mizener, Arthur. A Handbook for Use with "Modern
    Short Stories: The Uses of Imagination, Revised Edi-
    tion" (New York: Norton, 1966), 96–99.

"Tickets, Please"
  Trilling, Lionel. The Experience of Literature (New
    York: Holt, Rinehart & Winston, 1967), 672–674.

"The White Stocking"
  Mizener, Arthur. A Handbook for Use with "Modern
    Short Stories: The Uses of Imagination, Revised Edi-
    tion" (New York: Norton, 1966), 100–105.

"You Touched Me"
  Lerner, Laurence. The Truthtellers: Jane Austen,
    George Eliot, D. H. Lawrence (New York: Schocken,
    1967), 206–208.

                        HENRY LAWSON

"The Drover's Wife"
  Matthews, Brian. "'The Drover's Wife' Writ Large:
    One Measure of Lawson's Achievement," Meanjin Q,
    XXVII (1968), 54–66.

"Joe Wilson's Courtship"
  Wilkes, G. A. "Henry Lawson Reconsidered," Southerly,
    XXV (1965), 272–273.

"The Union Buries Its Dead"
  Wilkes, G. A. "Henry Lawson Reconsidered," Southerly,
    XXV (1965), 265–268.

"Water Them Geraniums"
  Wilkes, G. A. "Henry Lawson Reconsidered," Southerly,
    XXV (1965), 273–275.

SIEGFRIED LENZ

"Die Festung"
  Russ, C. A. "The Short Stories of Siegfried Lenz,"
    Germ Life & Letters, XIX (1966), 243.

"Der seelische Ratgeber"
  Russ, C. A. "The Short Stories of Siegfried Lenz,"
    Germ Life & Letters, XIX (1966), 243.

NICOLAI LESKOV

"Lady Macbeth of the Mtsensk District"
  Proffer, Carl R., Ed. From Karamzin to Bunin: An
    Anthology of Russian Short Stories (Bloomington:
    Indiana Univ. Press, 1969), 19–21.

DORIS LESSING

"The Day Stalin Died"
  Mizener, Arthur. A Handbook for Use with "Modern
    Short Stories: The Uses of Imagination, Revised Edi-
    tion" (New York: Norton, 1966), 38–39.

"The Nuisance"
    Bloom, Edward A., and Lillian D. Bloom, Eds. The
        Variety of Fiction: A Critical Anthology (New York:
        Odyssey, 1969), 385–388.

JACK LONDON

"In a Far Country"
    Shivers, Alfred S. "The Romantic in Jack London: Far
        Away Frozen Wilderness," Alaska R, I (Winter, 1963),
        39–40.

"To Build a Fire"
    Labor, Earle, and King Hendricks. "Jack London's Twice-
        Told Tale," Stud Short Fiction, IV (1967), 334–341.

"The White Silence"
    Frakes, James, and Isadore Traschen. Short Fiction:
        A Critical Collection (Englewood Cliffs: Prentice-Hall,
        1959), 21–23; Second edition (1969), 20–22.

"The Wife of a King"
    Shivers, Alfred S. "The Romantic in Jack London: Far
        Away Frozen Wilderness," Alaska R, I (Winter, 1963),
        40–41.

MALCOLM LOWRY

"Economic Conference, 1934"
    Edmonds, Dale. "The Short Fiction of Malcolm Lowry,"
        Tulane Stud Engl, XV (1967), 62–67.

"The Forest Path"
    Edmonds, Dale. "The Short Fiction of Malcolm Lowry,"
        Tulane Stud Engl, XV (1967), 79–80.

"Gin and Goldenrod"
    Edmonds, Dale. "The Short Fiction of Malcolm Lowry,"
        Tulane Stud Engl, XV (1967), 74–75.

"Hotel Room in Chartres"
    Edmonds, Dale. "The Short Fiction of Malcolm Lowry,"
      Tulane Stud Engl, XV (1967), 61.

"In Le Havre"
    Edmonds, Dale. "The Short Fiction of Malcolm Lowry,"
      Tulane Stud Engl, XV (1967), 60–61.

"Lunar Caustic"
    Edmonds, Dale. "The Short Fiction of Malcolm Lowry,"
      Tulane Stud Engl, XV (1967), 65–68.

"Through the Panama"
    Edmonds, Dale. "The Short Fiction of Malcolm Lowry,"
      Tulane Stud Engl, XV (1967), 78–79.

HARRIS MERTON LYON

"In the Black-and-Tan"
    Lyon, Zoë. "Harris Merton Lyon: Early American Re-
      alist," Stud Short Fiction, V (1968), 374–375.

"The Man with the Broken Fingers"
    Lyon, Zoë. "Harris Merton Lyon: Early American Re-
      alist," Stud Short Fiction, V (1968), 373–374.

"The Weaver Who Clad the Summer"
    Lyon, Zoë. "Harris Merton Lyon: Early American Re-
      alist," Stud Short Fiction, V (1968), 375–376.

ANDREW LYTLE

"Mister McGregor"
    Mizener, Arthur. A Handbook for Use with "Modern
      Short Stories: The Uses of Imagination, Revised Edi-
      tion" (New York: Norton, 1966), 166–170.

MARY McCARTHY

"The Cicerone"
  Grumbach, Doris. The Company She Kept (New York:
    Coward-McCann, 1967), 150–153.
  McKenzie, Barbara. "The Arid Plain of 'The Cicerone,'"
    in McKenzie, Barbara, Ed. The Process of Fiction
    (New York: Harcourt, Brace & World, 1969), 76–83.

"The Company Is Not Responsible"
  Grumbach, Doris. The Company She Kept (New York:
    Coward-McCann, 1967), 111–112.

"Cruel and Barbarous Treatment"
  Grumbach, Doris. The Company She Kept (New York:
    Coward-McCann, 1967), 93–95.
  McKenzie, Barbara. Mary McCarthy (New York: Twayne,
    1966), 86–89.

"The Friend of the Family"
  Grumbach, Doris. The Company She Kept (New York:
    Coward-McCann, 1967), 153–155.

"Genial Host"
  Grumbach, Doris. The Company She Kept (New York:
    Coward-McCann, 1967), 101–102.

"Ghostly Father, I Confess"
  Grumbach, Doris. The Company She Kept (New York:
    Coward-McCann, 1967), 106–108.
  McKenzie, Barbara. Mary McCarthy (New York: Twayne,
    1966), 92–95.
  Stock, Irvin. Mary McCarthy (Minneapolis: Univ. of
    Minnesota Press, 1968), 18–20.

"The Hounds of Summer"
  Grumbach, Doris. The Company She Kept (New York:
    Coward-McCann, 1967), 140–142.

"The Man in the Brooks Brothers Shirt"
  Grumbach, Doris. The Company She Kept (New York:
    Coward-McCann, 1967), 97–101.
  McKenzie, Barbara. Mary McCarthy (New York: Twayne,
    1966), 88–92.

"The Old Men"
  McKenzie, Barbara. Mary McCarthy (New York: Twayne,
    1966), 84–85.

"Portrait of the Intellectual as a Yale Man"
  Grumbach, Doris. The Company She Kept (New York:
    Coward-McCann, 1967), 102–106.

"Rogue's Gallery"
  Grumbach, Doris. The Company She Kept (New York:
    Coward-McCann, 1967), 95–97.

"The Unspoiled Reaction"
  Grumbach, Doris. The Company She Kept (New York:
    Coward-McCann, 1967), 112–114.
  Kreutz, Irving. "Mary McCarthy's 'The Unspoiled Re-
    action': Pejorative as Satire," Descant, XIII (1968),
    32–48.

"The Weeds"
  Grumbach, Doris. The Company She Kept (New York:
    Coward-McCann, 1967), 149–150.
  McKenzie, Barbara. Mary McCarthy (New York: Twayne,
    1966), 95–98.

CARSON McCULLERS

"The Ballad of the Sad Café"
  Evans, Oliver. "The Theme of Spiritual Isolation in
    Carson McCullers," New World Writing, No. 1 (1952),
    304–310.

—————. Carson McCullers: Her Life and Work
(London: Peter Owen, 1965), 127–138; American
edition entitled The Ballad of Carson McCullers
(New York: Coward-McCann, 1966), 127–138.
Griffith, Albert J. "Carson McCullers' Myth of the
Sad Cafe," Georgia R, XXI (1967), 46–56.
Hoffman, Frederick J. The Art of Southern Fiction: A
Study of Some Modern Novels (Carbondale: Southern
Illinois Univ. Press, 1967), 68–71.

"Sucker"
Evans, Oliver. Carson McCullers: Her Life and Work
(London: Peter Owen, 1965), 23–24; American edi-
tion entitled The Ballad of Carson McCullers (New
York: Coward-McCann, 1966), 23–24.

"A Tree. A Rock. A Cloud"
Evans, Oliver. Carson McCullers: Her Life and Work
(London: Peter Owen, 1965), 88–96; American edi-
tion entitled The Ballad of Carson McCullers (New
York: Coward-McCann, 1966), 88–96.

JOAQUIM M. MACHADO DE ASSIS

"Admiral's Night"
Nist, John. "The Short Stories of Machado de Assis,"
Arizona Q, XXIV (1968), 19–20.

"The Animal Game"
Nist, John. "The Short Stories of Machado de Assis,"
Arizona Q, XXIV (1968), 16.

"Education of a Stuffed Shirt"
Nist, John. "The Short Stories of Machado de Assis,"
Arizona Q, XXIV (1968), 12–13.

"Ernesto de Tal"
Virgillo, Carmelo. "Love and the 'Causa Secreta' in
the Tales of Machado de Assis," Hispania, XLIX
(1966), 779–780.

"Father versus Mother"
    Nist, John. "The Short Stories of Machado de Assis,"
        Arizona Q, XXIV (1968), 17–19.

"Final Request"
    Nist, John. "The Short Stories of Machado de Assis,"
        Arizona Q, XXIV (1968), 20–21.

"The Looking Glass"
    Nist, John. "The Short Stories of Machado de Assis,"
        Arizona Q, XXIV (1968), 14–15.

"Midnight Mass"
    Nist, John. "The Short Stories of Machado de Assis,"
        Arizona Q, XXIV (1968), 16–17.

"The Psychiatrist"
    Nist, John. "The Short Stories of Machado de Assis,"
        Arizona Q, XXIV (1968), 7–12.

"The Rod of Justice"
    Nist, John. "The Short Stories of Machado de Assis,"
        Arizona Q, XXIV (1968), 15–16.

"The Secret Heart"
    Nist, John. "The Short Stories of Machado de Assis,"
        Arizona Q, XXIV (1968), 15.

"A Woman's Arms"
    Nist, John. "The Short Stories of Machado de Assis,"
        Arizona Q, XXIV (1968), 13–14.

CLAUDE McKAY

"Truant"
    Turpin, Waters E. "Four Short Fiction Writers of the
        Harlem Renaissance: Their Legacy of Achievement,"
        Coll Lang Assoc J, XI (1967), 67–70.

BERNARD MALAMUD

"Angel Levine"
> Bloom, Edward A., and Lillian D. Bloom, Eds. The
> Variety of Fiction: A Critical Anthology (New York:
> Odyssey, 1969), 459–461.
> Richman, Sidney. Bernard Malamud (New York: Twayne,
> 1966), 105–106.

"Behold the Key"
> Richman, Sidney. Bernard Malamud (New York: Twayne,
> 1966), 113–115.

"The Bill"
> Richman, Sidney. Bernard Malamud (New York: Twayne,
> 1966), 107–109.

"Black Is My Favorite Color"
> Richman, Sidney. Bernard Malamud (New York: Twayne,
> 1966), 138–139.
> Skaggs, Merrill M. "A Complex Black-and-White Mat-
> ter," in McKenzie, Barbara, Ed. The Process of
> Fiction (New York: Harcourt, Brace & World, 1969),
> 384–391.

"A Choice of Profession"
> Richman, Sidney. Bernard Malamud (New York: Twayne,
> 1966), 133–134.

"The First Seven Years"
> Richman, Sidney. Bernard Malamud (New York: Twayne,
> 1966), 102–104.

"The German Refugee"
> Richman, Sidney. Bernard Malamud (New York: Twayne,
> 1966), 135–137.

"The Girl of My Dreams"
> Richman, Sidney. Bernard Malamud (New York: Twayne,
> 1966), 111–112.

"Idiots First"
    Richman, Sidney. Bernard Malamud (New York: Twayne,
        1966), 124–127.

"The Jewbird"
    Richman, Sidney. Bernard Malamud (New York: Twayne,
        1966), 125–127.

"The Lady of the Lake"
    Hill, John S. "Malamud's 'The Lady of the Lake'—a
        Lesson in Rejection," Univ R, XXXVI (1969), 149–
        150.
    Richman, Sidney. Bernard Malamud (New York: Twayne,
        1966), 114–115.

"The Last Mohican"
    Richman, Sidney. Bernard Malamud (New York: Twayne,
        1966), 115–118.

"Life Is Better Than Death"
    Richman, Sidney. Bernard Malamud (New York: Twayne,
        1966), 129–130.

"The Loan"
    Richman, Sidney. Bernard Malamud (New York: Twayne,
        1966), 106–109.

"The Magic Barrel"
    Gunn, Giles B. "Bernard Malamud and the High Cost
        of Living," in Scott, Nathan A., Ed. Adversity and
        Grace: Studies in Recent American Literature (Chi-
        cago: Univ. of Chicago Press, 1968), 83–84.
    Richman, Sidney. Bernard Malamud (New York: Twayne,
        1966), 118–123.
    Trilling, Lionel. The Experience of Literature (New
        York: Holt, Rinehart & Winston, 1967), 809–811.

"The Maid's Shoes"
    Richman, Sidney. Bernard Malamud (New York: Twayne,
        1966), 130–133.

"The Mourners"
    Richman, Sidney. Bernard Malamud (New York: Twayne,
        1966), 104–105.

"Naked Nude"
    Richman, Sidney. Bernard Malamud (New York: Twayne,
        1966), 128–129.

"The Prison"
    Richman, Sidney. Bernard Malamud (New York: Twayne,
        1966), 110–111.

"Still Life"
    Richman, Sidney. Bernard Malamud (New York: Twayne,
        1966), 127–128.

"A Summer's Reading"
    Dickinson, Leon T. Suggestions for Teachers of "Intro-
        duction to Literature" (New York: Holt, Rinehart &
        Winston, 1967), 70–71.

"Take Pity"
    Mizener, Arthur. A Handbook for Use with "Modern
        Short Stories: The Uses of Imagination, Revised Edi-
        tion" (New York: Norton, 1966), 124–127.
    Pinsker, Sanford. "A Note on Bernard Malamud's
        'Take Pity,'" Stud Short Fiction, VI (1969), 212–213.

ALBERT MALTZ

"Man on the Road"
    Eisinger, Chester E. "Character and Self in Fiction on
        the Left," in Madden, David, Ed. Proletarian Writers
        of the Thirties (Carbondale: Southern Illinois Univ.
        Press, 1968), 171–172.

THOMAS MANN

"At the Prophet's"
Heiney, Donald. Barron's Simplified Approach to
Thomas Mann (Woodbury: Barron, 1966), 36.

"The Blood of the Walsungs"
Heiney, Donald. Barron's Simplified Approach to
Thomas Mann (Woodbury: Barron, 1966), 37–38.

"Death in Venice"
Frey, John R. "'Die Stumme Begegnung,' Beobachtungen
zur Funktion des Blicks im 'Tod in Venedig,'" Germ
Q, XLI (1968), 177–195.
Heiney, Donald. Barron's Simplified Approach to
Thomas Mann (Woodbury: Barron, 1966), 39–42.
Howe, Irving, Ed. Classics of Modern Fiction (New
York: Harcourt, Brace & World, 1968), 323–334.
Kohut, Heinz. "'Death in Venice' by Thomas Mann: A
Story About Disintegration of Artistic Sublimation,"
Psychoanalytic Q, XXVI (1957), 206–228; reprinted
in Ruitenbeek, Hendrik M., Ed. Psychoanalysis and
Literature (New York: Dutton, 1964), 282–301.
Krotkoff, Hertha. "Zur Symbolik in Thomas Mann's
'Tod in Venedig,'" Mod Lang Notes, LXXXII (1967),
445–453.
McWilliams, J. R. "The Failure of a Repression:
Thomas Mann's 'Tod in Venedig,'" Germ Life &
Letters, XX (1967), 233–241.
Nicklas, Hans W. Thomas Manns Novelle "Der Tod in
Venedig": Analyse des Motivzusammenhangs und der
Erzählstruktur (Marburg: Elwert, 1968), passim.
Troy, William. "Myth as Progress," Nation, CXL
(May 22, 1935), 606; reprinted in William Troy: Se-
lected Essays, ed. Stanley E. Hyman (New Bruns-
wick: Rutgers Univ. Press, 1967), 219–223.

"The Dilettante"
Heiney, Donald. Barron's Simplified Approach to
Thomas Mann (Woodbury: Barron, 1966), 25–26.

"Disorder and Early Sorrow"
  Heiney, Donald. Barron's Simplified Approach to
    Thomas Mann (Woodbury: Barron, 1966), 43–45.
  Oliver, Clinton F. "Hemingway's 'The Killers' and
    Mann's 'Disorder and Early Sorrow,'" in Timko,
    Michael, and Clinton F. Oliver, Eds. Thirty-Eight
    Short Stories (New York: Knopf, 1968), 69–86.
  Trilling, Lionel. The Experience of Literature (New
    York: Holt, Rinehart & Winston, 1967), 707–709.

"The Fight Between Jappe and Do Escobar"
  Heiney, Donald. Barron's Simplified Approach to
    Thomas Mann (Woodbury: Barron, 1966), 38.

"Gladius Dei"
  Dickinson, Leon T. Suggestions for Teachers of "Intro-
    duction to Literature" (New York: Holt, Rinehart &
    Winston, 1967), 61–62.
  Heiney, Donald. Barron's Simplified Approach to
    Thomas Mann (Woodbury: Barron, 1966), 34–35.
  Hoffmann, Ernest F. "Thomas Mann's 'Gladius Dei,'"
    PMLA, LXXXIV (1968), 1353–1361.

"A Gleam"
  Heiney, Donald. Barron's Simplified Approach to
    Thomas Mann (Woodbury: Barron, 1966), 35–36.

"The Infant Prodigy"
  Heiney, Donald. Barron's Simplified Approach to
    Thomas Mann (Woodbury: Barron, 1966), 33–34.

"Little Herr Friedemann"
  Heiney, Donald. Barron's Simplified Approach to
    Thomas Mann (Woodbury: Barron, 1966), 24.
  Hollander, Robert, and Sidney E. Lind, Eds. The Art
    of the Story: An Introduction (New York: American
    Book, 1968), 241–242.

"Little Lizzie"
  Heiney, Donald. Barron's Simplified Approach to
  Thomas Mann (Woodbury: Barron, 1966), 26–27.

"A Man and His Dog"
  Heiney, Donald. Barron's Simplified Approach to
  Thomas Mann (Woodbury: Barron, 1966), 42–43.

"Mario and the Magician"
  Heiney, Donald. Barron's Simplified Approach to
  Thomas Mann (Woodbury: Barron, 1966), 45–46.
  Hunt, Joel E. "Thomas Mann and Faulkner: Portrait
  of a Magician," Wisconsin Stud Contemporary Lit,
  VIII (1967), 431–436.
  Lynskey, Winifred, Ed. Reading Modern Fiction (New
  York: Scribner, 1952), 367–373; Second edition
  (1957), 367–373; Third edition (1962), 367–373;
  Fourth edition (1968), 355–361.

"Railway Accident"
  Schorer, Mark, Ed. The Story: A Critical Anthology
  (New York: Prentice-Hall, 1950), 16–20; Second edition (Englewood Cliffs: Prentice-Hall, 1967), 13–16;
  reprinted in Matlaw, Myron, and Leonard Lief, Eds.
  Story and Critic (New York: Harper & Row, 1963),
  191–194.

"Tobias Mindernickel"
  Heiney, Donald. Barron's Simplified Approach to
  Thomas Mann (Woodbury: Barron, 1966), 26.

"Tonio Kröger"
  Heiney, Donald. Barron's Simplified Approach to
  Thomas Mann (Woodbury: Barron, 1966), 28–32.

"Tristan"
  Heiney, Donald. Barron's Simplified Approach to
  Thomas Mann (Woodbury: Barron, 1966), 32–33.

"The Wardrobe"
    Heiney, Donald. Barron's Simplified Approach to
        Thomas Mann (Woodbury: Barron, 1966), 27.

"The Way to the Churchyard"
    Heiney, Donald. Barron's Simplified Approach to
        Thomas Mann (Woodbury: Barron, 1966), 28.

"A Weary Hour"
    Daemmrich, Horst S. "Thomas Mann's 'Schwere
        Stunde' Reconsidered," Papers Lang & Lit, III (1967),
        34–41.
    Heiney, Donald. Barron's Simplified Approach to
        Thomas Mann (Woodbury: Barron, 1966), 36–37.

KATHERINE MANSFIELD

"Bliss"
    Lynskey, Winifred, Ed. Reading Modern Fiction, Sec-
        ond edition (New York: Scribner, 1952), 384–385;
        Third edition (1962), 384–385; Fourth edition (1968),
        372–373.

"A Cup of Tea"
    Hollander, Robert, and Sidney E. Lind, Eds. The Art
        of the Story: An Introduction (New York: American
        Book, 1968), 319–320.

"The Daughters of the Late Colonel"
    Steinmann, Martin, and Gerald Willen, Eds. Literature
        for Writing (Belmont: Wadsworth, 1962), 171–172;
        Second edition (1967), 163–164.

"The Fly"
    Shrodes, Caroline, Justine Van Gundy, and Joel Dorius.
        Instructor's Manual for "Reading for Understanding"
        (New York: Macmillan, 1968), 19–20.

"Her First Ball"
  Mizener, Arthur. A Handbook for Use with "Modern
    Short Stories: The Uses of Imagination, Revised Edi-
    tion" (New York: Norton, 1966), 121–123.

"An Ideal Family"
  Rees, Robert A., and Barry Menikoff. A Manual to Ac-
    company "The Short Story: An Introductory Anthology"
    (Boston: Little, Brown, 1969), 9–10.

"Miss Brill"
  Hull, Robert L. "Alienation in 'Miss Brill,'" Stud Short
    Fiction, V (1967), 74–76.

W. SOMERSET MAUGHAM

"A Bad Example"
  Cordell, Richard A. Somerset Maugham: A Biographical
    and Critical Study (Bloomington: Indiana Univ. Press,
    1961), 166; Second edition (1969), 166.

"Daisy"
  Cordell, Richard A. Somerset Maugham: A Biographical
    and Critical Study (Bloomington: Indiana Univ. Press,
    1961), 167; Second edition (1969), 167.

"The Fall of Edward Barnard"
  Cordell, Richard A. Somerset Maugham: A Biographical
    and Critical Study (Bloomington: Indiana Univ. Press,
    1961), 169; Second edition (1969), 169.

"The Force of Circumstance"
  Cordell, Richard A. Somerset Maugham: A Biographical
    and Critical Study (Bloomington: Indiana Univ. Press,
    1961), 176–177; Second edition (1969), 176–177.

"Mackintosh"
  Cordell, Richard A. Somerset Maugham: A Biographical
    and Critical Study (Bloomington: Indiana Univ. Press,
    1961), 168–169; Second edition (1969), 168–169.

"The Outstation"
  Cordell, Richard A. Somerset Maugham: A Biographical
    and Critical Study (Bloomington: Indiana Univ. Press,
    1961), 175–176; Second edition (1969), 175–176.
  Moskovit, Leonard. "Maugham's 'Outstation': A Single,
    Serious Effect," Univ Colorado Stud: Series in Lang
    and Lit, No. 10 (1966), 107–114.

"The Pool"
  Cordell, Richard A. Somerset Maugham: A Biographical
    and Critical Study (Bloomington: Indiana Univ. Press,
    1961), 170–171; Second edition (1969), 170–171.

"Rain"
  Cordell, Richard A. Somerset Maugham: A Biographical
    and Critical Study (Bloomington: Indiana Univ. Press,
    1961), 171–173; Second edition (1969), 171–173.
  —————. "The Trembling of a Leaf," in Jonas, Klaus
    W., Ed. The Maugham Enigma (New York: Citadel,
    1954), 174–176.

"Red"
  Cordell, Richard A. Somerset Maugham: A Biographical
    and Critical Study (Bloomington: Indiana Univ. Press,
    1961), 170; Second edition (1969), 170.

"The Treasure"
  Trilling, Lionel. The Experience of Literature (New
    York: Holt, Rinehart & Winston, 1967), 539–540.

GUY DE MAUPASSANT

"Amour"
  Lock, Peter W. "Pattern and Meaning in Maupassant's
    'Amour,'" French R, XLI (1967), 70–75.

"Bel-Ami"
  Bismut, Roger. "Quelques problèmes de création lit-
    téraire dans 'Bel-Ami,'" Revue d'Histoire Littéraire
    de la France, LXVII (1967), 577–589.

"Duchoux"
>   Trilling, Lionel. The Experience of Literature (New
>   York: Holt, Rinehart & Winston, 1967), 545–547.

"Moonlight"
>   Scholes, Robert. Elements of Fiction (New York: Ox-
>   ford Univ. Press, 1968), 50–55.

"Les Soeurs Rondoli"
>   Kirschner, Paul. "Conrad and Maupassant: Moral
>   Solitude and 'A Smile of Fortune,'" R Engl Lit,
>   VII (1966), 62–77.

"Tallow Ball"
>   Denommé, Robert T. "Maupassant's Use of Unanimism
>   in 'Boule de Suif,'" Revue de l'Université d'Ottawa,
>   XXXVII (1967), 159–166.

FRANÇOIS MAURIAC

"Thérèse Desqueyreux"
>   Gregor, Ian, and Brian Nicholas. The Moral and the
>   Story (London: Faber & Faber, 1962), 185–216.

HERMAN MELVILLE

"The Apple-Tree Table"
>   Magaw, Malcolm O. "Apocalyptic Imagery in Mel-
>   ville's 'The Apple-Tree Table,'" Midwest Q, VIII
>   (1967), 357–369.

"Bartleby the Scrivener"
>   Boies, J. J. "Existential Nihilism and Herman Mel-
>   ville," Trans Wisconsin Acad Sci, Arts & Letters,
>   L (1961), 313–315.
>   Browne, Ray B. "The Affirmation of 'Bartleby,'" in
>   Wilgus, D. K., Ed. Folklore International: Essays
>   in Traditional Literature, Belief, and Custom in

Honor of Wayland Debs Hand (Hatboro: Folklore
    Associates, 1967), 11–21.
Conarroe, Joel O. "Melville's Bartleby and Charles
    Lamb," Stud Short Fiction, V (1968), 113–118.
D'Avanzo, Mario L. "Melville's 'Bartleby' and Carlyle,"
    in Vincent, Howard P., Ed. Bartleby the Scrivener
    (Kent: Kent State Univ. Press, 1966), 113–139.
Dew, Marjorie. "The Attorney and the Scrivener: Quoth
    the Raven, 'Nevermore,'" in Vincent, Howard P., Ed.
    Bartleby the Scrivener (Kent: Kent State Univ. Press,
    1966), 94–103.
Felheim, Marvin. "Meaning and Structure in 'Bartleby,'"
    Coll Engl, XXIII (1962), 369–376; reprinted in Miller,
    James E., and Bernice Slote, Eds. The Dimensions
    of the Short Story (New York: Dodd, Mead, 1964),
    534–539; Miller, James E., and Bernice Slote, Eds.
    The Dimensions of Literature (New York: Dodd,
    Mead, 1967), 629–635.
Firchow, Peter E. "'Bartleby': Man and Metaphor,"
    Stud Short Fiction, V (1968), 342–348.
Friedman, Maurice. "Bartleby and the Modern Exile,"
    in Vincent, Howard P., Ed. Bartleby the Scrivener
    (Kent: Kent State Univ. Press, 1966), 64–81.
————. Problematic Rebel: An Image of Modern Man
    (New York: Random House, 1963), 93–95.
Guerard, Albert J., Ed. Stories of the Double (Phila-
    delphia: Lippincott, 1967), 10–12.
Hollander, Robert, and Sidney E. Lind, Eds. The Art
    of the Story: An Introduction (New York: American
    Book, 1968), 89–91.
Howard, Frances K. "The Catalyst of Language: Mel-
    ville's Symbol," Engl J, LVII (1968), 825–831.
Knox, G. A. "Communication and Communion in Mel-
    ville," Renascence, IX (1956), 28–30.
Marcus, Mordecai. "Melville's Bartleby as a Psycho-
    logical Double," Coll Engl, XXIII (1962), 365–368;
    reprinted in Miller, James E., and Bernice Slote,
    Eds. The Dimensions of the Short Story (New York:
    Dodd, Mead, 1964), 539–545; Miller, James E., and
    Bernice Slote, Eds. The Dimensions of Literature
    (New York: Dodd, Mead, 1967), 635–640.

Murray, Henry A. "Bartleby and I," in Vincent, Howard
P., Ed. Bartleby the Scrivener (Kent: Kent State
Univ. Press, 1966), 3–24.

Patrick, Walton R. "Melville's 'Bartleby' and the Doctrine of Necessity," Am Lit, XLI (1969), 39–54.

Plumstead, A. W. "Bartleby: Melville's Venture into
a New Genre," in Vincent, Howard P., Ed. Bartleby
the Scrivener (Kent: Kent State Univ. Press, 1966),
82–93.

Rees, Robert A., and Barry Menikoff. A Manual to Ac-
company "The Short Story: An Introductory Anthology"
(Boston: Little, Brown, 1969), 7–8.

Sedgwick, William E. Herman Melville: The Tragedy
of Mind (Cambridge: Harvard Univ. Press, 1944),
181–183; reprinted (New York: Russell & Russell,
1962), 181–183.

Springer, Norman. "Bartleby and the Terror of Limita-
tion," PMLA, LXXX (1965), 410–418; reprinted in
Levin, Gerald, Ed. The Short Story: An Inductive
Approach (New York: Harcourt, Brace & World, 1967),
488–501.

Stein, William B. "Bartleby: The Christian Conscience,"
in Vincent, Howard P., Ed. Bartleby the Scrivener
(Kent: Kent State Univ. Press, 1966), 104–112.

Stone, Geoffrey. Melville (New York: Sheed & Ward,
1949), 214–215.

Trilling, Lionel. The Experience of Literature (New
York: Holt, Rinehart & Winston, 1967), 466–468.

Walton, Patrick R. "Melville's 'Bartleby' and the Doctrine of Necessity," Am Lit, XLI (1969), 39–54.

"Benito Cereno"
Davis, O. B. Introduction to the Novel (New York: Hayden, 1969), 80–82.

Farnsworth, Robert M. "Slavery and Innocence in
'Benito Cereno,'" Emerson Soc Q, No. 44 (Third
Quarter, 1966), 94–96.

Galloway, David D. "Herman Melville's 'Benito Cereno':
An Anatomy," Texas Stud Lit & Lang, IX (1967), 239–
252.

Vanderhaar, Margaret M. "A Re-Examination of
'Benito Cereno,'" Am Lit, XL (1968), 179–191.
Widmer, Kingsley. "The Perplexity of Melville: 'Benito
Cereno,'" Stud Short Fiction, V (1968), 225–238.

"Billy Budd, Foretopman"
Brodtkorb, Paul. "The Definitive 'Billy Budd': 'But
Aren't It All Sham?'" PMLA, LXXXII (1967), 602–
612.
Chandler, Alice. "Captain Vere and the 'Tragedies of
the Palace,'" Mod Fiction Stud, XIII (1967), 259–261.
————. "The Name Symbolism of Captain Vere,"
Nineteenth-Century Fiction, XXII (1967), 86–89.
Duerksen, Roland A. "The Deep Quandary in 'Billy
Budd,'" New England Q, XLI (1968), 51–66.
Fite, Oliver. "Billy Budd, Claggart, and Schopenhauer,"
Nineteenth-Century Fiction, XXIII (1968), 336–343.
Fogle, Richard H. "'Billy Budd'—Acceptance or Irony,"
Tulane Stud Engl, VIII (1958), 107–113; reprinted in
Gordon, Walter K., Ed. Literature in Critical Per-
spectives: An Anthology (New York: Appleton-Century-
Crofts, 1969), 758–761; reprinted in part in Stafford,
William T., Ed. Melville's "Billy Budd" and the Cri-
tics (San Francisco: Wadsworth, 1961), 146–149.
————. "'Billy Budd': The Order of the Fall," Nine-
teenth-Century Fiction, XV (1960), 189–205.
Gaskins, Avery F. "Symbolic Nature of Claggart's
Name," Am Notes & Queries, VI (1967), 56.
Hudson, H. E. "Billy Budd: Adam or Christ?" Crane R,
VII (1965), 62–67; reprinted in Gordon, Walter K.,
Ed. Literature in Critical Perspectives: An An-
thology (New York: Appleton-Century-Crofts, 1969),
753–757.
Itofuji, Hiromi. "Another Aspect of 'Billy Budd,'"
Kyushu Am Lit, X (1967), 29–40.
Lemon, Lee T. "'Billy Budd': The Plot Against the
Story," Stud Short Fiction, II (1964), 32–43; re-
printed in Zitner, Sheldon P., James D. Kissane, and
M. M. Liberman, Eds. The Practice of Criticism
(Chicago: Scott, Foresman, 1966), 124–132; Gordon,

Walter K., Ed. Literature in Critical Perspectives:
An Anthology (New York: Appleton-Century-Crofts,
1969), 724–731.

Mitchell, Charles. "Melville and the Spurious Truth of
Legalism," Centennial R, XII (1968), 110–126.

Reich, Charles A. "The Tragedy of Justice in 'Billy
Budd,'" Yale R, LVI (1967), 368–389.

Rogers, Robert. "The 'Ineludible Gripe' of Billy Budd,"
Lit & Psych, XIV (1964), 9–22; reprinted in Gordon,
Walter K., Ed. Literature in Critical Perspectives:
An Anthology (New York: Appleton-Century-Crofts,
1969), 732–740.

Rosenberry, Edward H. "The Problem of 'Billy Budd,'"
PMLA, LXXX (1965), 489–498; reprinted in Gordon,
Walter K., Ed. Literature in Critical Perspectives:
An Anthology (New York: Appleton-Century-Crofts,
1969), 762–773.

Sedgwick, William E. Herman Melville: The Tragedy
of Mind (Cambridge: Harvard Univ. Press, 1944),
231–249; reprinted (New York: Russell & Russell,
1962), 231–249.

Stokes, Gary. "The Dansker, Melville's Manifesto on
Survival," Engl J, LVII (1968), 980–981.

Tindall, William Y. "The Ceremony of Innocence," in
MacIvor, R. M., Ed. Great Moral Dilemmas in Literature, Past and Present (New York: Harper, 1956),
73–81; reprinted in Gordon, Walter K., Ed. Literature in Critical Perspectives: An Anthology (New
York: Appleton-Century-Crofts, 1969), 719–723; reprinted in part in Stafford, William T., Ed. Melville's "Billy Budd" and the Critics (San Francisco:
Wadsworth, 1961), 125–131.

Willett, Ralph W. "Nelson and Vere: Hero and Victim
in 'Billy Budd, Sailor,'" PMLA, LXXXII (1967), 370–
376.

Wilson, G. R. "'Billy Budd' and Melville's Use of Dra-
matic Technique," Stud Short Fiction, IV (1967), 105–
111.

Zink, Karl E. "Herman Melville and the Forms—Irony
and Social Criticism in 'Billy Budd,'" Accent, XII

(1952), 131–139; reprinted in Gordon, Walter K.,
Ed. Literature in Critical Perspectives: An Anthology (New York: Appleton-Century-Crofts, 1969),
713–718.

"Cock-A-Doodle-Doo!"
Moss, Sidney P. "'Cock-A-Doodle-Doo!" and Some
Legends in Melville Scholarship," Am Lit, XL (1968),
192–210.

"The Paradise of Bachelors and the Tartarus of Maids"
Rowland, Beryl. "Melville's Bachelors and Maids: In-
terpretation Through Symbol and Metaphor," Am
Lit, XLI (1969), 389–405.
Sandberg, Alvin. "Erotic Patterns in 'The Paradise of
Bachelors and The Tartarus of Maids,'" Lit & Psych,
XVIII (1968), 2–8.

"The Piazza"
Breinig, Helmbrecht. "The Destruction of Fairyland:
Melville's 'Piazza' in the Tradition of the American
Imagination," Engl Lit Hist, XXXV (1968), 254–283.
Poenicke, Klaus. "A View from the Piazza: Herman
Melville and the Legacy of the European Sublime,"
Comp Lit Stud, IV (1967), 267–281.
Turner, Darwin T. "A View of Melville's 'Piazza,'"
Coll Lang Assoc J, VII (1963), 56–62.

GEORGE MEREDITH

"The Tale of Chloe"
Ketcham, Carl H. "Meredith at Work: 'The Tale of
Chloe,'" Nineteenth-Century Fiction, XXI (1966),
235–247.

CONRAD F. MEYER

"Der Heilige"
  Walker, Colin. "Unbelief and Martyrdom in C. F.
  Meyer's 'Der Heilige,'" Germ Life & Letters, XXI,
  N.S. (1968), 111-122.

ALBERTO MORAVIA

"Agostino"
  Heiney, Donald. Three Italian Novelists: Moravia,
  Pavese, Vittorini (Ann Arbor: Univ. of Michigan
  Press, 1968), 15-16.

"The Automaton"
  Heiney, Donald. Three Italian Novelists: Moravia,
  Pavese, Vittorini (Ann Arbor: Univ. of Michigan
  Press, 1968), 22-23.

"Disobedience" [same as "Luca"]
  Heiney, Donald. Three Italian Novelists: Moravia,
  Pavese, Vittorini (Ann Arbor: Univ. of Michigan
  Press, 1968), 16-17.

"Going to the People"
  Heiney, Donald. Three Italian Novelists: Moravia,
  Pavese, Vittorini (Ann Arbor: Univ. of Michigan
  Press, 1968), 21-22.

"Measurements"
  Ragusa, Olga. "Alberto Moravia: Voyeurism and Story-
  telling," Southern R, IV (1968), 137-138.

"The Negro and the Old Man with the Bill-Hook"
  Heiney, Donald. Three Italian Novelists: Moravia,
  Pavese, Vittorini (Ann Arbor: Univ. of Michigan
  Press, 1968), 19-21.

"Rain in May"
   Hollander, Robert, and Sidney E. Lind, Eds. The Art
   of the Story: An Introduction (New York: American
   Book, 1968), 358–359.

"Scatter-Brains"
   Ragusa, Olga. "Alberto Moravia: Voyeurism and Story-
   telling," Southern R, IV (1968), 136–137.

"A Sick Boy's Winter"
   Heiney, Donald. Three Italian Novelists: Moravia,
   Pavese, Vittorini (Ann Arbor: Univ. of Michigan
   Press, 1968), 13–15.

                        MARY N. MURFREE

"A-Playin' of Old Sledge at the Settlemint"
   Cary, Richard. Mary N. Murfree (New York: Twayne,
   1967), 63–64.

"Bushwhackers"
   Cary, Richard. Mary N. Murfree (New York: Twayne,
   1967), 129–130.

"The Casting Vote"
   Cary, Richard. Mary N. Murfree (New York: Twayne,
   1967), 72–73.

"The Dancin' Party at Harrison's Cove"
   Cary, Richard. Mary N. Murfree (New York: Twayne,
   1967), 56–57.

"Drifting Down Lost Creek"
   Cary, Richard. Mary N. Murfree (New York: Twayne,
   1967), 58–59.

"The Mystery of Witch-Face Mountain"
   Cary, Richard. Mary N. Murfree (New York: Twayne,
   1967), 76–77.

"The Panther of Jolton's Ridge"
   Cary, Richard. Mary N. Murfree (New York: Twayne,
   1967), 41–44.

"The Phantom of Bogue Holauba"
   Cary, Richard. Mary N. Murfree (New York: Twayne,
   1967), 165–166.

"The Phantoms of the Foot-Bridge"
   Cary, Richard. Mary N. Murfree (New York: Twayne,
   1967), 75–76.

"The Raid of the Guerilla"
   Cary, Richard. Mary N. Murfree (New York: Twayne,
   1967), 130–131.

"The Riddle of the Rocks"
   Cary, Richard. Mary N. Murfree (New York: Twayne,
   1967), 70–71.

"Taking the Blue Ribbon at the County Fair"
   Cary, Richard. Mary N. Murfree (New York: Twayne,
   1967), 39–41.

ROBERT MUSIL

"Grigia"
   Bedwell, Carol B. "Musil's 'Grigia': An Analysis of Cul-
   tural Dissolution," Seminar, III (1967), 117–126.
   Boa, Elizabeth J. "Austrian Ironies in Musil's 'Drei
   Frauen,'" Mod Lang R, LXIII (1968), 119–123.
   Tober, Karl. "Robert Musils 'Grigia,'" in Haslinger,
   Adolph, Ed. Sprachkunst als Weltgestaltung Fest-
   schrift für Herbert Seidler (Salzburg: Pustet, 1966),
   334–348.

"Die Portugiesin"
   Boa, Elizabeth J. "Austrian Ironies in Musil's 'Drei
   Frauen,'" Mod Lang R, LXIII (1968), 123–126.

"Tonka"
>   Boa, Elizabeth J. "Austrian Ironies in Musil's 'Drei
>   Frauen,'" Mod Lang R, LXIII (1968), 126–128.
>   Sokel, Walter H. "Kleist's Marquise of O., Kierke-
>   gaard's Abraham, and Musil's Tonka: Three Stages
>   of the Absurd as the Touchstone of Faith," Wiscon-
>   sin Stud Contemporary Lit, VIII (1967), 505–516.

VLADIMIR NABOKOV

"The Admiralty Needle"
>   Field, Andrew. Nabokov: His Life in Art (Boston:
>   Little, Brown, 1967), 98–99.

"An Affair of Honor" [originally entitled "The Scoundrel"]
>   Field, Andrew. Nabokov: His Life in Art (Boston:
>   Little, Brown, 1967), 237–238.

"The Assistant Producer"
>   Field, Andrew. Nabokov: His Life in Art (Boston:
>   Little, Brown, 1967), 206–208.

"Bachmann"
>   Field, Andrew. Nabokov: His Life in Art (Boston:
>   Little, Brown, 1967), 179–180.

"Bend Sinister"
>   Field, Andrew. Nabokov: His Life in Art (Boston:
>   Little, Brown, 1967), 198–203.
>   Lee, L. L. "'Bend Sinister': Nabokov's Political Dream,'
>   Wisconsin Stud Contemporary Lit, VIII (1967), 193–
>   203.

"A Christmas Story"
>   Field, Andrew. "The Artist as Failure in Nabokov's
>   Early Prose," Wisconsin Stud Contemporary Lit,
>   VIII (1967), 171–172; reprinted in his Nabokov: His
>   Life in Art (Boston: Little, Brown, 1967), 172–173;

Dembo, L. S., Ed. <u>Nabokov: The Man and His Work</u>
(Madison: Univ. of Wisconsin Press, 1967), 63–64.

"The Circle"
Field, Andrew. <u>Nabokov: His Life in Art</u> (Boston:
Little, Brown, 1967), 36–37.

"Cloud, Castle, Lake" [orignally entitled "Cloud, Lake,
Tower"]
Field, Andrew. <u>Nabokov: His Life in Art</u> (Boston:
Little, Brown, 1967), 196–198.

"A Dashing Fellow" [originally entitled "Khvat"]
Field, Andrew. <u>Nabokov: His Life in Art</u> (Boston:
Little, Brown, 1967), 334–335.

"The Defense" [originally entitled "The Luzhin Defense"]
Field, Andrew. <u>Nabokov: His Life in Art</u> (Boston:
Little, Brown, 1967), 175–179.

"The Doorbell"
Field, Andrew. <u>Nabokov: His Life in Art</u> (Boston:
Little, Brown, 1967), 145–146.

"Double Talk" [originally entitled "Conversation Piece,
1945"]
Field, Andrew. <u>Nabokov: His Life in Art</u> (Boston:
Little, Brown, 1967), 203–205.

"The Eye" [originally entitled "Soglyadatai"]
Field, Andrew. <u>Nabokov: His Life in Art</u> (Boston:
Little, Brown, 1967), 165–172.

"The Fight"
Field, Andrew. <u>Nabokov: His Life in Art</u> (Boston:
Little, Brown, 1967), 142–143.

"Guidebook to Berlin"
Field, Andrew. <u>Nabokov: His Life in Art</u> (Boston:
Little, Brown, 1967), 141–142.

"Letter to Russia"
      Field, Andrew. Nabokov: His Life in Art (Boston:
      Little, Brown, 1967), 115–116.

"Lips to Lips"
      Field, Andrew. "The Artist as Failure in Nabokov's
      Early Prose," Wisconsin Stud Contemporary Lit,
      VIII (1967), 172–173; reprinted in his Nabokov: His
      Life in Art (Boston: Little, Brown, 1967), 173–175;
      Dembo, L. S., Ed. Nabokov: The Man and His Work
      (Madison: Univ. of Wisconsin Press, 1967), 64–65.

"The Magician"
      Field, Andrew. Nabokov: His Life in Art (Boston:
      Little, Brown, 1967), 329–330.

"Music"
      Field, Andrew. Nabokov: His Life in Art (Boston:
      Little, Brown, 1967), 147–148.

"Notification"
      Field, Andrew. Nabokov: His Life in Art (Boston:
      Little, Brown, 1967), 240–241.

"The Offense"
      Field, Andrew. Nabokov: His Life in Art (Boston:
      Little, Brown, 1967), 48–50.

"Perfection"
      Field, Andrew. Nabokov: His Life in Art (Boston:
      Little, Brown, 1967), 239–240.

"Port"
      Field, Andrew. Nabokov: His Life in Art (Boston:
      Little, Brown, 1967), 144–145.

"The Potato Elf"
      Field, Andrew. Nabokov: His Life in Art (Boston:
      Little, Brown, 1967), 249–252.

"The Razor"
   Field, Andrew. Nabokov: His Life in Art (Boston:
      Little, Brown, 1967), 114–115.

"Recruitment"
   Field, Andrew. Nabokov: His Life in Art (Boston:
      Little, Brown, 1967), 143–144.

"The Return of Chorb"
   Field, Andrew. Nabokov: His Life in Art (Boston:
      Little, Brown, 1967), 146–147.

"Scenes from the Life of a Double Monster"
   Field, Andrew. Nabokov: His Life in Art (Boston:
      Little, Brown, 1967), 221–222.

"Spring in Fialta"
   Field, Andrew. Nabokov: His Life in Art (Boston:
      Little, Brown, 1967), 148–149.

"Terror"
   Field, Andrew. Nabokov: His Life in Art (Boston:
      Little, Brown, 1967), 222–223.

"That in Aleppo Once . . ."
   Field, Andrew. Nabokov: His Life in Art (Boston:
      Little, Brown, 1967), 149–150.
   Shrodes, Caroline, Justine Van Gundy, and Joel Dorius.
      Instructor's Manual for "Reading for Understanding"
      (New York: Macmillan, 1968), 30–32.

"Triangle in a Circle"
   Field, Andrew. Nabokov: His Life in Art (Boston:
      Little, Brown, 1967), 241–243.

"The Vane Sisters"
   Rees, Robert A., and Barry Menikoff. A Manual to Ac-
      company "The Short Story: An Introductory Anthology"
      (Boston: Little, Brown, 1969), 7.

"A Visit to a Museum"
>   Field, Andrew. Nabokov: His Life in Art (Boston:
>   Little, Brown, 1967), 123–125.

FLANNERY O'CONNOR

"The Artificial Nigger"
>   Frakes, James, and Isadore Traschen, Eds. Short Fic-
>   tion: A Critical Collection (Englewood Cliffs: Prentice
>   Hall, 1959), 118–121; Second edition (1969), 126–129.
>   Hays, Peter L. "Dante, Tobit, and 'The Artificial Nig-
>   ger,'" Stud Short Fiction, V (1968), 263–268.
>   Malin, Irving. "Flannery O'Connor and the Grotesque,"
>   in Friedman, Melvin J., and Lewis A. Lawson, Eds.
>   The Added Dimension: The Art and Mind of Flannery
>   O'Connor (New York: Fordham Univ. Press, 1966),
>   115–117.
>   Martin, Carter W. The True Country: Themes in the
>   Fiction of Flannery O'Connor (Nashville: Vanderbilt
>   Univ. Press, 1968), 112–116, 148–151.
>   Mizener, Arthur. A Handbook for Use with "Modern
>   Short Stories: The Uses of Imagination, Revised Edi-
>   tion" (New York: Norton, 1966), 41–43.
>   Mooney, Harry J. "Moments of Eternity: A Study in the
>   Short Stories of Flannery O'Connor," in Mooney,
>   Harry J., and Thomas F. Staley, Eds. The Shape-
>   less God: Essays on Modern Fiction (Pittsburgh:
>   Univ. of Pittsburgh Press, 1968), 128–130.

"The Capture"
>   Quinn, Sister M. Bernetta. "Flannery O'Connor, A Re-
>   alist of Distance," in Friedman, Melvin J., and
>   Lewis A. Lawson, Eds. The Added Dimension: The
>   Art and Mind of Flannery O'Connor (New York:
>   Fordham Univ. Press, 1966), 160–161.

"A Circle in the Fire"
>   Browning, Preston M. "Flannery O'Connor and the
>   Grotesque Recovery of the Holy," in Scott, Nathan A.,

Ed. Adversity and Grace: Studies in Recent American Literature (Chicago: Univ. of Chicago Press, 1968), 140–143.

Martin, Carter W. The True Country: Themes in the Fiction of Flannery O'Connor (Nashville: Vanderbilt Univ. Press, 1968), 34–37.

Mooney, Harry J. "Moments of Eternity: A Study in the Short Stories of Flannery O'Connor," in Mooney, Harry J., and Thomas F. Staley, Eds. The Shapeless God: Essays on Modern Fiction (Pittsburgh: Univ. of Pittsburgh Press, 1968), 118–119.

"The Comforts of Home"

Carlson, Thomas M. "Flannery O'Connor: The Manichean Dilemma," Sewanee R, LXXVII (1969), 261–262.

Martin, Carter W. The True Country: Themes in the Fiction of Flannery O'Connor (Nashville: Vanderbilt Univ. Press, 1968), 39–40.

Quinn, Sister M. Bernetta. "Flannery O'Connor, a Realist of Distance," in Friedman, Melvin J., and Lewis A. Lawson, Eds. The Added Dimension: The Art and Mind of Flannery O'Connor (New York: Fordham Univ. Press, 1966), 161–162.

"The Displaced Person"

Baldeshwiler, Eileen [formerly Sister M. Joselyn]. "Thematic Center in 'The Displaced Person,'" Stud Short Fiction, I (1964), 85–92; reprinted in McKenzie, Barbara, Ed. The Process of Fiction (New York: Harcourt, Brace & World, 1969), 529–537.

Malin, Irving. "Flannery O'Connor and the Grotesque," in Friedman, Melvin J., and Lewis A. Lawson, Eds. The Added Dimension: The Art and Mind of Flannery O'Connor (New York: Fordham Univ. Press, 1966), 117–118.

Martin, Carter W. The True Country: Themes in the Fiction of Flannery O'Connor (Nashville: Vanderbilt Univ. Press, 1968), 93–98.

Mooney, Harry J. "Moments of Eternity: A Study in
the Short Stories of Flannery O'Connor," in Mooney,
Harry J., and Thomas F. Staley, Eds. The Shapeless
God: Essays on Modern Fiction (Pittsburgh: Univ. of
Pittsburgh Press, 1968), 122–125.

"The Enduring Chill"
Carlson, Thomas M. "Flannery O'Connor: The Manichean Dilemma," Sewanee R, LXXVII (1969), 260–
261.

"Everything That Rises Must Converge"
Shrodes, Caroline, Justine Van Gundy, and Joel Dorius.
Instructor's Manual for "Reading for Understanding"
(New York: Macmillan, 1968), 44–46.
Smith, Oates J. "Ritual and Violence in Flannery O'Con-
nor," Thought, XLI (1966), 557–558.

"Good Country People"
Dickinson, Leon T. Suggestions for Teachers of "In-
troduction to Literature" (New York: Holt, Rinehart
& Winston, 1967), 71–72.
Huck, Wilbur, and William Shanahan, Eds. The Modern
Short Story (New York: American Book, 1968), 82–
84.
Martin, Carter W. The True Country: Themes in the
Fiction of Flannery O'Connor (Nashville: Vander-
bilt Univ. Press, 1968), 62–65.
Mooney, Harry J. "Moments of Eternity: A Study in the
Short Stories of Flannery O'Connor," in Mooney,
Harry J., and Thomas F. Staley, Eds. The Shapeless
God: Essays on Modern Fiction (Pittsburgh: Univ. of
Pittsburgh Press, 1968), 131–132.

"A Good Man Is Hard to Find"
Brittain, Joan T. "O'Connor's 'A Good Man Is Hard to
Find,'" Explicator, XXVI (1967), Item 1.
Browning, Preston M. "Flannery O'Connor and the Gro-
tesque Recovery of the Holy," in Scott, Nathan A.,

Ed. Adversity and Grace: Studies in Recent American Literature (Chicago: Univ. of Chicago Press, 1968), 143–147.

Carlson, Thomas M. "Flannery O'Connor: The Manichean Dilemma," Sewanee R, LXXVII (1969), 255–256.

Hamblen, Abigail A. "Flannery O'Connor's Study of Innocence and Evil," Univ R, XXXIV (1968), 295–297.

Malin, Irving. "Flannery O'Connor and the Grotesque," in Friedman, Melvin J., and Lewis A. Lawson, Eds. The Added Dimension: The Art and Mind of Flannery O'Connor (New York: Fordham Univ. Press, 1966), 113–115.

Martin, Carter W. The True Country: Themes in the Fiction of Flannery O'Connor (Nashville: Vanderbilt Univ. Press, 1968), 163–167.

Montgomery, Marion. "Miss Flannery's 'Good Man,'" Univ Denver Q, III (Autumn, 1968), 1–19.

"Greenleaf"

Asals, Frederick. "The Mythic Dimensions of Flannery O'Connor's 'Greenleaf,'" Stud Short Fiction, V (1968), 317–330.

Carlson, Thomas M. "Flannery O'Connor: The Manichean Dilemma," Sewanee R, LXXVII (1969), 266–269.

Martin, Carter W. The True Country: Themes in the Fiction of Flannery O'Connor (Nashville: Vanderbilt Univ. Press, 1968), 230–232.

Mooney, Harry J. "Moments of Eternity: A Study in the Short Stories of Flannery O'Connor," in Mooney, Harry J., and Thomas F. Staley, Eds. The Shapeless God: Essays on Modern Fiction (Pittsburgh: Univ. of Pittsburgh Press, 1968), 137–138.

"Judgement Day"

Martin, Carter W. The True Country: Themes in the Fiction of Flannery O'Connor (Nashville: Vanderbilt Univ. Press, 1968), 23–27.

"The Lame Shall Enter First"
> Carlson, Thomas M. "Flannery O'Connor: The Manichean Dilemma," Sewanee R, LXXVII (1969), 262–264.
>
> Lorch, Thomas M. "Flannery O'Connor: Christian Allegorist," Critique, X, No. 2 (1968), 75–76.
>
> Martin, Carter W. The True Country: Themes in the Fiction of Flannery O'Connor (Nashville: Vanderbilt Univ. Press, 1968), 167–171.
>
> Mooney, Harry J. "Moments of Eternity: A Study in the Short Stories of Flannery O'Connor," in Mooney, Harry J., and Thomas F. Staley, Eds. The Shapeless God: Essays on Modern Fiction (Pittsburgh: Univ. of Pittsburgh Press, 1968), 132–136.

"The Life You Save May Be Your Own"
> Martin, Carter W. The True Country: Themes in the Fiction of Flannery O'Connor (Nashville: Vanderbilt Univ. Press, 1968), 87–88.
>
> Mooney, Harry J. "Moments of Eternity: A Study in the Short Stories of Flannery O'Connor," in Mooney, Harry J., and Thomas F. Staley, Eds. The Shapeless God: Essays on Modern Fiction (Pittsburgh: Univ. of Pittsburgh Press, 1968), 132–133.

"Parker's Back"
> Browning, Preston. "'Parker's Back': Flannery O'Connor's Iconography of Salvation by Profanity," Stud Short Fiction, VI (1969), 525–535.
>
> Carlson, Thomas M. "Flannery O'Connor: The Manichean Dilemma," Sewanee R, LXXVII (1969), 269–278.
>
> Driskell, Leon. "'Parker's Back' vs. 'The Partridge Festival': Flannery O'Connor's Critical Choice," Georgia R, XXI (1967), 483–485.
>
> Fahey, William A. "Flannery O'Connor's 'Parker's Back,'" Renascence, XX (1968), 162–164, 166.
>
> Gordon, Caroline. "Heresy in Dixie," Sewanee R, LXXVI (1968), 263–297.

Martin, Carter W. The True Country: Themes in the
   Fiction of Flannery O'Connor (Nashville: Vander-
   bilt Univ. Press, 1968), 42–44.
Mooney, Harry J. "Moments of Eternity: A Study in the
   Short Stories of Flannery O'Connor," in Mooney,
   Harry J., and Thomas F. Staley, Eds. The Shapeless
   God: Essays on Modern Fiction (Pittsburgh: Univ. of
   Pittsburgh Press, 1968), 130–131.
Quinn, Sister M. Bernetta. "Flannery O'Connor, a Re-
   alist of Distance," in Friedman, Melvin J., and Lewis
   A. Lawson, Eds. The Added Dimension: The Art and
   Mind of Flannery O'Connor (New York: Fordham
   Univ. Press, 1966), 165–167.

"The Partridge Festival"
   Driskell, Leon. "'Parker's Back' vs. 'The Partridge
      Festival': Flannery O'Connor's Critical Choice,"
      Georgia R, XXI (1967), 485–489.
   Martin, Carter W. The True Country: Themes in the
      Fiction of Flannery O'Connor (Nashville: Vander-
      bilt Univ. Press, 1968), 227–230.
   Quinn, Sister M. Bernetta. "Flannery O'Connor, a Re-
      alist of Distance," in Friedman, Melvin J., and Lewis
      A. Lawson, Eds. The Added Dimension: The Art and
      Mind of Flannery O'Connor (New York: Fordham
      Univ. Press, 1966), 162–163.

"Revelation"
   Carlson, Thomas M. "Flannery O'Connor: The Mani-
      chean Dilemma," Sewanee R, LXXVII (1969), 264–
      266.
   Martin, Carter W. The True Country: Themes in the
      Fiction of Flannery O'Connor (Nashville: Vander-
      bilt Univ. Press, 1968), 40–41.
   Mooney, Harry J. "Moments of Eternity: A Study in the
      Short Stories of Flannery O'Connor," in Mooney,
      Harry J., and Thomas F. Staley, Eds. The Shapeless
      God: Essays on Modern Fiction (Pittsburgh: Univ. of
      Pittsburgh Press, 1968), 120–122.

"The River"
  Martin, Carter W. The True Country: Themes in the
    Fiction of Flannery O'Connor (Nashville: Vander-
    bilt Univ. Press, 1968), 46–47.
  Mooney, Harry J. "Moments of Eternity: A Study in
    the Short Stories of Flannery O'Connor," in Mooney,
    Harry J., and Thomas F. Staley, Eds. The Shape-
    less God: Essays on Modern Fiction (Pittsburgh:
    Univ. of Pittsburgh Press, 1968), 126–128.
  Smith, Oates J. "Ritual and Violence in Flannery
    O'Connor," Thought, XLI (1966), 556–557.

"A Stroke of Good Fortune"
  Montgomery, Marion. "Flannery O'Connor's 'Leaden
    Tract Against Complacency and Contraception,'"
    Arizona Q, XXIV (1968), 133–146.

"A Temple of the Holy Ghost"
  Martin, Carter W. The True Country: Themes in the
    Fiction of Flannery O'Connor (Nashville: Vander-
    bilt Univ. Press, 1968), 109–112.
  Quinn, Sister M. Bernetta. "Flannery O'Connor, a Re-
    alist of Distance," in Friedman, Melvin J., and
    Lewis A. Lawson, Eds. The Added Dimension: The
    Art and Mind of Flannery O'Connor (New York:
    Fordham Univ. Press, 1966), 163.

"A View of the Woods"
  Carlson, Thomas M. "Flannery O'Connor: The Mani-
    chean Dilemma," Sewanee R, LXXVII (1969), 258–
    260.
  Martin, Carter W. The True Country: Themes in the
    Fiction of Flannery O'Connor (Nashville: Vander-
    bilt Univ. Press, 1968), 75–76.
  Mooney, Harry J. "Moments of Eternity: A Study in
    the Short Stories of Flannery O'Connor," in Mooney,
    Harry J., and Thomas F. Staley, Eds. The Shape-
    less God: Essays on Modern Fiction (Pittsburgh:
    Univ. of Pittsburgh Press, 1968), 119–120.

FRANK O'CONNOR

"First Confession"
Lynskey, Winifred, Ed. Reading Modern Fiction, Second edition (New York: Scribner, 1957), 417–419; Third edition (1962), 432–434; Fourth edition (1968), 422–424.

"My Oedipus Complex"
Mizener, Arthur. A Handbook for Use with "Modern Short Stories: The Uses of Imagination, Revised Edition" (New York: Norton, 1966), 26–28.

SEAN O'FAOLAIN

"Admiring the Scenery"
Harmon, Maurice. Sean O'Faolain: A Critical Introduction (Notre Dame: Univ. of Notre Dame Press, 1966), 86–87.

"The Bombshop"
Doyle, Paul A. Sean O'Faolain (New York: Twayne, 1968), 28–29.

"A Born Genius"
Doyle, Paul A. Sean O'Faolain (New York: Twayne, 1968), 82–84.

"A Broken World"
Doyle, Paul A. Sean O'Faolain (New York: Twayne, 1968), 77–78.
Harmon, Maurice. Sean O'Faolain: A Critical Introduction (Notre Dame: Univ. of Notre Dame Press, 1966), 71–79.

"Childybawn"
Harmon, Maurice. Sean O'Faolain: A Critical Introduction (Notre Dame: Univ. of Notre Dame Press, 1966), 113–114.

"Discord"
     Doyle, Paul A. Sean O'Faolain (New York: Twayne,
         1968), 81–82.

"Fugue"
     Doyle, Paul A. Sean O'Faolain (New York: Twayne,
         1968), 26–28.

"The Fur Coat"
     Doyle, Paul A. Sean O'Faolain (New York: Twayne,
         1968), 94–95.

"I Remember! I Remember!"
     Doyle, Paul A. Sean O'Faolain (New York: Twayne,
         1968), 108–110.
     Harmon, Maurice. Sean O'Faolain: A Critical Introduc-
         tion (Notre Dame: Univ. of Notre Dame Press, 1966),
         134–136.

"Lady Lucifer"
     Harmon, Maurice. Sean O'Faolain: A Critical Introduc-
         tion (Notre Dame: Univ. of Notre Dame Press, 1966),
         94–95.

"Lilliput"
     Doyle, Paul A. Sean O'Faolain (New York: Twayne,
         1968), 31–34.

"Lovers of the Lake"
     Harmon, Maurice. Sean O'Faolain: A Critical Introduc-
         tion (Notre Dame: Univ. of Notre Dame Press, 1966),
         115–129.

"The Man Who Invented Sin"
     Doyle, Paul A. Sean O'Faolain (New York: Twayne,
         1968), 86–88.
     Harmon, Maurice. Sean O'Faolain: A Critical Introduc-
         tion (Notre Dame: Univ. of Notre Dame Press, 1966),
         95–100.

"Midsummer Night Madness"
    Doyle, Paul A. Sean O'Faolain (New York: Twayne,
        1968), 24–26.

"No Country for Old Men"
    Doyle, Paul A. Sean O'Faolain (New York: Twayne,
        1968), 116–118.

"The Old Master"
    Doyle, Paul A. Sean O'Faolain (New York: Twayne,
        1968), 78–81.

"One True Friend"
    Harmon, Maurice. Sean O'Faolain: A Critical Introduc-
        tion (Notre Dame: Univ. of Notre Dame Press, 1966),
        109–112.

"The Patriot"
    Harmon, Maurice. Sean O'Faolain: A Critical Introduc-
        tion (Notre Dame: Univ. of Notre Dame Press, 1966),
        66–68.

"A Shadow, Silent as a Cloud"
    Doyle, Paul A. Sean O'Faolain (New York: Twayne,
        1968), 112–114.

"The Silence of the Valley"
    Doyle, Paul A. Sean O'Faolain (New York: Twayne,
        1968), 90–91.
    Harmon, Maurice. Sean O'Faolain: A Critical Introduc-
        tion (Notre Dame: Univ. of Notre Dame Press, 1966),
        100–106.

"Sinners"
    Harmon, Maurice. Sean O'Faolain: A Critical Introduc-
        tion (Notre Dame: Univ. of Notre Dame Press, 1966),
        83–85.

"The Small Lady"
    Doyle, Paul A. Sean O'Faolain (New York: Twayne,
        1968), 31–33.

"The Sugawn Chair"
  Doyle, Paul A. Sean O'Faolain (New York: Twayne,
    1968), 110–112.

"Teresa"
  Doyle, Paul A. Sean O'Faolain (New York: Twayne,
    1968), 89–90.
  Harmon, Maurice. Sean O'Faolain: A Critical Introduc-
    tion (Notre Dame: Univ. of Notre Dame Press, 1966),
    89–90.
  Steinmann, Martin, and Gerald Willen, Eds. Literature
    for Writing (Belmont: Wadsworth, 1962), 213–214;
    Second edition (1967), 210–211.

"A Touch of Autumn in the Air"
  Doyle, Paul A. Sean O'Faolain (New York: Twayne,
    1968), 114–116.
  Harmon, Maurice. Sean O'Faolain: A Critical Introduc-
    tion (Notre Dame: Univ. of Notre Dame Press, 1966),
    131–132.

"Unholy Living and Half Dying"
  Harmon, Maurice. Sean O'Faolain: A Critical Introduc-
    tion (Notre Dame: Univ. of Notre Dame Press, 1966),
    112–113.

"Up the Bare Stairs"
  Doyle, Paul A. Sean O'Faolain (New York: Twayne,
    1968), 91–94.

                        LIAM O'FLAHERTY

"Spring Sowing"
  Murray, Michael H. "Liam O'Flaherty and the Speak-
    ing Voice," Stud Short Fiction, V (1968), 156.

JOHN O'HARA

"A Few Trips and Some Poetry"
  Sandberg, Peter L. "Conflicting Passions in Gibbs-
    ville, Pa., " Sat R, LI (November 30, 1968), 43, 58–
    59.

"The Girl on the Baggage Truck"
  Walcutt, Charles C. John O'Hara (Minneapolis: Univ.
    of Minnesota Press, 1969), 24–25.

"Horizon"
  Grebstein, Sheldon N. John O'Hara (New York: Twayne,
    1966), 127–130.

"Imagine Kissing Peter"
  Walcutt, Charles C. John O'Hara (Minneapolis: Univ.
    of Minnesota Press, 1969), 25–26.

"Radio"
  Grebstein, Sheldon N. John O'Hara (New York: Twayne,
    1966), 130–133.

"Summer's Day"
  Trilling, Lionel. The Experience of Literature (New
    York: Holt, Rinehart & Winston, 1967), 752–754.

"We're Friends Again"
  Walcutt, Charles C. John O'Hara (Minneapolis: Univ.
    of Minnesota Press, 1969), 26–28.

GEORGE ORWELL

"Animal Farm"
  Lee, Robert A. "The Uses of Form: A Reading of
    'Animal Farm,'" Stud Short Fiction, VI (1969), 557–
    573.

Thomas, Edward M. Orwell (Edinburgh: Oliver and
Boyd, 1965), 71–77; American edition (New York:
Barnes & Noble, 1967), 71–77.
Woodcock, George. The Crystal Spirit: A Study of
George Orwell (Boston: Little, Brown, 1966), 195–
198.

V. OVECHKIN

"One of the Many"
Gasiorowska, Xenia. Women in Soviet Fiction, 1917–
1964 (Madison: Univ. of Wisconsin Press, 1968),
65–66.

"Praskovya Maksimovna"
Gasiorowska, Xenia. Women in Soviet Fiction, 1917–
1964 (Madison: Univ. of Wisconsin Press, 1968),
65–66.

WALTER PATER

"Apollo in Picardy"
Court, Franklin E. "Change and Suffering in Pater's
Fictional Heroes," Mod Fiction Stud, XIII (1968),
451.
Monsman, Gerald C. Pater's Portraits: Mythic Pattern
in the Fiction of Walter Pater (Baltimore: Johns
Hopkins Press, 1967), 183–196.

"The Child in the House"
Gordon, Jan B. "The Beginning of Pater's Pilgrimage:
A Reading of 'The Child in the House,'" Tennessee
Stud Lit, XIII (1968), 17–25.
Monsman, Gerald C. Pater's Portraits: Mythic Pattern
in the Fiction of Walter Pater (Baltimore: Johns
Hopkins Press, 1967), 39–52.

"Denys L'Auxerrois"
> Court, Franklin E. "Change and Suffering in Pater's
> Fictional Heroes," Mod Fiction Stud, XIII (1968),
> 447–448.

"Duke Carl of Rosenmold"
> Court, Franklin E. "Change and Suffering in Pater's
> Fictional Heroes," Mod Fiction Stud, XIII (1968),
> 448–449.

"Emerald Uthwart"
> Court, Franklin E. "Change and Suffering in Pater's
> Fictional Heroes," Mod Fiction Stud, XIII (1968),
> 450–451.
> Gordon, Jan B. "Pater's Gioconda Smile: A Reading of
> 'Emerald Uthwart,'" Stud Short Fiction, VI (1969),
> 136–143.
> Monsman, Gerald C. Pater's Portraits: Mythic Pattern
> in the Fiction of Walter Pater (Baltimore: Johns
> Hopkins Press, 1967), 171–183.

"An English Poet"
> Monsman, Gerald C. Pater's Portraits: Mythic Pattern
> in the Fiction of Walter Pater (Baltimore: Johns
> Hopkins Press, 1967), 51–56.

"Gaudioso, the Second"
> Monsman, Gerald C. Pater's Portraits: Mythic Pattern
> in the Fiction of Walter Pater (Baltimore: Johns
> Hopkins Press, 1967), 198–200.

ITZHAK L. PERETZ

"The Adventures of a Melody"
> Rabinovich, Isaiah. Major Trends in Modern Hebrew
> Fiction, trans. M. Roston (Chicago: Univ. of Chicago
> Press, 1968), 32–33.

"Hear, O Israel"
Rabinovich, Isaiah. Major Trends in Modern Hebrew
Fiction, trans. M. Roston (Chicago: Univ. of Chicago
Press, 1968), 27-30.

"If Not Higher"
Clayton, John J. Saul Bellow: In Defense of Man
(Bloomington: Indiana Univ. Press, 1968), 146-147.

"The Kabbalists"
Rabinovich, Isaiah. Major Trends in Modern Hebrew
Fiction, trans. M. Roston (Chicago: Univ. of Chicago
Press, 1968), 33-34.

HAROLD PINTER

"Tea Party"
Canaday, Nicholas. "Harold Pinter's 'Tea Party': See-
ing and Not-Seeing," Stud Short Fiction, VI (1969),
580-585.

LUIGI PIRANDELLO

"La Camera in Attesa"
Starkie, Walter. Luigi Pirandello (Berkeley: Univ. of
California Press, 1965), 118-121.

"The Little Fan"
Starkie, Walter. Luigi Pirandello (Berkeley: Univ. of
California Press, 1965), 121-122.

"Il lume dell' alta casa"
Starkie, Walter. Luigi Pirandello (Berkeley: Univ. of
California Press, 1965), 116-118.

"Prima Notte"
Starkie, Walter. Luigi Pirandello (Berkeley: Univ. of
California Press, 1965), 115-116.

EDGAR ALLAN POE

"The Angel of the Odd: An Extravaganza"
  Gerber, Gerald E. "Poe's Odd Angel," Nineteenth-
    Century Fiction, XXIII (1968), 88-93.
  Richard, Claude. "Arrant Bubbles: Poe's 'The Angel
    of the Odd,'" Poe Newsletter, II (1969), 46-48.

"Berenice"
  Bonaparte, Marie. The Life and Works of Edgar Allan
    Poe: A Psycho-Analytic Interpretation [1933], trans.
    John Rodker (London: Imago, 1949), 213-219; re-
    printed in Ruitenbeek, Hendrik M., Ed. Psychoanaly-
    sis and Literature (New York: Dutton, 1964), 19-26.

"The Black Cat"
  Gargano, James W. "'The Black Cat': Perverseness
    Reconsidered," Texas Stud Lit & Lang, II (1960),
    172-178.
  ────────. "The Question of Poe's Narrators," Coll Engl,
    XXV (1963), 180-181; reprinted in Carlson, Eric W.,
    Ed. The Recognition of Edgar Allan Poe (Ann Arbor:
    Univ. of Michigan Press, 1966), 314-315; Regan,
    Robert, Ed. Poe: A Collection of Critical Essays
    (Englewood Cliffs: Prentice-Hall, 1967), 169-171.
  Martin, Terence. "The Imagination at Play: Edgar
    Allan Poe," Kenyon R, XXVIII (1966), 196-198.

"The Cask of Amontillado"
  Adler, Jacob H. "Are There Flaws in 'The Cask of
    Amontillado'?" Notes & Queries, CXCIX or N.S. I
    (1954), 32-34; reprinted in Freedman, Morris, and
    Paul B. Davis, Eds. Controversy in Literature
    (New York: Scribner, 1968), 53-56.
  Felheim, Marvin. "The Cask of Amontillado," Notes
    & Queries, CXCIX or N.S. I (1954), 447-448; re-
    printed in Freedman, Morris, and Paul B. Davis,
    Eds. Controversy in Literature (New York: Scrib-
    ner, 1968), 56-57.

Freehafer, John. "Poe's 'Cask of Amontillado': A Tale
   of Effect," Jahrbuch für Amerikastudien, No. 13
   (1968), 134–142.
Gargano, James W. "'The Cask of Amontillado': A
   Masquerade of Motive and Identity," Stud Short Fic-
   tion, IV (1967), 119–126.
————. "The Question of Poe's Narrators," Coll
   Engl, XXV (1963), 180; reprinted in Carlson, Eric
   W., Ed. The Recognition of Edgar Allan Poe (Ann
   Arbor: Univ. of Michigan Press, 1966), 313–314;
   Regan, Robert, Ed. Poe: A Collection of Critical
   Essays (Englewood Cliffs: Prentice-Hall, 1967),
   168–169.
Harris, Kathryn M. "Ironic Revenge in Poe's 'The
   Cask of Amontillado,'" Stud Short Fiction, VI (1969),
   333–335.
Martin, Terence. "The Imagination at Play: Edgar
   Allan Poe," Kenyon R, XXVIII (1966), 196–198.
Moon, Sam. "The Cask of Amontillado," Notes & Queries,
   CXCIX or N.S. I (1954), 448; reprinted in Freedman,
   Morris, and Paul B. Davis, Eds. Controversy in
   Literature (New York: Scribner, 1968), 57.
Nevi, Charles N. "Irony and 'The Cask of Amontillado,'"
   English J, LVI (1967), 461–463.
Pearce, Donald. "The Cask of Amontillado," Notes &
   Queries, CXCIX or N.S. I (1954), 448–449; reprinted
   in Freedman, Morris, and Paul B. Davis, Eds. Con-
   troversy in Literature (New York: Scribner, 1968),
   58.

"A Descent into the Maelstrom"
   Weber, Jean-Paul. "Edgar Poe or The Theme of the
      Clock," La Nouvelle Revue Française, VI (August-
      September, 1958), 498–499; reprinted in Regan,
      Robert, Ed. Poe: A Collection of Critical Essays
      (Englewood Cliffs: Prentice-Hall, 1967), 89–90.

"The Devil in the Belfry"
   Weber, Jean-Paul. "Edgar Poe or The Theme of the
      Clock," La Nouvelle Revue Française, VI (August-

September, 1958), 301–305; reprinted in Regan,
Robert, Ed. Poe: A Collection of Critical Essays
(Englewood Cliffs: Prentice-Hall, 1967), 79–83.

"Diddling Considered As One of the Exact Sciences"
Richard, Claude. "Poe and the Yankee Hero: An Interpretation of 'Diddling Considered As One of the Exact Sciences,'" Mississippi Q, XXI (1968), 93–109.

"Duc de L'Omelette"
Carson, David L. "Ortolans and Geese: The Origin of
Poe's 'Duc de L'Omelette,'" Coll Lang Assoc J, VIII
(1965), 277–283.

"Eleonora"
Benton, Richard P. "Platonic Allegory in Poe's
'Eleonora,'" Nineteenth-Century Fiction, XX (1967),
293–297.

"The Facts in the Case of M. Valdemar"
Falk, Doris V. "Poe and the Power of Animal Mag-
netism," PMLA, LXXXIV (1969), 536–546.

"The Fall of the House of Usher"
Abel, Darrel. "A Key to the House of Usher," Univ
Toronto Q, XVIII (1949), 176–185; reprinted in Feidel-
son, Charles, and Paul Brodtkorb, Eds. Interpretations
of American Literature (New York: Oxford Univ.
Press, 1959), 51–62; Woodson, Thomas, Ed. Twen-
tieth Century Interpretations of "The Fall of the
House of Usher" (Englewood Cliffs: Prentice-Hall,
1969), 43–55.
Beebe, Maurice. "The Universe of Roderick Usher,"
Personalist, XXXVII (1956), 147–160; reprinted in
his Ivory Towers and Sacred Founts (New York: New
York Univ. Press, 1964), 118–128; Regan, Robert,
Ed. Poe: A Collection of Critical Essays (Englewood
Cliffs: Prentice-Hall, 1967), 121–133; reprinted in
summary form in Beebe, Maurice. "The Fall of the
House of Pyncheon," Nineteenth-Century Fiction, XI
(1956), 4–8.

Bonaparte, Marie. The Life and Works of Edgar Allan Poe, trans. John Rodker (London: Imago, 1949), 249–250; reprinted in Woodson, Thomas, Ed. Twentieth Century Interpretations of "The Fall of the House of Usher" (Englewood Cliffs: Prentice-Hall, 1969), 26–27.

Booth, Wayne C. The Rhetoric of Fiction (Chicago: Univ. of Chicago Press, 1961), 201–203; reprinted in Woodson, Thomas, Ed. Twentieth Century Interpretations of "The Fall of the House of Usher" (Englewood Cliffs: Prentice-Hall, 1969), 33–34.

Brooks, Cleanth, and Robert P. Warren. Understanding Fiction (New York: Crofts, 1943), 202–205; reprinted in Woodson, Thomas, Ed. Twentieth Century Interpretations of "The Fall of the House of Usher" (Englewood Cliffs: Prentice-Hall, 1969), 23–26.

Davidson, Edward H. Poe: A Critical Study (Cambridge: Harvard Univ. Press, 1957), 196–198; reprinted in Feidelson, Charles, and Paul Brodtkorb, Eds. Interpretations of American Literature (New York: Oxford Univ. Press, 1959), 74–76; reprinted in Woodson, Thomas, Ed. Twentieth Century Interpretations of "The Fall of the House of Usher" (Englewood Cliffs: Prentice-Hall, 1969), 96–98.

Feidelson, Charles. Symbolism and American Literature (Chicago: Univ. of Chicago Press, 1953), 39–42; reprinted in Woodson, Thomas, Ed. Twentieth Century Interpretations of "The Fall of the House of Usher" (Englewood Cliffs: Prentice-Hall, 1969), 77–79.

Gordon, Caroline, and Allen Tate. The House of Fiction (New York: Scribner, 1950), 114–117; reprinted in Woodson, Thomas, Ed. Twentieth Century Interpretations of "The Fall of the House of Usher" (Englewood Cliffs: Prentice-Hall, 1969), 27–30.

Kendall, Lyle H. "The Vampire Motif in 'The Fall of the House of Usher,'" Coll Engl, XXIV (1963), 450–453; reprinted in Woodson, Thomas, Ed. Twentieth Century Interpretations of "The Fall of the House of Usher" (Englewood Cliffs: Prentice-Hall, 1969), 99–1

Lawrence, D. H. Studies in Classic American Literature (New York: Thomas Seltzer, 1923), 110–116; Anchor edition (Garden City: Doubleday, 1955), 85–89; Viking edition (New York: Viking, 1964), 76–79; Compass edition (New York: Viking, 1964), 76–79; reprinted in Wilson, Edmund, Ed. The Shock of Recognition (New York: Doubleday, Doran, 1943), 978–981; Matlaw, Myron, and Leonard Lief, Eds. Story and Critic (New York: Harper & Row, 1963), 97–100; Summers, Hollis, Ed. Discussions of the Short Story (Boston: Heath, 1963), 67–70; Carlson, Eric W., Ed. The Recognition of Edgar Allan Poe (Ann Arbor: Univ. of Michigan Press, 1966), 121–125; Woodson, Thomas, Ed. Twentieth Century Interpretations of "The Fall of the House of Usher" (Englewood Cliffs: Prentice-Hall, 1969), 38–42.

Levin, Harry. The Power of Blackness (New York: Knopf, 1958), 159–161; Vintage edition (1960), 159–161; reprinted in Woodson, Thomas, Ed. Twentieth Century Interpretations of "The Fall of the House of Usher" (Englewood Cliffs: Prentice-Hall, 1969), 31–32.

Lynen, John F. The Design of the Present: Essays on Time and Form in American Literature (New Haven: Yale Univ. Press, 1969), 229–238.

Quinn, Arthur H. Edgar Allan Poe: A Critical Biography (New York: Appleton-Century, 1941), 284–285; reprinted in Woodson, Thomas, Ed. Twentieth Century Interpretations of "The Fall of the House of Usher" (Englewood Cliffs: Prentice-Hall, 1969), 22–23.

Quinn, Patrick F. The French Face of Edgar Poe (Carbondale: Southern Illinois Univ. Press, 1957), 237–246; reprinted in Malin, Irving, Ed. Psychoanalysis and American Fiction (New York: Dutton, 1965), 77–85; Woodson, Thomas, Ed. Twentieth Century Interpretations of "The Fall of the House of Usher" (Englewood Cliffs: Prentice-Hall, 1969), 83–90.

Spitzer, Leo. "A Reinterpretation of 'The Fall of the House of Usher,'" Comp Lit, IV (1952), 351–363; reprinted in Woodson, Thomas, Ed. Twentieth Century

Interpretations of "The Fall of the House of Usher" (Englewood Cliffs: Prentice-Hall, 1969), 56–70.

Tate, Allen. "Our Cousin, Mr. Poe," Partisan R, XVI (1949), 1212–1214; reprinted in his The Forlorn Demon (Chicago: Regnery, 1953), 86–89; his Collected Essays (Denver: Swallow, 1959), 461–465; Phillips, William, and Philip Rahv, Eds. The New Partisan Reader, 1945–1953 (New York: Harcourt, Brace, 1953), 337–339; Regan, Robert, Ed. Poe: A Collection of Critical Essays (Englewood Cliffs: Prentice-Hall, 1967), 43–45; reprinted in part in Stallman, Robert W., and Arthur Waldhorn, Eds. American Literature: Readings and Critiques (New York: Putnam, 1961), 111–112.

————. "Three Commentaries: Poe, James, and Joyce," Sewanee R, LVIII (1950), 1–5; reprinted in Gordon, Caroline, and Allen Tate. The House of Fiction (New York: Scribner, 1950), 52–55.

Weber, Jean-Paul. "Edgar Poe or The Theme of the Clock," La Nouvelle Revue Française, VI (August-September, 1958), 309–311; reprinted in Regan, Robert, Ed. Poe: A Collection of Critical Essays (Englewood Cliffs: Prentice-Hall, 1967), 87–89.

Wilbur, Richard. "The House of Poe," in Regan, Robert, Ed. Poe: A Collection of Critical Essays (Englewood Cliffs: Prentice-Hall, 1967), 104–111.

"The Gold Bug"

Lynen, John F. The Design of the Present: Essays on Time and Form in American Literature (New Haven: Yale Univ. Press, 1969), 242–245.

"The Imp of the Perverse"

Kanjo, Eugene R. "'The Imp of the Perverse': Poe's Dark Comedy of Art and Death," Poe Newsletter, II (1969), 41–44.

"Ligeia"

Basler, Roy P. "The Interpretation of 'Ligeia,'" Coll Engl, V (1944), 363–372; reprinted in his Sex, Sym-

bolism and Psychology in Literature (New Bruns-
wick: Rutgers Univ. Press, 1948), 144–145; Stall-
man, Robert W., and R. E. Watters, Eds. The Cre-
ative Reader (New York: Ronald, 1954), 286–294;
Regan, Robert, Ed. Poe: A Collection of Critical
Essays (Englewood Cliffs: Prentice-Hall, 1967), 51–
63; reprinted in part in Frakes, James, and Isadore
Traschen, Eds. Short Fiction: A Critical Collection
(Englewood Cliffs: Prentice-Hall, 1959), 449.
Morrison, Claudia. "Poe's 'Ligeia': An Analysis,"
Stud Short Fiction, IV (1967), 234–244.
Ramakrishna, D. "The Conclusion of Poe's 'Liegeia,'"
Emerson Soc Q, No. 47 (Second Quarter, 1967), 69–
70.
Rea, J. "Classicism and Romanticism in Poe's 'Ligeia,'"
Ball State Univ Forum, VIII, i (1967), 25–29.

"Lionizing"
Arnold, John. "Poe's 'Lionizing': The Wound and the
Bawdry," Lit & Psych, XVII (1967), 52–54.
Benton, Richard P. "Poe's 'Lionizing': A Quiz on Wil-
lis and Lady Blessington," Stud Short Fiction, V
(1968), 239–244.

"Loss of Breath"
Bonaparte, Marie. The Life and Works of Edgar Allan
Poe: A Psycho-Analytic Interpretation [1933], trans.
John Rodker (London: Imago, 1949), 373–410; reprinted in Ruitenbeek, Hendrik M., Ed. Psychoanalysis and Literature (New York: Dutton, 1964), 26–
63.

"The Man That Was Used Up"
Mabbott, Thomas O. "Poe's 'The Man That Was Used
Up,'" Explicator, XXV (1967), Item 70.

"The Masque of the Red Death"
Henss, Hubert. "Edgar Allan Poe, 'The Masque of the
Red Death'; Ernest Hemingway, 'A Clean, Well-

Lighted Place,'" Die Neueren Sprachen, N.S. XVI
(1967), 327–338.
Hollander, Robert, and Sidney E. Lind, Eds. The Art
of the Story: An Introduction (New York: American
Book, 1968), 32–33.
Ropollo, Joseph P. "Meaning and 'The Masque of the
Red Death,'" Tulane Stud Engl, XIII (1963), 59–69;
reprinted in Regan, Robert, Ed. Poe: A Collection
of Critical Essays (Englewood Cliffs: Prentice-Hall,
1967), 134–144.
Weber, Jean-Paul. "Edgar Poe or The Theme of the
Clock," La Nouvelle Revue Française, VI (August-
September, 1958), 307–309; reprinted in Regan,
Robert, Ed. Poe: A Collection of Critical Essays
(Englewood Cliffs: Prentice-Hall, 1967), 85–87.
Wilbur, Richard. "The House of Poe," in Regan, Robert,
Ed. Poe: A Collection of Critical Essays (Englewood
Cliffs: Prentice-Hall, 1967), 118–119.

"Mesmeric Revelation"
Falk, Doris V. "Poe and the Power of Animal Mag-
netism," PMLA, LXXXIV (1969), 536–546.

"MS. Found in a Bottle"
Weber, Jean-Paul. "Edgar Poe or The Theme of the
Clock," La Nouvelle Revue Française, VI (August-
September, 1958), 499–501; reprinted in Regan,
Robert, Ed. Poe: A Collection of Critical Essays
(Englewood Cliffs: Prentice-Hall, 1967), 90–92.

"The Narrative of Arthur Gordon Pym"
Covici, Pascal. "Toward a Reading of Poe's 'Narrative
of A. Gordon Pym,'" Mississippi Q, XXI (1968), 111–
118.
Lee, Helen. "Possibilities of 'Pym,'" English J, LV
(1966), 1149–1154.
Levine, Richard A. "The Downward Journey of Purga-
tion: Notes on an Imagistic Leitmotif in 'The Narrative of Arthur Gordon Pym,'" Poe Newsletter, II
(1969), 29–31.

Lynen, John F. The Design of the Present: Essays on
Time and Form in American Literature (New Haven:
Yale Univ. Press, 1969), 266–267.

Martin, Terence. "The Imagination at Play: Edgar
Allan Poe," Kenyon R, XXVIII (1966), 203–204.

Moss, Sydney P. "'Arthur Gordon Pym,' or the Fal-
lacy of Thematic Interpretation," Univ R, XXXIII
(1967), 299–306.

Stroupe, John H. "Poe's Imaginary Voyage: Pym As
Hero," Stud Short Fiction, IV (1967), 315–321.

"Never Bet the Devil Your Head"
Glassheim, Eliot. "A Dogged Interpretation of 'Never
Bet the Devil Your Head,'" Poe Newsletter, II (1969),
44–45.

"The Pit and the Pendulum"
Bonaparte, Marie. The Life and Works of Edgar Allan
Poe: A Psycho-Analytic Interpretation [1933], trans.
John Rodker (London: Imago, 1949), 575–593; reprinted in Ruitenbeek, Hendrik M., Ed. Psychoanalysis and Literature (New York: Dutton, 1964), 81–
99.

Hirsch, David H. "The Pit and the Apocalypse," Sewanee
R, LXXVI (1968), 632–652.

Lundquist, James. "The Moral of Averted Descent: The
Failure of Sanity in 'The Pit and the Pendulum,'" Poe
Newsletter, II (1969), 25–26.

Lynen, John F. The Design of the Present: Essays on
Time and Form in American Literature (New Haven:
Yale Univ. Press, 1969), 215–217.

Weber, Jean-Paul. "Edgar Poe or The Theme of the
Clock," La Nouvelle Revue Française, VI (August-
September, 1958), 503–507; reprinted in Regan,
Robert, Ed. Poe: A Collection of Critical Essays
(Englewood Cliffs: Prentice-Hall, 1967), 94–97.

"A Predicament"
Martin, Terence. "The Imagination at Play: Edgar Allan
Poe," Kenyon R, XXVIII (1966), 199–202.

"The Scythe of Time"
    Weber, Jean-Paul. "Edgar Poe or The Theme of the
        Clock," La Nouvelle Revue Française, VI (August-
        September, 1958), 306–307; reprinted in Regan,
        Robert, Ed. Poe: A Collection of Critical Essays
        (Englewood Cliffs: Prentice-Hall, 1967), 84–85.

"Shadow—A Parable"
    De Falco, Joseph M. "The Source of Terror in Poe's
        'Shadow—A Parable,'" Stud Short Fiction, VI (1969),
        643–648.

"A Tale of the Ragged Mountains"
    Falk, Doris V. "Poe and the Power of Animal Magnet-
        ism," PMLA, LXXXIV (1969), 536–546.
    Thompson, G. R. "Is Poe's 'A Tale of the Ragged Mount-
        ains' A Hoax?" Stud Short Fiction, VI (1969), 454–
        460.

"The Tell-Tale Heart"
    Bonaparte, Marie. The Life and Works of Edgar Allan
        Poe: A Psycho-Analytic Interpretation [1933], trans.
        John Rodker (London: Imago, 1949), 491–504; re-
        printed in Ruitenbeek, Hendrik M., Ed. Psychoan-
        alysis and Literature (New York: Dutton, 1964), 67–
        80.
    Gargano, James W. "The Question of Poe's Narrators,"
        Coll Engl, XXV (1963), 178–180; reprinted in Carlson,
        Eric W., Ed. The Recognition of Edgar Allan Poe
        (Ann Arbor: Univ. of Michigan Press, 1966), 311–312;
        Regan, Robert, Ed. Poe: A Collection of Critical Es-
        says (Englewood Cliffs: Prentice-Hall, 1967), 167–
        168.
    —————. "The Theme of Time in 'The Tell-Tale
        Heart,'" Stud Short Fiction, V (1968), 378–382.
    Weber, Jean-Paul. "Edgar Poe or The Theme of the
        Clock," La Nouvelle Revue Française, VI (August-
        September, 1958), 502–503; reprinted in Regan,
        Robert, Ed. Poe: A Collection of Critical Essays
        (Englewood Cliffs: Prentice-Hall, 1967), 92–94.

"The Unparalleled Adventures of One Hans Pfaall"
    Wilkinson, Ronald S. "Poe's 'Hans Pfaall' Recon-
    sidered," Notes & Queries, XIII (1966), 333–337.

"Von Kempelen and His Discovery"
    Pollin, Burton R. "'Von Kempelen and His Discovery':
    Sources and Significance," Etudes Anglaises, XX
    (1967), 12–23.

"William Wilson"
    Gargano, James W. "The Question of Poe's Narrators,"
    Coll Engl, XXV (1963), 179–180; reprinted in Carl-
    son, Eric W., Ed. The Recognition of Edgar Allan
    Poe (Ann Arbor: Univ. of Michigan Press, 1966), 312–
    313; Regan, Robert, Ed. Poe: A Collection of Criti-
    cal Essays (Englewood Cliffs: Prentice-Hall, 1967),
    167–168.
    —————. "'William Wilson': The Wildest Sublunary
    Vision," Washington & Jefferson Lit J, I (1967), 9–
    16.

                    HAL PORTER

"Otto Ruff"
    Barnes, John. "New Tracks to Travel: The Stories of
    White, Porter and Cowan," Meanjin Q, XXV (1966),
    162.

                KATHERINE ANNE PORTER

"The Circus"
    Emmons, Winfred S. Katherine Anne Porter: The Re-
    gional Stories (Austin: Steck-Vaughn, 1967), 19–20.

"The Cracked Looking Glass"
    Warren, Robert P. "Irony with a Center: Katherine
    Anne Porter," Kenyon R, IV (1942), 41–42; reprinted

in his Selected Essays (New York: Random House,
1958), 148–149; Guth, Hans P., Ed. Literature, Second edition (Belmont: Wadsworth, 1968), 277.

"The Downward Path to Wisdom"
Hartley, Lodwick. "Stephen's Lost World: The Background of Katherine Anne Porter's 'The Downward
Path to Wisdom,'" Stud Short Fiction, VI (1969), 574–
579.

"The Fig Tree"
Emmons, Winfred S. Katherine Anne Porter: The Re-
gional Stories (Austin: Steck-Vaughn, 1967), 20–23.

"Flowering Judas"
Emmons, Winfred S. Katherine Anne Porter: The Re-
gional Stories (Austin: Steck-Vaughn, 1967), 8–9.
Gottfried, Leon. "Death's Other Kingdom: Dantesque
and Theological Symbolism in 'Flowering Judas,'"
PMLA, LXXXIV (1969), 112–124.
Huck, Wilbur, and William Shanahan, Eds. The Modern
Short Story (New York: American Book, 1968), 102–
103.
Redden, Dorothy S. "'Flowering Judas': Two Voices,"
Stud Short Fiction, VI (1969), 194–204.
Steinmann, Martin, and Gerald Willen, Eds. Literature
for Writing (Belmont: Wadsworth, 1962), 183–184;
Second edition (1967), 176–177.
Van Zyl, John. "Surface Elegance, Grotesque Content
—A Note on the Short Stories of Katherine Anne
Porter," Engl Stud Africa, IX (1966), 172–173.
Warren, Robert P. "Irony with a Center: Katherine Anne
Porter," Kenyon R, IX (1942), 32–35; reprinted in his
Selected Essays (New York: Random House, 1958),
140–143; Knoll, Robert E. Contrasts, Second edition
(New York: Harcourt, Brace, 1959), 495–497; McCal-
lum, John H., Ed. Prose and Criticism (New York:
Harcourt, Brace & World, 1966), 677–681; Guth, Hans
P., Ed. Literature, Second edition (Belmont: Wads-
worth, 1968), 272–274.

"The Grave"
> Emmons, Winfred S. Katherine Anne Porter: The Regional Stories (Austin: Steck-Vaughn, 1967), 23–25.
> Mizener, Arthur. A Handbook for Use with "Modern Short Stories: The Uses of Imagination, Revised Edition" (New York: Norton, 1966), 30–32.
> Prater, William. "'The Grave': Form and Symbol," Stud Short Fiction, VI (1969), 336–338.

"He"
> Emmons, Winfred S. Katherine Anne Porter: The Regional Stories (Austin: Steck-Vaughn, 1967), 26–28.

"Holiday"
> Emmons, Winfred S. Katherine Anne Porter: The Regional Stories (Austin: Steck-Vaughn, 1967), 34–36.

"The Jilting of Granny Weatherall"
> Becker, Laurence A. "'The Jilting of Granny Weatherall': The Discovery of a Pattern," Engl J, LV (1966), 1164–1169.
> Wolfe, Peter. "The Problem of Granny Weatherall," Coll Lang Assoc J, XI (1967), 142–148.

"The Last Leaf"
> Emmons, Winfred S. Katherine Anne Porter: The Regional Stories (Austin: Steck-Vaughn, 1967), 15–18.

"Maria Concepción"
> Lynskey, Winifred, Ed. Reading Modern Fiction, Second edition (New York: Scribner, 1957), 435; Fourth edition (1968), 440.
> Robinson, Cecil. With the Ears of Strangers: The Mexican in American Literature (Tucson: Univ. of Arizona Press, 1963), 210–212.

"Noon Wine"
> Baker, Howard. "The Upward Path: Notes on the Work of Katherine Anne Porter," Southern R, IV (1968), 12–14.

Emmons, Winfred S. Katherine Anne Porter: The Re-
gional Stories (Austin: Steck-Vaughn, 1967), 28–34.
Hoffman, Frederick J. The Art of Southern Fiction: A
Study of Some Modern Novels (Carbondale: Southern
Illinois Univ. Press, 1967), 44–47.
Leiter, Louis. "The Expense of Spirit in a Waste of
Shame: Motif, Montage, and Structure in 'Noon Wine,'"
in Clerc, Charles, and Louis Leiter, Eds. Seven
Contemporary Short Novels (Glenview: Scott, Fores-
man, 1969), 186–219.
Walsh, Thomas F. "The 'Noon Wine' Devils," Georgia
R, XXII (1968), 90–96.
Warren, Robert P. "Irony with a Center: Katherine Anne
Porter," Kenyon R, IV (1942), 40–41; reprinted, with
additions, in his Selected Essays (New York: Random
House, 1958), 143–148; Current-Garcia, Eugene, and
Walton R. Patrick, Eds. Realism and Romanticism
in Fiction (Chicago: Scott, Foresman, 1962), 490–494;
Guth, Hans P., Ed. Literature, Second edition (Bel-
mont: Wadsworth, 1968), 274–277.
Wescott, Glenway. "Praise," Southern R, V (1939), 161–
173; reprinted in his Images of Truth (New York:
Harper & Row, 1962), 38–44; reprinted, in part, in
Current-Garcia, Eugene, and Walton R. Patrick, Eds.
Realism and Romanticism in Fiction (Chicago: Scott,
Foresman, 1962), 487–490.

"Old Mortality"
Emmons, Winfred S. Katherine Anne Porter: The Re-
gional Stories (Austin: Steck-Vaughn, 1967), 6–7.
Hoffman, Frederick J. The Art of Southern Fiction: A
Study of Some Modern Novels (Carbondale: Southern
Illinois Univ. Press, 1967), 41–44.
Warren, Robert P. "Irony with a Center: Katherine
Anne Porter," Kenyon R, IV (1942), 35–40; reprinted
in his Selected Essays (New York: Random House,
1958), 149–154; Knoll, Robert E., Ed. Contrasts,
Second edition (New York: Harcourt, Brace, 1959),
497–501; Guth, Hans P., Ed. Literature, Second edi-
tion (Belmont: Wadsworth, 1968), 278–281.

————. "Uncorrupted Consciousness: The Stories
of Katherine Anne Porter," Yale R, LV (1966), 281–
284.

"The Old Order"
Emmons, Winfred S. Katherine Anne Porter: The Re-
gional Stories (Austin: Steck-Vaughn, 1967), 12–15.

"Pale Horse, Pale Rider"
Shrodes, Caroline, Justine Van Gundy, and Joel Dorius.
Instructor's Manual for "Reading for Understanding"
(New York: Macmillan, 1968), 23–24.
Van Zyl, John. "Surface Elegance, Grotesque Content
—A Note on the Short Stories of Katherine Anne
Porter," Engl Stud Africa, IX (1966), 173–174.
Yannella, Philip R. "The Problems of Dislocation in
'Pale Horse, Pale Rider,'" Stud Short Fiction, VI
(1969), 637–642.

"Theft"
Givner, Joan. "A Re-Reading of Katherine Anne Porter's 'Theft,'" Stud Short Fiction, VI (1969), 463–465.

J. F. POWERS

"The Blessing"
Hagopian, John V. J. F. Powers (New York: Twayne,
1968), 43–44.

"Blue Island"
Hagopian, John V. J. F. Powers (New York: Twayne,
1968), 55–58.

"Dawn"
Boyle, Robert. "To Look Outside: The Fiction of J. F.
Powers," in Mooney, Harry J., and Thomas F. Staley,
Eds. The Shapeless God: Essays on Modern Fiction
(Pittsburgh: Univ. of Pittsburgh Press, 1968), 94–95.

Hagopian, John V. J. F. Powers (New York: Twayne,
    1968), 107–108.

"Death of a Favorite"
    Hagopian, John V. J. F. Powers (New York: Twayne,
    1968), 83–85.

"Defection of a Favorite"
    Hagopian, John V. J. F. Powers (New York: Twayne,
    1968), 85–87.

"The Devil Was the Joker"
    Hagopian, John V. J. F. Powers (New York: Twayne,
    1968), 109–113.

"The Forks"
    Boyle, Robert. "To Look Outside: The Fiction of J. F.
        Powers," in Mooney, Harry J., and Thomas F. Staley,
        Eds. The Shapeless God: Essays on Modern Fiction
        (Pittsburgh: Univ. of Pittsburgh Press, 1968), 92–93.
    Hagopian, John V. "The Forks," in Hagopian, John V.,
        and Martin Dolch, Eds. Insight I: Analyses of Ameri-
        can Literature (Frankfurt: Hirschgraben, 1962), 221–
        225; reprinted, with slight changes, in his J. F. Powers
        (New York: Twayne, 1968), 95–99.
    Huck, Wilbur, and William Shanahan, Eds. The Modern
        Short Story (New York: American Book, 1968), 40–42.
    Twombly, Robert G. "Hubris, Health, and Holiness: The
        Despair of J. F. Powers," in Whitbread, Thomas B.,
        Ed. Seven Contemporary Authors (Austin: Univ. of
        Texas Press, 1966), 144.

"He Don't Plant Cotton"
    Hagopian, John V. J. F. Powers (New York: Twayne,
    1968), 37–39.

"Interlude in a Bookshop"
    Hagopian, John V. J. F. Powers (New York: Twayne,
    1968), 42–43.

"Jamesie"
   Boyle, Robert. "To Look Outside: The Fiction of J. F.
   Powers," in Mooney, Harry J., and Thomas F. Staley,
   Eds. The Shapeless God: Essays on Modern Fiction
   (Pittsburgh: Univ. of Pittsburgh Press, 1968), 97.
   Hagopian, John V. J. F. Powers (New York: Twayne,
   1968), 53–55.

"The Keystone"
   Boyle, Robert. "To Look Outside: The Fiction of J. F.
   Powers," in Mooney, Harry J., and Thomas F. Staley,
   Eds. The Shapeless God: Essays on Modern Fiction
   (Pittsburgh: Univ. of Pittsburgh Press, 1968), 94.
   Hagopian, John V. J. F. Powers (New York: Twayne,
   1968), 113–119.
   Kaufman, Maynard. "J. F. Powers and Secularity," in
   Scott, Nathan A., Ed. Adversity and Grace: Studies
   in Recent American Literature (Chicago: Univ. of
   Chicago Press, 1968), 180–181.

"Lions, Harts, and Leaping Does"
   Boyle, Robert. "To Look Outside: The Fiction of J. F.
   Powers," in Mooney, Harry J., and Thomas F. Staley,
   Eds. The Shapeless God: Essays on Modern Fiction
   (Pittsburgh: Univ. of Pittsburgh Press, 1968), 97–98.
   Hagopian, John V. "The Fathers of J. F. Powers," Stud
   Short Fiction, V (1968), 139–148; reprinted in his
   J. F. Powers (New York: Twayne, 1968), 67–78.
   Twombly, Robert G. "Hubris, Health, and Holiness: The
   Despair of J. F. Powers," in Whitbread, Thomas B.,
   Ed. Seven Contemporaries (Austin: Univ. of Texas
   Press, 1966), 160–161.

"Look How the Fish Live"
   Hagopian, John V. J. F. Powers (New York: Twayne,
   1968), 62–66.

"The Lord's Day"
   Boyle, Robert. "To Look Outside: The Fiction of J. F.
   Powers," in Mooney, Harry J., and Thomas F. Staley,

Eds. The Shapeless God: Essays on Modern Fiction
(Pittsburgh: Univ. of Pittsburgh Press, 1968), 96.
Hagopian, John V. J. F. Powers (New York: Twayne,
1968), 92–95.

"A Losing Game"
Hagopian, John V. J. F. Powers (New York: Twayne,
1968), 104–105.
Mizener, Arthur. A Handbook for Use with "Modern
Short Stories: The Uses of Imagination, Revised Edi-
tion" (New York: Norton, 1966), 79–82.

"The Old Bird, A Love Story"
Hagopian, John V. J. F. Powers (New York: Twayne,
1968), 51–53.

"The Poor Thing"
Hagopian, John V. J. F. Powers (New York: Twayne,
1968), 58–62.

"Presence of Grace"
Hagopian, John V. J. F. Powers (New York: Twayne,
1968), 99–103.

"Prince of Darkness"
.Boyle, Robert. "To Look Outside: The Fiction of J. F.
Powers," in Mooney, Harry J., and Thomas F. Staley,
Eds. The Shapeless God: Essays on Modern Fiction
(Pittsburgh: Univ. of Pittsburgh Press, 1968), 93–94.
Hagopian, John V. "The Fathers of J. F. Powers," Stud
Short Fiction, V (1968), 148–153; reprinted in his
J. F. Powers (New York: Twayne, 1968), 77–82.
Twombly, Robert G. "Hubris, Health, and Holiness: The
Despair of J. F. Powers," in Whitbread, Thomas B.,
Ed. Seven Contemporary Authors (Austin: Univ. of
Texas Press, 1966), 145.

"Renner"
Hagopian, John V. J. F. Powers (New York: Twayne,
1968), 45–51.

"The Trouble"
  Boyle, Robert. "To Look Outside: The Fiction of J. F.
  Powers," in Mooney, Harry J., and Thomas F.
  Staley, Eds. The Shapeless God: Essays on Modern
  Fiction (Pittsburgh: Univ. of Pittsburgh Press,
  1968), 97.
  Hagopian, John V. J. F. Powers (New York: Twayne,
  1968), 39–43.

"The Valiant Woman"
  Boyle, Robert. "To Look Outside: The Fiction of J. F.
  Powers," in Mooney, Harry J., and Thomas F.
  Staley, Eds. The Shapeless God: Essays on Modern
  Fiction (Pittsburgh: Univ. of Pittsburgh Press,
  1968), 96–97.
  Hagopian, John V. J. F. Powers (New York: Twayne,
  1968), 87–92.
  Lynskey, Winifred, Ed. Reading Modern Fiction, Sec-
  ond edition (New York: Scribner, 1957), 445; Third
  edition (1962), 460; Fourth edition (1968), 449–450.

"Zeal"
  Hagopian, John V. J. F. Powers (New York: Twayne,
  1968), 105–107.

                     REYNOLDS PRICE

"Uncle Grant"
  Hoffman, Frederick J. The Art of Southern Fiction: A
  Study of Some Modern Novels (Carbondale: Southern
  Illinois Univ. Press, 1967), 140–141.
  Mizener, Arthur. A Handbook for Use with "Modern
  Short Stories: The Uses of Imagination, Revised Edi-
  tion" (New York: Norton, 1966), 176–178.

JAMES PURDY

"Daddy Wolf"
  Burris, Shirley W. "The Emergency in Purdy's 'Daddy
    Wolf,'" Renascence, XX (1968), 94–98, 103.

"Why Can't They Tell You Why?"
  Skaggs, Calvin. "The Sexual Nightmare of 'Why Can't
    They Tell You Why?'," in McKenzie, Barbara, Ed.
    The Process of Fiction (New York: Harcourt, Brace
    & World, 1969), 305–310.

ALEXANDER PUSHKIN

"The Queen of Spades"
  Proffer, Carl R., Ed. From Karamzin to Bunin: An
    Anthology of Russian Short Stories (Bloomington:
    Indiana Univ. Press, 1969), 7–12.

"The Station Master"
  Proffer, Carl R., Ed. From Karamzin to Bunin: An
    Anthology of Russian Short Stories (Bloomington:
    Indiana Univ. Press, 1969), 4–6.

MARJORIE KINNAN RAWLINGS

"The Enemy"
  Bigelow, Gordon E. Frontier Eden: The Literary
    Career of Marjorie Kinnan Rawlings (Gainesville:
    Univ. of Florida Press, 1966), 118–119.

GUIMARÃES ROSA

"Buriti"
  Harss, Luis, and Barbara Dohmann. Into the Main-
    stream (New York: Harper & Row, 1967), 162–164.

"A Love Story"
   Harss, Luis, and Barbara Dohmann. Into the Main-
      stream (New York: Harper & Row, 1967), 161–162.

"Message from the Mountain"
   Harss, Luis, and Barbara Dohmann. Into the Main-
      stream (New York: Harper & Row, 1967), 160–161.

"My People"
   Harss, Luis, and Barbara Dohmann. Into the Main-
      stream (New York: Harper & Row, 1967), 155–156.

"The Return of the Prodigal Husband"
   Harss, Luis, and Barbara Dohmann. Into the Main-
      stream (New York: Harper & Row, 1967), 154–155.

"The Third Bank of the River"
   Harss, Luis, and Barbara Dohmann. Into the Main-
      stream (New York: Harper & Row, 1967), 170–171.

"The Time and Turn of Augusto Matraga"
   Harss, Luis, and Barbara Dohmann. Into the Main-
      stream (New York: Harper & Row, 1967), 156.

PHILIP ROTH

"The Conversion of the Jews"
   Deer, Irving, and Harriet Deer. "Philip Roth and the
      Crisis in American Fiction," Minnesota R, VI (1966),
      356–358.

"Defender of the Faith"
   Deer, Irving, and Harriet Deer. "Philip Roth and the
      Crisis in American Fiction," Minnesota R, VI (1966),
      355–356.
   Mizener, Arthur. A Handbook for Use with "Modern
      Short Stories: The Uses of Imagination, Revised Edi-
      tion" (New York: Norton, 1966), 75–78.

"Eli, the Fanatic"
> Deer, Irving, and Harriet Deer. "Philip Roth and the
> Crisis in American Fiction," Minnesota R, VI (1966),
> 356–358.
> Hollis, James R. "Eli Agonistes: Philip Roth's Knight
> of Faith," in McKenzie, Barbara, Ed. The Process
> of Fiction (New York: Harcourt, Brace & World,
> 1969), 241–245.

"Goodbye, Columbus"
> Clerc, Charles. "Goodbye to All That: Theme, Char-
> acter, and Symbol in 'Goodbye, Columbus,'" in
> Clerc, Charles, and Louis Leiter, Eds. Seven Con-
> temporary Short Novels (Glenview: Scott, Foresman,
> 1969), 106–133.
> Deer, Irving, and Harriet Deer. "Philp Roth and the
> Crisis in American Fiction," Minnesota R, VI (1966),
> 358–359.

J. D. SALINGER

"De Daumier-Smith's Blue Period"
> Harper, Howard M. Desperate Faith (Chicago: Univ.
> of Chicago Press, 1967), 76–80.

"For Esmé—With Love and Squalor"
> Bryan, James. "A Reading of Salinger's 'For Esmé—
> With Love and Squalor,'" Criticism, IX (1967), 275–
> 288.
> Harper, Howard M. Desperate Faith (Chicago: Univ.
> of Chicago Press, 1967), 74–76.

"Franny"
> Livingston, James T. "J. D. Salinger: The Artist's
> Struggle to Stand on Holy Ground," in Scott, Nathan
> A., Ed. Adversity and Grace: Studies in Recent
> American Literature (Chicago: Univ. of Chicago
> Press, 1968), 123–133.

Schulz, Max F. Radical Sophistication: Studies in Contemporary Jewish-American Novelists (Athens: Ohio Univ. Press, 1969), 198–201.

Wiegand, William. "Salinger and Kierkegaard," Minnesota R, V (1965), 141–144.

"Hapworth 16, 1924"

Harper, Howard M. Desperate Faith (Chicago: Univ. of Chicago Press, 1967), 84–85.

"Just Before the War with the Eskimos"

Harper, Howard M. Desperate Faith (Chicago: Univ. of Chicago Press, 1967), 72.

"The Laughing Man"

Harper, Howard M. Desperate Faith (Chicago: Univ. of Chicago Press, 1967), 72–73.

"A Perfect Day for Bananafish"

Hamilton, Kenneth. J. D. Salinger: A Critical Essay (Grand Rapids: Eerdmans, 1967), 28–31.

Harper, Howard M. Desperate Faith (Chicago: Univ. of Chicago Press, 1967), 85–87.

Livingston, James T. "J. D. Salinger: The Artist's Struggle to Stand on Holy Ground," in Scott, Nathan A., Ed. Adversity and Grace: Studies in Recent American Literature (Chicago: Univ. of Chicago Press, 1968), 110–117.

Schulz, Max F. Radical Sophistication: Studies in Contemporary Jewish-American Novelists (Athens: Ohio Univ. Press, 1969), 199–203.

"Pretty Mouth and Green My Eyes"

Hamilton, Kenneth. "Hell in New York: J. D. Salinger's 'Pretty Mouth and Green My Eyes,'" Dalhousie R, XLVII (1967), 394–399.

"Raise High the Roofbeam, Carpenters"

Wiegand, William. "Salinger and Kierkegaard," Minnesota R, V (1965), 151–156.

"Seymour: An Introduction"
  Schulz, Max F. "Epilogue to 'Seymour: An Introduc-
    tion': Salinger and the Crisis of Consciousness,"
    Stud Short Fiction, V (1968), 128–138.
  ————————. Radical Sophistication: Studies in Contem-
    porary Jewish-American Novelists (Athens: Ohio
    Univ. Press, 1969), 204–211.
  Wiegand, William. "Salinger and Kierkegaard," Min-
    nesota R, V (1965), 151–156.

"Teddy"
  Bryan, James. "A Reading of Salinger's 'Teddy,'" Am
    Lit, XL (1968), 352–369.
  Harper, Howard M. Desperate Faith (Chicago: Univ. of
    Chicago Press, 1967), 80–82.
  Perrine, Laurence. "Teddy? Booper? or Blooper?"
    Stud Short Fiction, IV (1967), 217–224.

"Zooey"
  Livingston, James T. "J. D. Salinger: The Artist's Strug-
    gle to Stand on Holy Ground," in Scott, Nathan A., Ed.
    Adversity and Grace: Studies in Recent American
    Literature (Chicago: Univ. of Chicago Press, 1968),
    123–133.
  Seitzman, Daniel. "Therapy and Antitherapy in Salinger's
    'Zooey,'" Am Imago, XXV (1968), 140–162.
  Wiegand, William. "Salinger and Kierkegaard," Minne-
    sota R, V (1965), 144–150.

                    WILLIAM SAROYAN

"The Journey to Hanford"
  Fabritius, Rudolf. "Charakterkomik in William Saroyans
    Erzählung 'The Journey to Hanford,'" Die Neueren
    Sprachen, XVII (1968), 127–131.

ARTHUR SCHNITZLER

"Casanova's Homecoming"
  Rey, Willy H. "Schnitzlers Erzählung 'Casanovas Heim-
    fahrt': Eine Strukturanalyse," in Schwarz, Egon,
    Hunter G. Hannum, and Edgar Lohner, Eds. Fest-
    schrift für Bernhard Blume: Aufsätze zur deutschen
    und europäischen Literatur (Göttingen: Vandenhoeck
    & Ruprecht, 1967), 195–217.

"Leutnant Gustl"
  Stern, J. P., Ed. Arthur Schnitzler: "Liebelei," "Leut-
    nant Gustl," "Die Letzten Masken" (London: Cam-
    bridge Univ. Press, 1966), 28–40.
  Swales, M. W. "Arthur Schnitzler as a Moralist," Mod
    Lang R, LXII (1967), 468–469.

MARK SCHORER

"What We Don't Know Hurts Us"
  Bluefarb, Sam. "What We Don't Know Can Hurt Us,"
    Stud Short Fiction, V (1968), 163–170.

DELMORE SCHWARTZ

"In Dreams Begin Responsibilities"
  Shrodes, Caroline, Justine Van Gundy, and Joel Dorius.
    Instructor's Manual for "Reading for Understanding"
    (New York: Macmillan, 1968), 42–43.

MARY SHELLEY

"The Parvenue"
  Pollin, Burton. "Mary Shelley as the Parvenue," R Engl
    Lit, VIII (July, 1967), 9–21.

GERSHON SHOFFMAN

"The Barrier"
   Rabinovich, Isaiah. Major Trends in Modern Hebrew
      Fiction, trans. M. Roston (Chicago: Univ. of Chicago
      Press, 1968), 112–114.

"No"
   Rabinovich, Isaiah. Major Trends in Modern Hebrew
      Fiction, trans. M. Roston (Chicago: Univ. of Chicago
      Press, 1968), 115–116.

"The Ticket"
   Rabinovich, Isaiah. Major Trends in Modern Hebrew
      Fiction, trans. M. Roston (Chicago: Univ. of Chicago
      Press, 1968), 119–121.

MIKHAIL SHOLOKHOV

"Alien Blood"
   Stewart, D. H. Mikhail Sholokhov: A Critical Introduc-
      tion (Ann Arbor: Univ. of Michigan Press, 1967), 29–
      32.

"The Birthmark"
   Stewart, D. H. Mikhail Sholokhov: A Critical Introduc-
      tion (Ann Arbor: Univ. of Michigan Press, 1967),
      26–28.

ALAN SILLITOE

"On Saturday Afternoon"
   Isaacs, Neil D. "No Man in His Humour: A Note on
      Sillitoe," Stud Short Fiction, IV (1967), 350–351.
   Penner, Allen R. "'What Are Yo' Looking So Bleddy
      Black For?': Survival and Bitters in 'On Saturday
      Afternoon,'" Stud Short Fiction, IV (1967), 300–307.

ISAAC SINGER

"Caricature"
  Malin, Irving. <u>Critical Views of Isaac Bashevis Singer</u>
  (New York: New York Univ. Press, 1969), 215–217.

"The Fast"
  Buchen, Irving. <u>Isaac Bashevis Singer and the Eternal</u>
  <u>Past</u> (New York: New York Univ. Press, 1968), 136–
  138.

"Getzel the Monkey"
  Buchen, Irving. <u>Isaac Bashevis Singer and the Eternal</u>
  <u>Past</u> (New York: New York Univ. Press, 1968), 125–
  126.

"Gimpel the Fool"
  Frakes, James, and Isadore Traschen, Eds. <u>Short Fic-</u>
  <u>tion: A Critical Collection</u> (Englewood Cliffs: Prentice-
  Hall, 1959), 133–134; Second edition (1969), 141–143.

"The Shadow of a Crib"
  Buchen, Irving. <u>Isaac Bashevis Singer and the Eternal</u>
  <u>Past</u> (New York: New York Univ. Press, 1968), 135–
  136.

"The Spinoza of Market Street"
  Buchen, Irving. <u>Isaac Bashevis Singer and the Eternal</u>
  <u>Past</u> (New York: New York Univ. Press, 1968), 133–
  135.
  Malin, Irving. <u>Critical Views of Isaac Bashevis Singer</u>
  (New York: New York Univ. Press, 1969), 207–215.

"Taibele and Her Demon"
  Buchen, Irving. <u>Isaac Bashevis Singer and the Eternal</u>
  <u>Past</u> (New York: New York Univ. Press, 1968), 132–
  133.

"The Unseen"
> Buchen, Irving. <u>Isaac Bashevis Singer and the Eternal
> Past</u> (New York: New York Univ. Press, 1968), 139–
> 140.

"Yentl the Yeshiva Boy"
> Buchen, Irving. <u>Isaac Bashevis Singer and the Eternal
> Past</u> (New York: New York Univ. Press, 1968), 123–
> 125, 126–129.

MURIEL SPARK

"Bang, Bang—You're Dead"
> Stanford, Derek. <u>Muriel Spark: A Biographical and Cri-
> tical Study</u> (Fontwell: Centaur, 1963), 111–113.

"Come Along, Marjorie"
> Stanford, Derek. <u>Muriel Spark: A Biographical and Cri-
> tical Study</u> (Fontwell: Centaur, 1963), 109–111.

"The Go-Away Bird"
> Stanford, Derek. <u>Muriel Spark: A Biographical and Cri-
> tical Study</u> (Fontwell: Centaur, 1963), 118–119.

"The Portobello Road"
> Stanford, Derek. <u>Muriel Spark: A Biographical And Cri-
> tical Study</u> (Fontwell: Centaur, 1963), 113–116.

"The Seraph and the Zambesi"
> Rees, Robert A., and Barry Menikoff. <u>A Manual to Ac-
> company "The Short Story: An Introductory Anthology"</u>
> (Boston: Little, Brown, 1969), 2–3.
> Stanford, Derek. <u>Muriel Spark: A Biographical and Cri-
> tical Study</u> (Fontwell: Centaur, 1963), 116–118.

JOHN STEINBECK

"The Chrysanthemums"
> Dietrich, R. F., and Roger H. Sundell. <u>Instructor's
> Manual for "The Art of Fiction"</u> (New York: Holt,
> Rinehart & Winston, 1967), 33–40.

McMahan, Elizabeth E. "'The Chrysanthemums': Study
of a Woman's Sexuality," Mod Fiction Stud, XIV
(1969), 453–458.

Shrodes, Caroline, Justine Van Gundy, and Joel Dorius.
Instructor's Manual for "Reading for Understanding"
(New York: Macmillan, 1968), 33–34.

"Flight"
Anderson, Hilton. "Hawthorne's 'Roger Malvin's Burial,"
Explicator, XXVIII (1969), Item 12.

ROBERT LOUIS STEVENSON

"Markheim"
Egan, Joseph J. "'Markheim': A Drama of Moral Psychology," Nineteenth-Century Fiction, XX (1966), 377–
384.

Saposnik, Irving S. "Stevenson's 'Markheim': A Fictional Christmas Sermon," Nineteenth-Century Fiction,
XXI (1966), 277–282.

"The Strange Case of Dr. Jekyll and Mr. Hyde"
Girling, H. K. "The Strange Case of Dr. James and Mr.
Stevenson," Wascana R, III (1968), 65–79.

Guerard, Albert J., Ed. Stories of the Double (Philadelphia: Lippincott, 1967), 8–10.

ADALBERT STIFTER

"Forest Path"
Fuerst, Norbert. The Victorian Age of German Liter-
ature (University Park: Pennsylvania State Univ.
Press, 1966), 60–63.

"Limestone"
Fuerst, Norbert. The Victorian Age of German Liter-
ature (University Park: Pennsylvania State Univ.
Press, 1966), 63–64.

THEODOR STORM

"Aquis Submersus"
    Bernd, Clifford A. Theodor Storm's Craft of Fiction:
      The Torment of a Narrator (Chapel Hill: Univ. of
      North Carolina Press, 1963), 11–53; Second edition
      (1966), 11–53.
    Menhennet, A. "The Time Element in Storm's Later
      Novellen," Germ Life & Letters, XX (1966), 46–48.

"In St. Jürgen"
    Bernd, Clifford A. Theodor Storm's Craft of Fiction:
      The Torment of a Narrator (Chapel Hill: Univ. of
      North Carolina Press, 1963), 57–72; Second edition
      (1966), 57–72.

JESSE STUART

"Angel in the Pasture"
    Blair, Everetta L. Jesse Stuart: His Life and Works
      (Columbia: Univ. of South Carolina Press, 1967),
      119–123.

"Another April"
    Blair, Everetta L. Jesse Stuart: His Life and Works
      (Columbia: Univ. of South Carolina Press, 1967),
      96–97.

"Another Hanging"
    Foster, Ruel E. Jesse Stuart (New York: Twayne, 1968),
      81–83.

"Battle Keaton Dies"
    Blair, Everetta L. Jesse Stuart: His Life and Works
      (Columbia: Univ. of South Carolina Press, 1967),
      89–93.

"The Bellin' of the Bride"
    Blair, Everetta L. Jesse Stuart: His Life and Works
      (Columbia: Univ. of South Carolina Press, 1967),
      93.

"Betwixt Life and Death"
    Foster, Ruel E. Jesse Stuart (New York: Twayne,
    1968), 83–84.

"Clearing in the Sky"
    Blair, Everetta L. Jesse Stuart: His Life and Works
    (Columbia: Univ. of South Carolina Press, 1967),
    103–104.

"Frog Trouncin' Contest"
    Dietrich, R. F., and Roger H. Sundell. Instructor's
    Manual for "The Art of Fiction" (New York: Holt,
    Rinehart & Winston, 1967), 20–24.

"Hair"
    Blair, Everetta L. Jesse Stuart: His Life and Works
    (Columbia: Univ. of South Carolina Press, 1967),
    86–88.

"Huey, the Engineer"
    Blair, Everetta L. Jesse Stuart: His Life and Works
    (Columbia: Univ. of South Carolina Press, 1967),
    126–129.

"Nest Egg"
    Blair, Everetta L. Jesse Stuart: His Life and Works
    (Columbia: Univ. of South Carolina Press, 1967),
    98–99.

"The Slipover Sweater"
    Blair, Everetta L. Jesse Stuart: His Life and Works
    (Columbia: Univ. of South Carolina Press, 1967),
    101–102.

"The Storm"
    Blair, Everetta L. Jesse Stuart: His Life and Works
    (Columbia: Univ. of South Carolina Press, 1967),
    97–98.

"Sylvania Is Dead"
  Blair, Everetta L. Jesse Stuart: His Life and Works
    (Columbia: Univ. of South Carolina Press, 1967),
    108–112.
  Foster, Ruel E. Jesse Stuart (New York: Twayne,
    1968), 84–85.

"Tim"
  Blair, Everetta L. Jesse Stuart: His Life and Works
    (Columbia: Univ. of South Carolina Press, 1967),
    123–126.

"Uncle Jeff"
  Blair, Everetta L. Jesse Stuart: His Life and Works
    (Columbia: Univ. of South Carolina Press, 1967),
    116–119.

"Zeke Hammertight"
  Blair, Everetta L. Jesse Stuart: His Life and Works
    (Columbia: Univ. of South Carolina Press, 1967),
    112–115.

WILLIAM STYRON

"The Long March"
  Asselineau, Roger. "En suivant 'La Marche de Nuit,'"
    Revue des Lettres Moderne, CLVII/CLIX (1967),
    73–83.
  Brandriff, Welles T. "The Role of Order and Disorder
    in 'The Long March,'" Engl J, LVI (1967), 54–59.
  Bryant, Jerry H. "The Hopeful Stoicism of William
    Styron," So Atlantic Q, LXII (1963), 544–547.
  Carver, Wayne. "The Grand Inquisitor's Long March,"
    Univ Denver Q, I (1966), 49–57.
  Davis, Robert G. "The American Individualist Tradi-
    tion: Bellow and Styron," in Balakian, Nona, and
    Charles Simmons, Eds. The Creative Present
    (Garden City: Doubleday, 1963), 134–135.

Friedman, Melvin J. "William Styron: An Interim Appraisal," Engl J, L (1961), 155–156.

Galloway, David D. "The Absurd Man as a Tragic Hero: The Novels of William Styron, " Texas Stud Lit & Lang, VI (1965), 519–522; reprinted in his The Absurd Hero in American Fiction (Austin: Univ. of Texas Press, 1966), 61–64.

Geismar, Maxwell. American Moderns: From Rebellion to Conformity (New York: Hill & Wang, 1958), 246–250.

Hays, Peter. "The Nature of Rebellion in The Long March," Critique, VIII, ii (1966), 70–74.

Hoffman, Frederick J. The Art of Southern Fiction: A Study of Some Modern Novels (Carbondale: Southern Illinois Univ. Press, 1967), 146–148.

McNamara, Eugene. "William Styron's Long March: Absurdity and Authority," Western Hum R, XV (1961), 267–272.

Mudrick, Marvin. "Mailer and Styron: Guests of the Establishment," Hudson R, XVII (1964), 350–353.

Nigro, August. "The Long March: The Expansive Hero in a Closed World," Critique, IX, iii (1967), 103–112.

O'Connell, Shaun. "Expense of Spirit: The Vision of William Styron," Critique, VIII, ii (1966), 25–27.

RUTH SUCKOW

"Auntie Bissel"
Kissane, Leedice M. Ruth Suckow (New York: Twayne, 1969), 131–132.

"Eltha"
Kissane, Leedice M. Ruth Suckow (New York: Twayne, 1969), 136–137.

"Four Generations"
Kissane, Leedice M. Ruth Suckow (New York: Twayne, 1969), 31–32.

"Golden Wedding"
    Kissane, Leedice M. Ruth Suckow (New York: Twayne,
        1969), 37–38.

"Good Pals"
    Kissane, Leedice M. Ruth Suckow (New York: Twayne,
        1969), 91–92.

"A Homecoming"
    Kissane, Leedice M. Ruth Suckow (New York: Twayne,
        1969), 32–33.

"A Little Girl's World"
    Kissane, Leedice M. Ruth Suckow (New York: Twayne,
        1969), 58–59.

"Mame"
    Kissane, Leedice M. Ruth Suckow (New York: Twayne,
        1969), 36–37.

"Mrs. Vogel and Ollie"
    Kissane, Leedice M. Ruth Suckow (New York: Twayne,
        1969), 134–135.

"Uprooted"
    Kissane, Leedice M. Ruth Suckow (New York: Twayne,
        1969), 38–40.

"The Valentine Box"
    Kissane, Leedice M. Ruth Suckow (New York: Twayne,
        1969), 86–87.

"What Have I"
    Kissane, Leedice M. Ruth Suckow (New York: Twayne,
        1969), 116–118.

ITALO SVEVO

"Argo and His Master"
    Furbank, P. N. Italo Svevo: The Man and the Writer
        (Berkeley: Univ. of California Press, 1966), 193–194.

"The Hoax"
   Furbank, P. N. <u>Italo Svevo: The Man and the Writer</u>
     (Berkeley: Univ. of California Press, 1966), 135–137.
   Nelson, Lowry. "A Survey of Svevo," <u>Italian Q</u>, III
     (Summer, 1959), 27–28.

"The Story of the Nice Old Man and the Pretty Girl"
   Furbank, P. N. <u>Italo Svevo: The Man and the Writer</u>
     (Berkeley: Univ. of California Press, 1966), 204–206.
   Nelson, Lowry. "A Survey of Svevo," <u>Italian Q</u>, III
     (Summer, 1959), 26–27.

"This Indolence of Mine"
   Nelson, Lowry. "A Survey of Svevo," <u>Italian Q</u>, III
     (Summer, 1959), 27.

RABINDRANATH TAGORE

"A Lapse of Judgment"
   Lago, Mary M. "Modes of Questioning in Tagore's
     Short Stories," <u>Stud Short Fiction</u>, V (1967), 32–36.

"Punishment"
   Lago, Mary M. "Modes of Questioning in Tagore's
     Short Stories," <u>Stud Short Fiction</u>, V (1967), 28–32.

PETER TAYLOR

"The Fancy Woman"
   Lynskey, Winifred, Ed. <u>Reading Modern Fiction</u>, Fourth
     edition (New York: Scribner, 1968), 494–499.

"Miss Leonora When Last Seen"
   Schuler, Barbara. "The House of Peter Taylor,"
     <u>Critique</u>, IX, iii (1967), 15–17.

"Skyline"
   Schuler, Barbara. "The House of Peter Taylor," <u>Cri</u>-
     <u>tique</u>, IX, iii (1967), 10–11.

"The Throughway"
  Schuler, Barbara. "The House of Peter Taylor, Critique, IX, iii (1967), 15.

"What You Hear from 'Em?"
  Mizener, Arthur. A Handbook for Use with "Modern Short Stories: The Uses of Imagination, Revised Edition" (New York: Norton, 1966), 171–174.

ABRAM TERTZ

"Graphomaniacs"
  Dickinson, Leon T. Suggestions for Teachers of "Introduction to Literature" (New York: Holt, Rinehart & Winston, 1967), 72–73.

DYLAN THOMAS

"The Followers"
  Bloom, Edward A., and Lillian D. Bloom, Eds. The Variety of Fiction: A Critical Anthology (New York: Odyssey, 1969), 245–248.

"One Warm Saturday"
  Kelly, Richard. "The Lost Vision in Dylan Thomas' 'One Warm Saturday,'" Stud Short Fiction, VI (1969), 205–209.

"The Peaches"
  Mosher, Harold F. "The Structure of Dylan Thomas's 'The Peaches,'" Stud Short Fiction, VI (1969), 536–547.

"A Story"
  Mizener, Arthur. A Handbook for Use with "Modern Short Stories: The Uses of Imagination, Revised Edition" (New York: Norton, 1966), 24–25.

THOMAS B. THORPE

"The Big Bear of Arkansas"
  Simoneaux, Katherine G. "Symbolism in Thorpe's
  'The Big Bear of Arkansas,'" Arkansas Hist Q, XXV
  (1966), 240–247.

JAMES THURBER

"The Catbird Seat"
  Shrodes, Caroline, Justine Van Gundy, and Joel Dorius.
  Instructor's Manual for "Reading for Understanding"
  (New York: Macmillan, 1968), 21–22.

"A Couple of Hamburgers"
  Mizener, Arthur, Ed. Modern Short Stories: The Uses
  of Imagination, Revised edition (New York: Norton,
  1967), 201–206.

"The Secret Life of Walter Mitty"
  Fitzgerald, Gregory. "An Example of Associationism
  as an Organizational Technique from Thurber's
  'Walter Mitty,'" Coll Engl Assoc Critic, XXXI (Janu-
  ary, 1969), 11.
  Sundell, Carl. "The Architecture of Walter Mitty's
  Secret Life," Engl J, LVI (1967), 1284–1287.

LEO TOLSTOY

"The Death of Ivan Ilych"
  Dietrich, R. F., and Roger H. Sundell. Instructor's
  Manual for "The Art of Fiction" (New York: Holt,
  Rinehart & Winston, 1967), 71–78.
  Hirschberg, W. R. "Tolstoy's 'The Death of Ivan Ilych,'"
  Explicator, XXVIII (1969), Item 26.
  Howe, Irving, Ed. Classics of Modern Fiction (New
  York: Harcourt, Brace & World, 1968), 113–121.

Proffer, Carl R., Ed. From Karamzin to Bunin: An
Anthology of Russian Short Stories (Bloomington:
Indiana Univ. Press, 1969), 25–31.
Simmons, Ernest J. Introduction to Tolstoy's Writings
(Chicago: Univ. of Chicago Press, 1968), 148–150.
Trilling, Lionel. The Experience of Literature (New
York: Holt, Rinehart & Winston, 1967), 525–527.

"God Sees the Truth, but Waits"
Proffer, Carl R., Ed. From Karamzin to Bunin: An
Anthology of Russian Short Stories (Bloomington:
Indiana Univ. Press, 1969), 24–25.

"Hadji Murad"
Bayley, John, Ed. Great Short Works of Leo Tolstoy
(New York: Harper & Row, 1967), xvi–xviii.

"The Two Hussars"
Simmons, Ernest J. Introduction to Tolstoy's Writings
(Chicago: Univ. of Chicago Press, 1968), 31–32.

JEAN TOOMER

"Blood-Burning Moon"
Turpin, Waters E. "Four Short Fiction Writers of the
Harlem Renaissance: Their Legacy of Achievement,"
Coll Lang Assoc J, XI (1967), 59–62.

F. ORLIN TREMAINE

"The Escape"
Sapiro, Leland. "The Mystic Renaissance: A Survey of
F. Orlin Tremaine's Astounding Stories, Part III,"
Riverside Q, II (1966), 272–274.

LIONEL TRILLING

"Of This Time, Of That Place"
    Shrodes, Caroline, Justine Van Gundy, and Joel Dorius.
        Instructor's Manual for "Reading for Understanding"
        (New York: Macmillan, 1968), 35-37.
    Trilling, Lionel. The Experience of Literature (New
        York: Holt, Rinehart & Winston, 1967), 781-784.

IVAN TURGENEV

"Bezhin Meadow"
    Proffer, Carl R., Ed. From Karamzin to Bunin: An
        Anthology of Russian Short Stories (Bloomington:
        Indiana Univ. Press, 1969), 17-19.

MARK TWAIN

"Captain Stormfield's Visit to Heaven"
    Baldanza, Frank. Mark Twain: An Introduction and In-
        terpretation (New York: Barnes & Noble, 1961), 128-
        131.

"The Invalid's Story"
    Horowitz, Floyd R. "The Invalid's Story: An Early
        Mark Twain Commentary on Institutional Christian-
        ity," Midcontinent Am Stud J, VII (Spring, 1966), 37-
        44.

"The Man That Corrupted Hadleyburg"
    Baldanza, Frank. Mark Twain: An Introduction and In-
        terpretation (New York: Barnes & Noble, 1961), 135-
        138.
    Foner, Philip S. Mark Twain, Social Critic (New York:
        International Publishers, 1958), 140-142.
    Malin, Irving. "Mark Twain: The Boy as Artist," Lit
        & Psych, XI (1961), 81-82.

Rule, Henry B. "The Role of Satan in 'The Man That Corrupted Hadleyburg,'" Stud Short Fiction, VI (1969), 619–629.

"The Mysterious Stranger"

Baldanza, Frank. Mark Twain: An Introduction and Interpretation (New York: Barnes & Noble, 1961), 138–140.

Bellamy, Gladys C. Mark Twain as a Literary Artist (Norman: Univ. of Oklahoma Press, 1950), 352–362; reprinted in Tuckey, John S., Ed. Mark Twain's "The Mysterious Stranger" and the Critics (Belmont: Wadsworth, 1968), 168–173.

Covici, Pascal. Mark Twain's Humor: The Image of a World (Dallas: Southern Methodist Univ. Press, 1962), 227–236.

Cox, James M. Mark Twain: The Fate of Humor (Princeton: Princeton Univ. Press, 1966), 272–284; reprinted in Tuckey, John S., Ed. Mark Twain's "The Mysterious Stranger" and the Critics (Belmont: Wadsworth, 1968), 212–220.

De Voto, Bernard. Mark Twain at Work (Cambridge: Harvard Univ. Press, 1942), 127–130; reprinted in Tuckey, John S., Ed. Mark Twain's "The Mysterious Stranger" and the Critics (Belmont: Wadsworth, 1968), 107–108.

————, Ed. The Portable Mark Twain (New York: Viking, 1946), 25.

Fiedler, Leslie. Love and Death in the American Novel (New York: Criterion Books, 1960), 437–440.

Foner, Philip S. Mark Twain, Social Critic (New York: International Publishers, 1958), 63–64.

Fussell, E. S. "The Structural Problem of 'The Mysterious Stranger,'" Stud Philol, XLIV (1952), 95–104; reprinted in Tuckey, John S., Ed. Mark Twain's "The Mysterious Stranger" and the Critics (Belmont: Wadsworth, 1968), 75–83.

Glick, Wendell. "The Epistemological Theme in 'The Mysterious Stranger,'" in Browne, Ray B., and

Donald Pizer, Eds. Themes and Directions in
American Literature (Lafayette: Purdue Univ.
Studies, 1969), 130–147.

Malin, Irving. "Mark Twain: The Boy as Artist," Lit
& Psych, XI (1961), 82–83.

Salomon, Roger B. Twain and the Image of History
(New Haven: Yale Univ. Press, 1961), 201–210; re-
printed in Tuckey, John S., Ed. Mark Twain's "The
Mysterious Stranger" and the Critics (Belmont:
Wadsworth, 1968), 176–182.

Sherman, Stuart P. "The Misanthropy of Mark Twain,"
Nation, CIII (December 21, 1916), 588–589.

Smith, Henry N. Mark Twain: The Development of a
Writer (Cambridge: Harvard Univ. Press, 1962),
185–188; reprinted in Tuckey, John S., Ed. Mark
Twain's "The Mysterious Stranger" and the Critics
(Belmont: Wadsworth, 1968), 192–194.

Stone, Albert E. The Innocent Eye: Childhood in Mark
Twain's Imagination (New Haven: Yale Univ. Press,
1961), 242–250; reprinted in Tuckey, John S., Ed.
Mark Twain's "The Mysterious Stranger" and the
Critics (Belmont: Wadsworth, 1968), 186–191.

MIGUEL DE UNAMUNO

"Abel Sanchez"
Ilie, Paul. "Moral Psychology in Unamuno," in Barcia,
José R., and M. A. Zeitlin, Eds. Unamuno: Creator
and Creation (Berkeley: Univ. of California Press,
1967), 78–79.

————. Unamuno: An Existential View of Self and
Society (Madison: Univ. of Wisconsin Press, 1967),
94–95.

Marias, Julian. Miguel de Unamuno (Cambridge: Harvard Univ. Press, 1966), 94–101.

"Aunt Tula"
Marias, Julian. Miguel de Unamuno (Cambridge: Harvard Univ. Press, 1966), 104–113.

"Love and Pedagogy"
  Marias, Julian. Miguel de Unamuno (Cambridge: Harvard Univ. Press, 1966), 85–88.

"Saint Manuel Bueno Martyr"
  Arroyo, Ciriaco Morón. "'San Manuel Bueno, mártir'
  y el 'sistema' de Unamuno," Hispanic R, XXXII (1964),
  227–246.
  Barcia, José R. "Unamuno the Man," in Barcia, José R.,
  and M. A. Zeitlin, Eds. Unamuno: Creator and Creation (Berkeley: Univ. of California Press, 1967), 19–
  20.
  Marias. Julian. Miguel de Unamuno (Cambridge: Harvard Univ. Press, 1966), 113–118.

                    JOHN UPDIKE

"Flight"
  Samuels, Charles T. John Updike (Minneapolis: Univ.
  of Minnesota Press, 1969), 20–21.

"A Gift from the City"
  Warner, John M. "Charity in 'A Gift from the City,'"
  in McKenzie, Barbara, Ed. The Process of Fiction
  (New York: Harcourt, Brace & World, 1969), 118–123.

"Lifeguard"
  Hamilton, Alice, and Kenneth Hamilton. John Updike:
  A Critical Essay (Grand Rapids: Eerdmans, 1967),
  29–30.

"Packed Dirt, Churchgoing, A Dying Cat, A Traded Car"
  Hamilton, Alice, and Kenneth Hamilton. John Updike:
  A Critical Essay (Grand Rapids: Eerdmans, 1967),
  27–29.

"The Persistence of Desire"
  Samuels, Charles T. John Updike (Minneapolis: Univ.
  of Minnesota Press, 1969), 21–22.

"Pigeon Feathers"
    Hamilton, Alice, and Kenneth Hamilton. John Updike:
       A Critical Essay (Grand Rapids: Eerdmans, 1967),
       27–29.

"A Sense of Shelter"
    Mizener, Arthur. A Handbook for Use with "Modern
       Short Stories: The Uses of Imagination, Revised Edi-
       tion" (New York: Norton, 1966), 34–37.
       ————, Ed. Modern Short Stories: The Uses of Imagi-
       nation, Revised edition (New York: Norton, 1967),
       427–430.

"Tomorrow and Tomorrow and So Forth"
    Rees, Robert A., and Barry Menikoff. A Manual to Ac-
       company "The Short Story: An Introductory Anthol-
       ogy" (Boston: Little, Brown, 1969), 2.

"Toward Evening"
    Hamilton, Alice, and Kenneth Hamilton. John Updike:
       A Critical Essay (Grand Rapids: Eerdmans, 1967),
       24–26.

GIOVANNI VERGA

"In Piazza della Scala"
    Ragusa, Olga. Verga's Milanese Tales (New York:
       Vanni, 1964), 54–58.

"The Last Day"
    Erickson, John D. "A Milanese Tale by Giovanni Verga,"
       Symposium, XX (1966), 7–13.
    Ragusa, Olga. Verga's Milanese Tales (New York: Van-
       ni, 1964), 58–62.

"Liberty"
    Dickinson, Leon T. Suggestions for Teachers of "In-
       troduction to Literature" (New York: Holt, Rinehart
       & Winston, 1967), 56–57.

"Temptation"
    Ragusa, Olga. Verga's Milanese Tales (New York:
        Vanni, 1964), 69–77.

"Via Crucis"
    Ragusa, Olga. Verga's Milanese Tales (New York:
        Vanni, 1964), 63–69.

ALFRED DE VIGNY

"La Canne de jonc"
    Doolittle, James. Alfred de Vigny (New York: Twayne,
        1967), 119–124.

"Laurette, ou le cachet rouge"
    Doolittle, James. Alfred de Vigny (New York: Twayne,
        1967), 117–118.

"La Veillée de Vincennes"
    Doolittle, James. Alfred de Vigny (New York: Twayne,
        1967), 118–119.

ELIO VITTORINI

"The Lady of the Station"
    Heiney, Donald. Three Italian Novelists: Moravia,
        Pavese, Vittorini (Ann Arbor: Univ. of Michigan
        Press, 1968), 157–158.

"My War"
    Heiney, Donald. Three Italian Novelists: Moravia,
        Pavese, Vittorini (Ann Arbor: Univ. of Michigan
        Press, 1968), 158–160.

DAVID WAGONER

"The Spinning Ladies"
    Schafer, William J. "David Wagoner's Fiction: In the
        Mills of Satan," Critique, IX (1967), 83–84.

ROBERT WALSER

"The Battle of Sempach"
Avery, George C. Inquiry and Testament: A Study of
the Novels and Short Prose of Robert Walser (Philadelphia: Univ. of Pennsylvania Press, 1968), 202–
203.

"Tobold"
Avery, George C. Inquiry and Testament: A Study of
the Novels and Short Prose of Robert Walser (Philadelphia: Univ. of Pennsylvania Press, 1968), 200–
202.

"A Young Girl from Berlin"
Avery, George C. Inquiry and Testament: A Study of
the Novels and Short Prose of Robert Walser (Philadelphia: Univ. of Pennsylvania Press, 1968), 199–200.

ROBERT PENN WARREN

"Blackberry Winter"
Davidson, Richard A. "Physical Imagery in Robert Penn
Warren's 'Blackberry Winter,'" Georgia R, XXII
(1968), 487–488.

"When the Light Gets Green"
Mizener, Arthur. A Handbook for Use with "Modern
Short Stories: The Uses of Imagination, Revised Edi-
tion" (New York: Norton, 1966), 151–156.

FRANK WEDEKIND

"The Fire at Egliswyl"
Gittleman, Sol. Frank Wedekind (New York: Twayne,
1969), 127–129.

"The Hoary Suitor"
Gittleman, Sol. Frank Wedekind (New York: Twayne,
1969), 123–125.

"Princess Russalka"
    Gittleman, Sol. <u>Frank Wedekind</u> (New York: Twayne,
       1969), 121–122.

"The Scapegoat"
    Gittleman, Sol. <u>Frank Wedekind</u> (New York: Twayne,
       1969), 122–123.

H. G. WELLS

"The Beautiful Suit"
    Costa, Richard H. <u>H. G. Wells</u> (New York: Twayne,
       1967), 57–58.

"The Country of the Blind"
    Costa, Richard H. <u>H. G. Wells</u> (New York: Twayne,
       1967), 59–63.

"The Desert Daisy"
    Costa, Richard H. <u>H. G. Wells</u> (New York: Twayne,
       1967), 19–20.

"The Door in the Wall"
    Buckley, Jerome H. <u>The Triumph of Time: A Study of
       Victorian Concepts of Time, History, and Decadence</u>
       (Cambridge: Harvard Univ. Press, 1966), 113–114.
    Costa, Richard H. <u>H. G. Wells</u> (New York: Twayne,
       1967), 58–59.

"The Lord of the Dynamos"
    Costa, Richard H. <u>H. G. Wells</u> (New York: Twayne,
       1967), 54–56.

"The Man Who Could Work Miracles"
    Costa, Richard H. <u>H. G. Wells</u> (New York: Twayne,
       1967), 53–54.

"The Remarkable Case of Davidson's Eyes"
    Costa, Richard H. <u>H. G. Wells</u> (New York: Twayne,
       1967), 56–57.

"The Stolen Bacillus"
    Costa, Richard H. H. G. Wells (New York: Twayne,
        1967), 52–53.

"The Time Machine"
    Philmus, Robert M. "'The Time Machine'; or, The
        Fourth Dimension as Prophecy," PMLA, LXXXIV
        (1969), 530–535.

EUDORA WELTY

"At the Landing"
    Bryant, J. A. Eudora Welty (Minneapolis: Univ. of Min-
        nesota Press, 1968), 16.

"The Bride of Innisfallen"
    Bryant, J. A. Eudora Welty (Minneapolis: Univ. of Min-
        nesota Press, 1968), 40–41.

"The Burning"
    Bryant, J. A. Eudora Welty (Minneapolis: Univ. of Min-
        nesota Press, 1968), 38–39.

"Clytie"
    Hoffman, Frederick J. The Art of Southern Fiction: A
        Study of Some Modern Novels (Carbondale: Southern
        Illinois Univ. Press, 1967), 56–58.

"A Curtain of Green"
    Bryant, J. A. Eudora Welty (Minneapolis: Univ. of Min-
        nesota Press, 1968), 12.

"Death of a Traveling Salesman"
    Hoffman, Frederick J. The Art of Southern Fiction: A
        Study of Some Modern Novels (Carbondale: Southern
        Illinois Univ. Press, 1967), 58–59.
    Jones, William M. "The Plot As Search," Stud Short
        Fiction, V (1967), 38.

Schorer, Mark, Ed. The Story: A Critical Anthology
(New York: Prentice-Hall, 1950), 354–357; Second
edition (Englewood Cliffs: Prentice-Hall, 1967),
285–287.

"The Demonstrators"
Bryant, J. A. Eudora Welty (Minneapolis: Univ. of Min-
nesota Press, 1968), 44.
Vande Kieft, Ruth M. "Demonstrators in a Stricken
Land," in McKenzie, Barbara, Ed. The Process of
Fiction (New York: Harcourt, Brace & World, 1969),
342–349.

"First Love"
Curley, Daniel. "Eudora Welty and the Quondam Ob-
struction," Stud Short Fiction, V (1968), 211–213.
Lynskey, Winifred, Ed. Reading Modern Fiction (New
York: Scribner, 1952), 483–485; Second edition
(1957), 483–485; Third edition (1962), 498–499;
Fourth edition (1968), 532–534.

"Going to Naples"
Bryant, J. A. Eudora Welty (Minneapolis: Univ. of Minnesota Press, 1968), 40.

"June Recital"
Bryant, J. A. Eudora Welty (Minneapolis: Univ. of Min-
nesota Press, 1968), 29.
Hoffman, Frederick J. The Art of Southern Fiction: A
Study of Some Modern Novels (Carbondale: Southern
Illinois Univ. Press, 1967), 63–64.
Jones, William M. "The Plot As Search," Stud Short
Fiction, V (1967), 40–41.

"Keela, the Outcast Indian Maiden"
Bryant, J. A. Eudora Welty (Minneapolis: Univ. of Minnesota Press, 1968), 11.

"The Key"
Curley, Daniel. "Eudora Welty and the Quondam Ob-
struction," Stud Short Fiction, V (1968), 214–215.

"Kin"
    Bryant, J. A. Eudora Welty (Minneapolis: Univ. of Min-
        nesota Press, 1968), 37–38.

"Ladies in Spring"
    Bryant, J. A. Eudora Welty (Minneapolis: Univ. of Min-
        nesota Press, 1968), 36–37.

"Livvie"
    Bryant, J. A. Eudora Welty (Minneapolis: Univ. of Min-
        nesota Press, 1968), 15–16.
    Shrodes, Caroline, Justine Van Gundy, and Joel Dorius.
        Instructor's Manual for "Reading for Understanding"
        (New York: Macmillan, 1968), 38–39.
    Smith, Julian. "'Livvie'—Eudora Welty's Song of Solo-
        mon," Stud Short Fiction, V (1967), 73–74.

"A Memory"
    Bryant, J. A. Eudora Welty (Minneapolis: Univ. of Min-
        nesota Press, 1968), 7–8.

"Moon Lake"
    Bryant, J. A. Eudora Welty (Minneapolis: Univ. of Min-
        nesota Press, 1968), 29–30.
    Jones, William M. "The Plot As Search," Stud Short
        Fiction, V (1967), 41–42.

"Music from Spain"
    Bryant, J. A. Eudora Welty (Minneapolis: Univ. of Min-
        nesota Press, 1968), 28–29.

"No Place for You, My Love"
    Bryant, J. A. Eudora Welty (Minneapolis: Univ. of Min-
        nesota Press, 1968), 41–42.

"Petrified Man"
    Cochran, Robert W. "Welty's 'Petrified Man,'" Expli-
        cator, XXVII (1968), Item 25.
    Huck, Wilbur, and William Shanahan, Eds. The Modern
        Short Story (New York: American Book, 1968), 26–27.

"A Piece of News"
   Bryant, J. A. Eudora Welty (Minneapolis: Univ. of Minnesota Press, 1968), 10–11.

"Powerhouse"
   Kirkpatrick, Smith. "The Anointed Powerhouse,'"
   Sewanee R, LXXVII (1969), 94–108.

"A Still Moment"
   Bryant, J. A. Eudora Welty (Minneapolis: Univ. of Minnesota Press, 1968), 14.
   Curley, Daniel. "Eudora Welty and the Quondam Ob-
   struction," Stud Short Fiction, V (1968), 220–224.

"A Visit of Charity"
   May, Charles E. "The Difficulty of Loving in 'A Visit
   of Charity,'" Stud Short Fiction, VI (1969), 338–341.
   Toole, William B. "The Texture of 'A Visit of Charity,'"
   Mississippi Q, XX (1967), 43–46.

"The Wanderers"
   Bryant, J. A. Eudora Welty (Minneapolis: Univ. of Min-
   nesota Press, 1968), 30–33.
   Jones, William M. "The Plot As Search," Stud Short
   Fiction, V (1967), 42–43.

"Why I Live at the P. O."
   Bryant, J. A. Eudora Welty (Minneapolis: Univ. of Min-
   nesota Press, 1968), 8–9.
   Hoffman, Frederick J. The Art of Southern Fiction: A
   Study of Some Modern Novels (Carbondale: Southern
   Illinois Univ. Press, 1967), 55–56.

"The Wide Net"
   Bryant, J. A. Eudora Welty (Minneapolis: Univ. of Minnesota Press, 1968), 16–17.
   Curley, Daniel. "Eudora Welty and the Quondam Ob-
   struction," Stud Short Fiction, V (1968), 213–214.

"A Worn Path"
   Mizener, Arthur. A Handbook for Use with "Modern
      Short Stories: The Uses of Imagination, Revised Edi-
      tion" (New York: Norton, 1966), 163–165.

GLENWAY WESCOTT

"The Pilgrim Hawk"
   Moss, Howard. "Love Birds of Prey," New Yorker,
      XLIII (March 11, 1967), 184–191.

NATHANAEL WEST

"A Cool Million"
   Edenbaum, Robert I. "A Surfeit of Shoddy: Nathanael
      West's 'A Cool Million,'" Southern Hum R, II (1968),
      427–439.
   Reid, Randall. The Fiction of Nathanael West (Chicago:
      Univ. of Chicago Press, 1967), 106–115.
   Schulz, Max F. Radical Sophistication: Studies in Con-
      temporary Jewish-American Novelists (Athens: Ohio
      Univ. Press, 1969), 44–48.
   Widmer, Kingsley. "The Sweet Savage Prophecies of
      Nathanael West," in French, Warren, Ed. The Thirties:
      Fiction, Poetry, Drama (Deland: Everett Edwards,
      1967), 102–103.

"The Dream Life of Balso Snell"
   Klein, Marcus. "The Roots of Radicals: Experience in
      the Thirties," in Madden, David, Ed. Proletarian
      Writers of the Thirties (Carbondale: Southern Illinois
      Univ. Press, 1968), 142–144.
   Reid, Randall. The Fiction of Nathanael West (Chicago:
      Univ. of Chicago Press, 1967), 13–40.
   Schulz, Max F. Radical Sophistication: Studies in Con-
      temporary Jewish-American Novelists (Athens: Ohio
      Univ. Press, 1969), 36–41.

Widmer, Kingsley. "The Sweet Savage Prophecies of
Nathanael West," in French, Warren, Ed. The
Thirties: Fiction, Poetry, Drama (Deland: Everett
Edwards, 1967), 98–99.

"Miss Lonelyhearts"
Abrahams, Roger D. "Androgynes Bound: Nathanael
West's 'Miss Lonelyhearts,'" in Whitbread, Thomas
B., Ed. Seven Contemporaries (Austin: Univ. of
Texas Press, 1966), 51–72.
Bush, C. W. "This Stupendous Fabric: The Metaphysics
of Order in Melville's Pierre and Nathanael West's
'Miss Lonelyhearts,'" J Am Stud, I (1967), 269–274.
Edenbaum, Robert I. "To Kill God and Build a Church:
Nathanael West's 'Miss Lonelyhearts,'" Coll Engl
Assoc Critic, XXIX (June, 1967), 5–7, 11.
Lorch, Thomas M. "Religion and Art in 'Miss Lonely-
hearts,'" Renascence, XX (1967), 11–17.
Reid, Randall. The Fiction of Nathanael West (Chicago:
Univ. of Chicago Press, 1967), 41–105.
Richardson, Robert D. "'Miss Lonelyhearts,'" Univ R,
XXXIII (1966), 151–157.
Schulz, Max F. Radical Sophistication: Studies in Con-
temporary Jewish-American Novelists (Athens:
Ohio Univ. Press, 1969), 41–44.
Smith, Marcus. "Religious Experience in 'Miss Lonely-
hearts,'" Contemporary Lit, IX (1968), 172–188.
Widmer, Kingsley. "The Sweet Savage Prophecies of
Nathanael West," in French, Warren, Ed. The Thir-
ties: Fiction, Poetry, Drama (Deland: Everett Ed-
wards, 1967), 99–102.

EDITH WHARTON

"Ethan Frome"
Bernard, Kenneth. "Imagery and Symbolism in 'Ethan
Frome,'" Coll Engl, XXIII (1961), 178–184; reprinted
in Nevius, Blake, Ed. Edith Wharton's "Ethan Frome"
(New York: Scribner, 1968), 107–113.

Brennan, Joseph X. "'Ethan Frome': Structure and Metaphor," Mod Fiction Stud, VII (1961), 347–356; reprinted in Nevius, Blake, Ed. Edith Wharton's "Ethan Frome" (New York: Scribner, 1968), 114–120.

Bruce, Charles. "Circularity: Theme and Structure in 'Ethan Frome,'" Stud & Critiques (Arlington) [no vol. or number] (1966), 78–81.

De Voto, Bernard. "Introduction," Ethan Frome (New York: Scribner, 1938), v–xviii; reprinted in Nevius, Blake, Ed. Edith Wharton's "Ethan Frome" (New York: Scribner, 1968), 91–95.

Lubbock, Percy. "The Novels of Edith Wharton," Quarterly R, CCXXIII (1915), 193–195; reprinted in Nevius, Blake, Ed. Edith Wharton's "Ethan Frome" (New York: Scribner, 1968), 81–82.

Nevius, Blake. "'Ethan Frome' and the Themes of Edith Wharton's Fiction," New England Q, XXIV (1951), 204–207; reprinted, with additions, in his Edith Wharton: A Study of Her Fiction (Berkeley: Univ. of California Press, 1953), 117–124; 127–129; Howe, Irving, Ed. Edith Wharton: A Collection of Critical Essays (Englewood Cliffs: Prentice-Hall, 1962), 130–136; Nevius, Blake, Ed. Edith Wharton's "Ethan Frome" (New York: Scribner, 1968), 96–100.

Ransom, John C. "Characters and Character: A Note on Fiction," Am R, VI (1936), 271–275; reprinted in Nevius, Blake, Ed. Edith Wharton's "Ethan Frome" (New York: Scribner, 1968), 88–90.

Sergeant, Elizabeth S. "Idealized New England," New Republic, III (May 8, 1915), 20–21; reprinted in Nevius, Blake, Ed. Edith Wharton's "Ethan Frome" (New York: Scribner, 1968), 83–85.

Trilling, Lionel. "The Morality of Inertia," in MacIver, R. M., Ed. Great Moral Dilemmas in Literature, Past and Present (New York: Harper, 1956), 37–46; reprinted in Trilling, Lionel. A Gathering of Fugitives (Boston: Beacon Press, 1956), 31–40; Hepburn, James G., and Robert A. Greenberg, Eds. Modern Essays: A Rhetorical Approach (New York:

Macmillan, 1962), 189–199; Howe, Irving, Ed.
Edith Wharton: A Collection of Critical Essays
(Englewood Cliffs: Prentice-Hall, 1962), 137–146;
Nevius, Blake, Ed. Edith Wharton's "Ethan Frome"
(New York: Scribner, 1968), 101–106.
Wharton, Edith. A Backward Glance (New York: Ap-
pleton-Century, 1934), 293, 295–296; reprinted in
Nevius, Blake, Ed. Edith Wharton's "Ethan Frome"
(New York: Scribner, 1968), 74–75.
————. Ethan Frome (New York: Scribner, 1922),
v–x; reprinted in Nevius, Blake, Ed. Edith Wharton's
"Ethan Frome" (New York: Scribner, 1968), 70–71.
————. "The Writing of 'Ethan Frome,'" Colophon,
III, Part 11, [1–4]; reprinted in Adler, E., et al.
Breaking Into Print (New York: Simon and Schuster,
1937), 187–191; Targ, William, Ed. Reader for
Writers (New York: Hermitage, 1951), 145–147;
Nevius, Blake, Ed. Edith Wharton's "Ethan Frome"
(New York: Scribner, 1968), 72–73.

"Roman Fever"
Mizener, Arthur. A Handbook for Use with "Modern
Short Stories: The Uses of Imagination, Revised Edi-
tion" (New York: Norton, 1966), 61–66.

E. B. WHITE

"The Second Tree from the Corner"
Lynskey, Winifred, Ed. Reading Modern Fiction, Third
edition (New York: Scribner, 1962), 505–507; Fourth
edition (1968), 539–541.
Timko, Michael. "Kafka's 'A Country Doctor,' Williams'
'The Use of Force,' and White's 'The Second Tree
from the Corner,'" in Timko, Michael, and Clinton
F. Oliver, Eds. Thirty-Eight Short Stories (New
York: Knopf, 1968), 86–101.

PATRICK WHITE

"Down at the Dump"
Barnes, John. "New Tracks to Travel: The Stories of White, Porter and Cowan," Meanjin Q, XXV (1966), 157–158.

WILLIAM CARLOS WILLIAMS

"The Accident"
Guimond, James. The Art of William Carlos Williams (Urbana: Univ. of Illinois Press, 1968), 144–145.

"Jean Beicke"
Dickinson, Leon T. Suggestions for Teachers of "Introduction to Literature" (New York: Holt, Rinehart & Winston, 1967), 65–66.
Guimond, James. The Art of William Carlos Williams (Urbana: Univ. of Illinois Press, 1968), 140–141.

"A Night in June"
Guimond, James. The Art of William Carlos Williams (Urbana: Univ. of Illinois Press, 1968), 165–166.

"Old Doc Rivers"
Guimond, James. The Art of William Carlos Williams (Urbana: Univ. of Illinois Press, 1968), 142–144.

"Pink and Blue"
Guimond, James. The Art of William Carlos Williams (Urbana: Univ. of Illinois Press, 1968), 139–140.

"The Use of Force"
Dietrich, R. F., and Roger H. Sundell. Instructor's Manual for "The Art of Fiction" (New York: Holt, Rinehart & Winston, 1967), 1–8.
Slate, J. E. "William Carlos Williams and the Modern Short Story," Southern R, IV (1968), 647–664.

Timko, Michael. "Kafka's 'A Country Doctor,' Williams'
'The Use of Force,' and White's 'The Second Tree
from the Corner,'" in Timko, Michael, and Clinton
F. Oliver, Eds. Thirty-Eight Short Stories (New
York: Knopf, 1968), 86–101.
Wagner, Linda W. "Williams' 'The Use of Force': An
Expansion," Stud Short Fiction, IV (1967), 351–353.

EDMUND WILSON

"Ellen Terhune"
Paul, Sherman. Edmund Wilson: A Study of Literary
Vocation in Our Time (Urbana: Univ. of Illinois Press,
1965), 151–153.

"Glimpses of Wilbur Flick"
Paul, Sherman. Edmund Wilson: A Study of Literary
Vocation in Our Time (Urbana: Univ. of Illinois
Press, 1965), 153–154.

"The Man Who Shot Snapping Turtles"
Paul, Sherman. Edmund Wilson: A Study of Literary
Vocation in Our Time (Urbana: Univ. of Illinois
Press, 1965), 150–151.

"The Milhollands and Their Damned Soul"
Paul, Sherman. Edmund Wilson: A Study of Literary
Vocation in Our Time (Urbana: Univ. of Illinois
Press, 1965), 160–162.

"Mr. and Mrs. Blackburn at Home"
Paul, Sherman. Edmund Wilson: A Study of Literary
Vocation in Our Time (Urbana: Univ. of Illinois
Press, 1965), 162–164.

"The Princess with the Golden Hair"
Paul, Sherman. Edmund Wilson: A Study of Literary
Vocation in Our Time (Urbana: Univ. of Illinois
Press, 1965), 155–159.

THEODORE WINTHROP

"Saccharissa Mellasys"
Colby, Elbridge. Theodore Winthrop (New York:
Twayne, 1965), 102–103.

THOMAS WOLFE

"God's Lonely Man"
Hartley, Lois. "Theme in Thomas Wolfe's 'The Lost
Boy' and 'God's Lonely Man,'" Georgia R, XV (1961),
230–235; reprinted in Field, Leslie A., Ed. Thomas
Wolfe: Three Decades of Criticism (New York: New
York Univ. Press, 1968), 261–267.

"The Lost Boy"
Forssberg, William. "Part Two of 'The Lost Boy':
Theme and Intention," Stud Short Fiction, IV (1967),
167–169.
Hartley, Lois. "Theme in Thomas Wolfe's 'The Lost
Boy' and 'God's Lonely Man,'" Georgia R, XV (1961),
230–235; reprinted in Field, Leslie A., Ed. Thomas
Wolfe: Three Decades of Criticism (New York: New
York Univ. Press, 1968), 261–267.
Stegner, Wallace. "Analysis of 'The Lost Boy,'" in
Stegner, Wallace, Richard Snowcroft, and Boris
Ilyin, Eds. The Writer's Art (Boston: Heath, 1950),
178–183; reprinted in Field, Leslie A., Ed. Thomas
Wolfe: Three Decades of Criticism (New York: New
York Univ. Press, 1968), 255–260.

"No Door"
Eichelberger, Clayton L. "Wolfe's 'No Door' and the
Brink of Discovery," Georgia R, XXI (1967), 319–327.

"Only the Dead Know Brooklyn"
Bloom, Edward A. The Order of Fiction (New York:
Odyssey, 1964), 143–146; reprinted in Field, Leslie
A., Ed. Thomas Wolfe: Three Decades of Criticism
(New York: New York Univ. Press, 1968), 269–272.

"The String Quartet"
　　Bloom, Edward A., and Lillian D. Bloom, Eds. The
　　　　Variety of Fiction: A Critical Anthology (New York:
　　　　Odyssey, 1969), 340-342.

RICHARD WRIGHT

"Down by the Riverside"
　　Hand, Clifford. "The Struggle to Create Life in the
　　　　Fiction of Richard Wright," in French, Warren, Ed.
　　　　The Thirties: Fiction, Poetry, Drama (Deland:
　　　　Everett Edwards, 1967), 81-87.

"Long Black Song"
　　Hand, Clifford. "The Struggle to Create Life in the
　　　　Fiction of Richard Wright," in French, Warren, Ed.
　　　　The Thirties: Fiction, Poetry, Drama (Deland:
　　　　Everett Edwards, 1967), 84.

ÉMILE ZOLA

"Les coquillages de M. Chabre"
　　Baguley, D. "Maupassant avant la lettre? A Study of a
　　　　Zola Short Story: 'Les coquillages de M. Chabre,'"
　　　　Nottingham French Stud, VI (1967), 77-86.

MIKHAIL M. ZOSHCHENKO

"Adventures of a Monkey"
　　Mihailovich, Vasa D. "Zoshchenko's 'Adventures of a
　　　　Monkey' as an Allegory," Satire Newsletter, IV
　　　　(1967), 84-89.

"Healing and Psychics"
　　Von Wiren-Garczynski, Vera. "Zoscenko's Psycho-
　　　　logical Interests," Slavic and East European J, XI
　　　　(1967), 7.

INDEX OF SHORT STORY WRITERS

AGEE, JAMES, 1
AGNON, SCHMUEL YOSEF,
1-9
AICHINGER, ILSE, 9
ANDERSON, SHERWOOD,
9-17
AUSTIN, MARY, 17

BABEL, ISAAC, 17
BALDWIN, JAMES, 18
BALZAC, HONORÉ DE, 18
BARBEY D'AUREVILLY,
18-19
BECKETT, SAMUEL, 19-20
BELLOW, SAUL, 20-23
BENÉT, STEPHEN VINCENT,
23
BERGENGRUEN, WERNER,
23
BERKOVITZ, ITZHAK D.
23
BIERCE, AMBROSE, 24
BÖLL, HEINRICH, 24
BORGES, JORGE L., 24-30
BOWEN, ELIZABETH, 30
BOYLE, KAY, 31
BÜCHNER, GEORG, 31
BUNIN, IVAN, 31

CABELL, JAMES BRANCH,
31-32
CABLE, GEORGE W., 32-33
CALLAGHAN, MORLEY,
33-35
CAMUS, ALBERT, 35-37
CASSILL, R. V., 37
CATHER, WILLA, 37-39

CHAMISSO, ADELBERT
VON, 39
CHEEVER, JOHN, 40
CHEKHOV, ANTON, 40-42
CHOPIN, KATE, 42-43
CLARK, WALTER VAN
TILBURG, 44
CONRAD, JOSEPH, 44-54
CONROY, JACK, 54
CONSTANT, BENJAMIN,
54
COWAN, PETER, 54
CRANE, STEPHEN, 55-60

DINESEN, ISAK, 60-61
DOSTOEVSKY, FYODOR,
61-64
DREISER, THEODORE,
64-65
DROSTE-HÜLSHOFF,
ANNETTE VON, 65
DUNSANY, LORD, 65

EDGEWORTH, MARIA, 65
ELIOT, GEORGE, 65

FAULKNER, WILLIAM,
66-69
FEIERBERG, MORDEKHAI
ZE'EV, 69
FIEDLER, LESLIE, 70
FISHER, RUDOLPH, 70
FITZGERALD, F. SCOTT,
70-72
FLAUBERT, GUSTAVE,
72-73
FORSTER, E. M., 73-76

FREEMAN, MARY E.
  WILKINS, 76
FUENTES, CARLOS, 77

GARCÍA MÁRQUEZ,
  GABRIEL, 77
GARSHIN, VSEVOLOD
  M., 77
GAUTIER, THÉOPHILE,
  77-78
GIDE, ANDRÉ, 78-80
GOGOL, NIKOLAI,
  80-81
GOLD, HERBERT, 81
GOODMAN, PAUL, 81
GORDON, CAROLINE,
  82
GORKI, MAXIM, 82-84
GOYEN, WILLIAM, 85
GRASS, GÜNTER, 85
GREENE, GRAHAM, 85
GRIGOROVICH, DMITRI
  V., 85-86
GRILLPARZER, FRANZ,
  86

HARBEN, WILL N., 86
HARDY, THOMAS, 86-87
HARTE, BRET, 87
HAWTHORNE, NATHANIEL,
  87-96
HAZAZ, HAIYIM, 96-97
HEINLEIN, ROBERT, 97
HEMINGWAY, ERNEST, 97-
  112
HESSE, HERMANN, 112-113
HOFFMANN, E. T. A., 113
HUGHES, LANGSTON, 113

IRVING, WASHINGTON,
  113-114

JACOBSON, DAN, 114
JAMES, HENRY, 114-130
JEWETT, SARAH ORNE,
  130-131
JOHNSON, UWE, 131
JOHNSTON, RICHARD
  MALCOLM, 131
JOYCE, JAMES, 131-142

KAFKA, FRANZ, 143-147
KARAMZIN, NIKOLAI, 147
KELLER, GOTTFRIED,
  147-148
KIPLING, RUDYARD, 148-
  150
KLEIST, HEINRICH VON,
  151-152
KOLLONTAY, A., 153
KOROLENKO, VLADIMIR,
  153
KUPRIN, ALEXANDER, 153

LARDNER, RING, 153
LAWRENCE, D. H., 153-
  156
LAWSON, HENRY, 156-
  157
LENZ, SIEGFRIED, 157
LESKOV, NICOLAI, 157
LESSING, DORIS, 157-158
LONDON, JACK, 158
LOWRY, MALCOLM, 158-
  159
LYON, HARRIS MERTON,
  159
LYTLE, ANDREW, 159

McCARTHY, MARY, 160-
  161
McCULLERS, CARSON,
  161-162

MACHADO DE ASSIS,
 JOAQUIM M., 162–163
McKAY, CLAUDE, 163
MALAMUD, BERNARD,
 164–166
MALTZ, ALBERT, 166
MANN, THOMAS, 167–170
MANSFIELD, KATHERINE,
 170–171
MAUGHAM, W. SOMERSET,
 171–172
MAUPASSANT, GUY DE, 172–
 173
MAURIAC, FRANÇOIS, 173
MELVILLE, HERMAN, 173–
 178
MEREDITH, GEORGE, 178
MEYER, CONRAD F., 179
MORAVIA, ALBERTO, 179–
 180
MURFREE, MARY N., 180–
 181
MUSIL, ROBERT, 181–182

NABOKOV, VLADIMIR,
 182–186

O'CONNOR, FLANNERY,
 186–192
O'CONNOR, FRANK, 193
O'FAOLAIN, SEAN, 193–196
O'FLAHERTY, LIAM, 196
O'HARA, JOHN, 197
ORWELL, GEORGE, 197–
 198
OVECHKIN, V., 198

PATER, WALTER, 198–199
PERETZ, ITZHAK L., 199–
 200

PINTER, HAROLD, 200
PIRANDELLO, LUIGI, 200
POE, EDGAR ALLAN, 201–
 211
PORTER, HAL, 211
PORTER, KATHERINE
 ANNE, 211–215
POWERS, J. F., 215–219
PRICE, REYNOLDS, 219
PURDY, JAMES, 220
PUSHKIN, ALEXANDER,
 220

RAWLINGS, MARJORIE
 KINNAN, 220
ROSA, GUIMÁRAES, 220–
 221
ROTH, PHILIP, 221–222

SALINGER, J. D., 222–224
SAROYAN, WILLIAM, 224
SCHNITZLER, ARTHUR,
 225
SCHORER, MARK, 225
SCHWARTZ, DELMORE,
 225
SHELLEY, MARY, 225
SHOFFMAN, GERSHON,
 226
SHOLOKHOV, MIKHAIL,
 226
SILLITOE, ALAN, 226
SINGER, ISAAC, 227–228
SPARK, MURIEL, 228
STEINBECK, JOHN, 228–
 229
STEVENSON, ROBERT
 LOUIS, 229
STIFTER, ADALBERT,
 229

STORM, THEODOR, 230
STUART, JESSE, 230-232
STYRON, WILLIAM, 232-233
SUCKOW, RUTH, 233-234
SVEVO, ITALO, 234-235

TAGORE, RABINDRANATH,
   235
TAYLOR, PETER, 235-236
TERTZ, ABRAM, 236
THOMAS, DYLAN, 236
THORPE, THOMAS B., 237
THURBER, JAMES, 237
TOLSTOY, LEO, 237-238
TOOMER, JEAN, 238
TREMAINE, F. ORLIN, 238
TRILLING, LIONEL, 239
TURGENEV, IVAN, 239
TWAIN, MARK, 239-241

UNAMUNO, MIGUEL DE, 241-
   242
UPDIKE, JOHN, 242-243

VERGA, GIOVANNI, 243-244

VIGNY, ALFRED DE, 244
VITTORINI, ELIO, 244

WAGONER, DAVID, 244
WALSER, ROBERT, 245
WARREN, ROBERT PENN,
   245
WEDEKIND, FRANK, 245-
   246
WELLS, H. G., 246-247
WELTY, EUDORA, 247-251
WESCOTT, GLENWAY, 251-25:
WEST, NATHANAEL, 251
WHARTON, EDITH, 252-254
WHITE, E. B., 254
WHITE, PATRICK, 255
WILLIAMS, WILLIAM
   CARLOS, 255-256
WILSON, EDMUND, 256
WINTHROP, THEODORE, 257
WOLFE, THOMAS, 257-258
WRIGHT, RICHARD, 258

ZOLA, ÉMILE, 258
ZOSHCHENKO, MIKHAIL M., 25